Latin American Monographs

Second Series

The Embattled Colossus

Economic Nationalism and United States Investors in Latin America

16

Center for Latin American Studies
University of Florida

The Embattled Colossus

Economic Nationalism and United States Investors in Latin America

Robert H. Swansbrough

A University of Florida Book

The University Presses of Florida
Gainesville / 1976

A University of Florida Book
sponsored by the
Center for Latin American Studies

Printed by
Rose Printing Company, Incorporated
Tallahassee, Florida

Typography by Canon Graphics
Tallahassee, Florida

Library of Congress Cataloging in Publication Data

Swansbrough, Robert H 1938–
The embattled colossus.

(Latin American monographs; 2d ser., no. 16)
"A University of Florida book."
Bibliography: p.
1. Latin America—Foreign economic relations—United States. 2. United States—Foreign economic relations—Latin America. 3. Nationalism—Latin America. 4. Investments, American—Latin America. I. Title. II. Series: Florida. University, Gainesville. Center for Latin American Studies. Latin American monographs; 2d ser., no. 16.
HF1480.5.S9 332.6'7373'08 75-43994
ISBN 0-8130-0409-8

Contents

Introduction

A NEW WAVE of economic nationalism is growing throughout Latin America. As a result, policy makers and corporate executives in the United States have been forced to grapple with the expropriation of American properties in Peru and Bolivia, the "nationalization by agreement" of Anaconda in Chile and subsequent nationalization of U.S. interests by Socialist President Salvador Allende, and recent restrictions in other hemispheric capitals and the Andean Common Market. But why are these events in Latin America important to the U.S. government?

U.S. policies toward Latin America have been formulated to achieve a broad range of perceived national interests: strategic defense, economic prosperity, promotion of democracy, encouragement of private enterprise, and protection of American citizens. The Soviet introduction of missiles into Cuba brought the world to the brink of nuclear war and thus illustrated the importance of Latin America to the security of the United States. The American economy, buffeted by an adverse balance of payments, is strengthened by favorable trade and investment flows with Latin America. The nationalization of American properties results in financial losses for American business, and the establishment of state enterprises in the hemisphere challenges the ideology of free enterprise. Disputes over the property and fishing rights of American citizens have contributed to the growing opposition of Latin American republics to the positions of the United States in the Organization of American States and the United Nations. Clearly, economic nationalism has affected the strategic, economic, political, and ideological interests of the United States in Latin America.

This study analyzes the phenomenon of economic nationalism, its emergence in Latin America, and the inevitable clash with American investors. It also examines the tensions between Latin American and U.S. perceptions of the role of private enterprise in the development process and assesses current American policies to promote and protect foreign private investment in the developing countries. It clarifies the issue by focusing on the psychological and political roots of economic nationalism in Latin America and offers policy proposals to avoid investment disputes between the United States and Latin America.

Chapters 1 and 2 explore the evolution of economic nationalism in the industrialized Western countries and its relationship to the less-developed countries. The following questions are considered: How have memories of the interventionist policies of the United States during the heyday of Dollar Diplomacy affected Latin American perceptions of the United States and its investors today? What cultural differences separate the American and Latin American views of the role of the state and the private sector in the development process? How do the "psychological rewards" of economic nationalism militate against a "rational" assessment of the contributions of private capital to the economic growth of a country?

The central question considered in chapters 3 and 4 is whether the conflicting positions of the United States and Latin Americans on the advantages and disadvantages of foreign investment in the development process can be reconciled, or whether the efforts of American corporations to become good corporate citizens in their host countries are doomed to failure. The Economic Commission for Latin America (ECLA) maintains that foreign investment creates a drain on the balance of payments of the host country and exerts an influence on its domestic politics—a charge that is countered by the rebuttals of American spokesmen who stress the attendant benefits which private capital brings to the recipient country. Likewise, ECLA's call for industrialization policies promoted by the state and recent restrictions on the type and mode of foreign investment are balanced by the views of U.S. officials and businessmen who insist on a favorable investment climate so that private capital can act as the catalyst for economic growth.

The role of private enterprise in the foreign assistance program of the United States since World War II is examined in chapters 5, 6, and 7. Major issues include whether the perceptions of American policy makers changed as Latin American hostility to foreign investment grew, and whether the patterns of U.S. investment and the orientation of the foreign assistance program were altered to cope with a less hospitable investment climate. This examination encompasses the traditional emphasis on the private sector as the key element in the development process (called the "gospel of private enterprise" by some enthusiastic proponents); the Alliance for Progress and its heavy reliance on governmental assistance to encourage social and economic reforms; and the reassertion of the central role of private enterprise in the U.S. aid effort. Statements by administration officials, presidential task force reports on foreign assistance and U.S. economic policies, and congressional hearings indicate the rationale employed to justify to Congress foreign aid and the role of private enterprise in the program.

Have U.S. programs and policies to encourage and protect private investment safeguarded American properties in Latin America or have they embroiled the U.S. government deeply in investment disputes which jeopardize other American interests in the host country and throughout the hemisphere? Have the recent expropriations of insured U.S. investments in Chile affected the policies of the Overseas Private Investment Corporation (OPIC) to promote foreign investment in the developing countries? These questions are considered in chapter 8, which evaluates the legislative history and effectiveness of investment guaranty agreements and the Hickenlooper Amendment, which cuts off all U.S. assistance to a country that expropriates American property without prompt and adequate compensation. An examination of the creation of OPIC in the Foreign Assistance Act of 1969 is based upon an analysis of congressional documents and interviews conducted in the fall of 1969 with officials of the State Department, Agency for International Development (AID), Commerce Department, and congressional offices. Additional interviews were conducted in October 1971 at the Department of State Scholar-Diplomat Seminar on Latin American Affairs.

Chapters 9 and 10 present the views of the American business community on economic nationalism in the hemisphere, the individual firm's greatest concerns over its investment in the area, and possible actions the United States can take to cope with the phenomenon, based on a 1970 survey of the Council of the Americas, whose members comprise about 85 per cent of U.S. investment in Latin America. The following questions are discussed: Do American companies fear that their investments will be expropriated and that the Hickenlooper Amendment will not effectively deter nationalization? Are petroleum and mining firms, with their higher profiles and investments in sensitive sectors of the economy of a nation, more worried about economic nationalism than manufacturing investors? Has their greater exposure led to new corporate policies to meet local demands or reinforced a hard-line approach to investment disputes? Is the larger investor or firm, with more years of experience in Latin America, more or less concerned over the hostility to private enterprise than smaller investors and corporate newcomers to the region? The U.S. investors' perception of why Latin Americans resent foreign capital and what policies they think would safeguard the interests of American companies in the hemisphere are compared with Latin American demands for greater control over foreign investment and the current policies of the U.S. government.

The conclusion notes the history of U.S. economic nationalism in the late nineteenth century, which was directed against British investments in the United States and Britain's economic and political dominance of the Western Hemisphere; similarities to Latin American economic nationalism are pointed out. The conflicting views of foreign investment are evaluated and policy recommendations offered on how the U.S. government and American firms can meet the challenge posed by economic nationalism in Latin America.

This study focuses primarily on the role of U.S. direct foreign private investment in the economic development of Latin America; however, references are made to programs directed toward promoting private enterprise in the less-developed countries in general. Therefore, questions relating to U.S. trade with Latin America, the tying of foreign assistance to the procurement of U.S. goods and services, technical assistance, and the Public Law 480 "Food for Peace" program are discussed only peripherally. The examination of the U.S. foreign assistance program is thus concerned with the role that private enterprise is expected to perform in the development process, rather than an overall assessment of the social and economic goals of the Alliance for Progress and the limitations of the program. For literary reasons, the terms "U.S. foreign investment" or "U.S. capital" refer to U.S. direct foreign private investment, not portfolio investment or governmental investment, unless so indicated. While the United States is only one of the countries of the Americas, with due respect to the Latin Americans, the term "American" is employed to describe U.S. policies or investors.

1. Economic Nationalism

Its Meaning and Significance in Latin America

TODAY, economic nationalism is widely viewed by the American press, politicians, and business sector as some sort of illegitimate manifestation of irrational behavior in the less-developed countries. It is excoriated as a major impediment to a more rational international order based on the free flow of trade and private enterprise to all corners of the globe, with the attendant benefits of economic growth and improved standards of living. But this bias for a laissez-faire international investment climate ignores the birth of "offensive" economic nationalism in the Western industrialized countries, the root cause of the "defensive" economic nationalism in the developing nations.

NATIONALISM—A WESTERN DERIVATIVE

Scholars have not agreed upon a single definition of nationalism; some have simply refused to define this important phenomenon of the modern world. It has been variously described as a state of mind calling for exclusive loyalty to the state,[1] the fusion of pa-

1. Hans Kohn, *The Idea of Nationalism: A Study of Its Origins and Background*, p. 10.

triotism with the consciousness of nationality,[2] a set of demands derived from patriotism which incline the individual to personal sacrifices and action on behalf of his government,[3] and the assertion of a particular "we" against a "they" which includes the rest of the world.[4] The term "nationalism" may have three connotations—an ideology, a social movement, and a form of group consciousness.[5] One definition has attempted to incorporate all three: "Nationalism is the active solidarity of a larger human collectivity which shares a common culture, or a common fund of human experiences and interests, conceives of itself as a nation, and strives for political unity and self-government."[6] This description highlights the psychological and social-movement features of nationalism which will be examined in this study.

While there is controversy over the proper definition of nationalism, most scholars agree that the French Revolution was the first expression of this idea, which was to have such a dramatic impact upon mankind. Nationalism developed from the idea of popular sovereignty advanced by the bourgeoisie to challenge the absolute power of the crown. The existence or ideal of the centralized state was important for the development of this secular mass phenomenon. A common language, culture, or history often stimulated nationalism, but astute leadership and a shared will to form a nation were crucial for the realization of its aims. Nationalism was also a response to crisis, rapid change, tension, or conflict. In Europe it was an outgrowth of the Industrial Revolution, and in the less-developed countries it has been a reaction to colonialism and a means to achieve modernization and independence.[7] The breakup of traditional society and the emergence of the bourgeoisie have also contributed to the rise of nationalism in the Third World.[8]

Nationalism arose in Europe after the establishment of centralized government by absolute monarchs. The monarch's will was considered the national interest and his person represented

2. Carlton J. H. Hayes, *Nationalism: A Religion*, p. 2.

3. Leonard W. Doob, *Patriotism and Nationalism: Their Psychological Foundations*, p. 6.

4. Rupert Emerson, *From Empire to Nation: The Rise to Self-Assertion of Asian and African Peoples*, p. 213.

5. Konstantin Symmons-Symonolewicz, *Modern Nationalism*, p. 26.

6. Ibid., p. 27.

7. Ibid., p. 31.

8. Emerson, *From Empire to Nation*, p. 93.

the nation. The European monarchs consolidated their power with the assistance of merchants who desired the greater security and wider economic opportunities of a centralized government and a single legal system. The use of an official language and the Hundred Years War nurtured popular feelings of a separate national identity and loyalty, and the Reformation brought about the creation of national churches, breaking the hold of the universal Church. The monarchs adopted mercantilism in their domestic and foreign policies to advance the power of the state by enriching the royal coffers, thus providing the necessary resources for war. However, while both mercantilism and the subsequent policy of laissez-faire were concerned with national goals, the key difference was that mercantilism reflected the belief that the interest of the nation was identical with the interest of its monarch.[9]

The idea of democratic nationalism espoused by Jean-Jacques Rousseau was manifest in the French Revolution. The bourgeoisie, which had collaborated with the European monarchs against the nobility, came to power imbued with a liberal belief in individualism and a laissez-faire view of the role of the state. The bourgeoisie in the major Western countries agreed on the need for free trade to expand the international economy and shared a fear that the masses would challenge the rights of property. But despite this faith in laissez-faire, there was a close nexus between political power and economic power, best exemplified by the role of the British navy in bolstering English economic interests.[10] The Industrial Revolution intensified nationalism and the economic rivalry in the overseas search for markets and resources. The entire system of laissez-faire began to crumble after Germany adopted a protective tariff in 1879; soon other nations enacted tariffs and restrictions on foreign immigration. "But even more important was the new tendency towards a gradual amalgamation of the aims of commercial policy with the expansionist aspirations of the Great Powers, which more and more implied close cooperation between their diplomatic and military machinery and the leading financial and industrial interests."[11] According to Carlton Hayes, the aggressive imperialism of 1874–1914 was not primarily motivated by economic considerations but was a nationalistic phenomenon which

9. Edward Hallett Carr, *Nationalism and After*, p. 6.
10. Ibid., p. 16.
11. Royal Institute of International Affairs, *Nationalism*, p. 233.

reflected a "psychological reaction, an ardent desire on the part of statesmen to maintain or recover national prestige."[12] It was this political and economic challenge to the status quo which led to World War I.

One result of World War I was that national integration, even in economic policies, became the major concern of governments. This development coincided with the growth of mass democracy, the enhanced authority of the nation-state, and the increase in the number of nations. The popularization of the state through mass education, extension of the franchise, and the trade union movement created pressures on the state to defend wages and employment against foreign competition and to assume a welfare role: "The socialization of the nation has as its natural corollary the nationalization of socialism. . . ."[13] Beginning with the unification of Germany and Italy after 1871, the number of independent nations increased, spurred by nationalism and the principle of self-determination. These new nations employed economic nationalism to challenge the international division of labor which benefited a few Western European nations. The intense nationalism after World War I was related to economic weakness; depression caused unrest and a demand for strong governments to enforce unity, and the economic weakness of a regime compelled it to utilize political power to obtain commercial goals abroad.

From this brief discussion, certain features in the development of nationalism in the European context stand out. There has always been a close relationship between the economic and political manifestations of nationalism. The European middle class supported nationalism as a means to bolster their interests through economic liberalism. Then the laissez-faire economic order began to fall as the democratization of the nation-state led to calls for protectionism and social services. Nationalism stimulated the rise of new states like Germany and Italy, which rejected the existing division of labor and markets. The Industrial Revolution accentuated the international rivalry and spread the idea of nationalism. Industrialization became a national goal and a means to achieve political and economic independence. The economic weakness of a country tended to intensify nationalism, which led to an increase in the power of the central government over domes-

12. Hayes, *Nationalism: A Religion*, p. 97.
13. Carr, *Nationalism and After*, p. 19.

tic affairs and an assertive foreign policy. These developments were also present in the rise of nationalism in Latin America.

Economic Nationalism—A Matter of Perception

The definition of economic nationalism suggested by William E. Rappard will be employed in this study. He described it as "a doctrine destined to serve the nation by making it not richer, but freer, by promoting not its material welfare, but its independence of foreign influences. Economic nationalism is the policy of national self-sufficiency."[14] Another scholar elaborated on this definition by distinguishing between autarchy as an objective of economic nationalism and self-sufficiency as a by-product of policies which seek to achieve other goals. Self-sufficiency may be preliminary to engaging in aggressive warfare, a policy of insulating the domestic economy from the vicissitudes of the world economy, or a policy to diversify production and achieve a balanced national economy for prosperity and national power.[15] This latter objective appears to be the major consideration of Latin Americans.

The model of economic nationalism advanced by Harry Johnson in 1967 is perhaps the most applicable to Latin America; it offers a means to understand the motivations behind economic nationalism in the developing areas and how apparent irrational decisions by their governments may have a positive value in relation to their own political systems.[16] He argues that nationalism tends to produce a psychological income in the form of nationalistic satisfaction, which could offset the loss or deferment of material income. Under the emotional banner of nationalism the workers and peasants of a country might make great sacrifices for national prestige and independence, although economic nationalism might actually slow the real pace of economic development. Needed foreign capital might be barred, enterprises with high symbolic value encouraged, inefficient national industries protected, and public control and ownership expanded to allocate more jobs to nationals. A study of economic

14. Quoted in Michael A. Heilperin, *Studies in Economic Nationalism*, p. 18.

15. Ibid., pp. 19–20.

16. Harry G. Johnson, ed., *Economic Nationalism in Old and New States*, pp. 14–15.

nationalism in Mexico reaches a similar conclusion: "Economic nationalism may be a necessary input for economic development, and what superficially by the rules of immediate optimal allocation appears counter-productive may be the best investment that a developing nation can make. An investment in symbols, in national mythology, if successful in motivating persons to strive for economic ends and to forego consumption, is an important investment in human beings. . . ."[17]

The idea of psychological satisfaction is especially relevant to the current wave of economic nationalism in Latin America. It enables one to comprehend better the limitations of arguments by U.S. policy makers concerning the necessity of a favorable investment climate for economic growth, the inadequacy and perhaps futility of efforts to publicize the contributions of American private investment to economic growth, and the difficult path which must be navigated to formulate policies which mesh the private and public sectors in the development process of the hemisphere.

One examination of the psychological facet of nationalism notes that a sense of insecurity could lead to nationalistic attacks on outside groups.[18] The perceived threat of outside groups could give rise to economic nationalism regardless of the facts of the situation. However, a sense of security and satisfaction with their society would reduce the likelihood of hostile actions against outsiders. Nationalist attacks on the United States intensified as the political, economic, and cultural preeminence of the United States increased, belying juridical notions of equality or sovereignty. The interventions of the United States in hemispheric affairs made the Latin Americans "psychologically allergic" to past humiliations, and they responded angrily to any perceived affront or demeaning situation.[19]

The Unique Imperialism of the United States

There is considerable controversy over historical interpretations of the overseas expansion of the United States in the late nineteenth century, stemming from the various concepts of empire embraced by historians. While the United States did acquire

17. Manning Nash, "Economic Nationalism in Mexico," p. 84.
18. Doob, *Patriotism and Nationalism*, p. 258.
19. Everett E. Hagen, *On the Theory of Social Change*, p. 431.

and administer new territories during this period—the manifestations of a formal empire—the heart of the issue concerns the motivations behind American policy. Was the underlying policy of the United States to create a formal empire similar to those of the European powers, or to establish an informal empire relying on trade and economic penetration to achieve national objectives?

One school of thought argues that after 1861, under the impact of the Industrial Revolution, the United States was compelled to search for overseas markets. The economic depression of the 1890s emphasized the urgency of finding new outlets for American manufactured products and raised the specter of domestic political unrest and revolution in the minds of some national leaders. The fabled market potential of China appeared to be the solution to the problem of overproduction, which led to the adoption of the Open Door policy: "Instead of closed doors, open markets; instead of political dominion, economic hegemony; instead of large scale colonialism, informal empire. In short, a most interesting hybrid of anti-colonialism and economic imperialism."[20]

The notion of an informal empire reflected both America's faith in its economic superiority over European competitors (which would allow domination of the Chinese market through the access of the Open Door) and the fact that the United States lacked a political base in China. Such a policy also avoided the unsatisfactory alternatives of joining in the partition of China or a military alliance with England and Japan, which could involve the United States in an unpopular war in the Far East. Even antiannexationists agreed on the need for economic expansion. Informal empire through trade meant "that America could reap the material rewards of expansion without paying its prices or bearing its burdens."[21] The annexation of Hawaii, purchase of Alaska and the Midway Islands, and acquisition of Puerto Rico, the Philippines, and Cuba from Spain were not for their intrinsic economic worth or for the fulfillment of Manifest Destiny; they were deemed important because they provided access to and protection for the China market through the establishment of a network of coaling, cable, and naval stations along the trade route. According to this interpretation, U.S. interest in the Isthmian

20. Thomas J. McCormick, *China Market: America's Quest for Informal Empire, 1893–1901*, p. 128.
21. Ibid., p. 194.

canal in the 1890s was economic rather than strategic, since control of the canal would facilitate commercial expansion into Asia.[22]

Julius Pratt argues that American colonial policy of this period, though not perfect, was benevolent toward those living under it.[23] He stresses the American aims of material and educational improvement of the colonial people and development of their capacity for self-government. While Filipinos did rise up against U.S. rule, they later acquiesced to temporary American control until granted independence by the United States. American businessmen were at first skeptical about the need for colonies, which might be difficult and expensive to administer and could involve the United States in war. However, their attitude changed in 1898 when the territorial acquisitions from Spain appeared to open the China market to U.S. industry. Other individuals and groups hostile to colonialism also had second thoughts after the victories in the Spanish-American War. Although Spain's inability to end the Cuban war affected American economic interests—the United States had $40–50 million invested in Cuba and trade fell from $60 million in 1895 to $15 million in 1896—American intervention was seen as motivated by humanitarian rather than economic reasons.[24] Some businessmen informed the State Department that they would suffer more from a war with Spain than from the chaos of the Cuban rebellion against Spanish dominance. The Caribbean policy of the United States was thus based upon political and strategic considerations, rather than economic goals: ". . . in none of the five republics except Cuba were American financial interests large or important."[25] The objectives were to defend the Panama Canal and to encourage democratic processes.

The belief that strategic and political factors were the principal motivations behind U.S. imperialist policies in the hemisphere is also embraced by other scholars. They point out that American interventions were largely confined to the Caribbean, Central America, and Mexico; the geographic proximity of this area made it important for continental security. Early American diplomatic efforts sought to prevent the exclusive control of an

22. Walter La Feber, *The New Empire: An Interpretation of American Expansion, 1860–1898*, and William Appleman Williams, *The Tragedy of American Diplomacy*.

23. Julius W. Pratt, *America's Colonial Experiment*, p. 3.

24. Ibid., p. 43.

25. Ibid., p. 116.

Isthmian canal by any European power, but in the 1880s strategic and commercial incentives led the United States to pursue a policy to obtain exclusive control over an interoceanic canal. The ideas of Admiral Alfred T. Mahan on the need for a two-ocean navy for national defense bolstered the case for controlling such a canal. Fear that the financial delinquency of the Caribbean republics could lead to European intervention, sanctioned under international law, pushed the United States toward a policy of "preventive imperialism."[26] With the exception of Cuba, American trade and investment in the Caribbean were not significant compared to other parts of the world. The State Department solicited American banks to extend loans to Caribbean republics for the stabilization of their economies, rather than U.S. banking interests appealing for government intervention on their behalf—the conventional image of Dollar Diplomacy. Financial control was considered necessary to achieve the political and strategic objective of preventing foreign involvement in hemispheric affairs.[27]

The United States established protectorates in the five Caribbean republics to stabilize their economies and prevent European action to collect debts. Another goal, especially under President Woodrow Wilson, was to substitute democratic procedures for the violent politics of the region. During this period of overt hegemony, the United States tried to bring order to their finances, constructed schools and roads, established health and sanitation facilities, and created professional military forces and constabularies. Despite these efforts to institute fiscal responsibility and democratic government, matters often reverted back to the original chaotic situation after the United States withdrew. Sometimes the United States was invited back by local governments unable to maintain control, or was compelled to intervene again to reinstitute financial order.

The different interpretations of this period of U. S. "imperialism" indicate that U.S. policy sought to achieve a number of diverse objectives. Conflicts and contradictions among these goals reflected the lack of a consistent, coherent American policy

26. J. Lloyd Mecham, *A Survey of United States–Latin American Relations*, p. 69.

27. Other scholars who support the view that strategic considerations were more important than economic factors are Edwin Lieuwen, *U.S. Policy in Latin America*, p. 35; Norman A. Bailey, *Latin America in World Politics*, p. 53; and Federico G. Gil, *Latin American–United States Relations*, p. 88.

in the hemisphere. Instead of a single, unifying theme in U.S.–Latin American relations, U.S. foreign policy manifested the diversity of American interests. Some groups felt a strong economic need to search for overseas markets, while others were more concerned about the capacity of the United States to defend its territory. Certainly America's faith in democracy and belief in social justice were factors in the decisions to intervene abroad.

Given the lack of a unifying purpose in U.S. policy toward Latin America, it is reasonable to assume that Latin American countries had their own perceptions of U.S. intentions in the region. The Latin American interpretation of U.S. intervention in the domestic affairs of hemispheric republics will be discussed next.

Blossoming of Latin American Economic Nationalism

Arthur Whitaker has observed that at its inception Latin American nationalism performed an integrative function by filling the void created by the independence movement of 1810–25. A similar situation existed in the thirteen colonies when British authority was severed.[28] The first phase of Latin American nationalism, which lasted throughout most of the nineteenth century, emulated the liberal nationalism of Europe and the United States, and manifestations of economic nationalism were only rudimentary.[29] Foreign capital was welcomed, often on very favorable terms. In fact, it was the warm *abrazo* and close collaboration between the traditional elites and foreign investors which subsequently gave rise to economic nationalism. The turbulence of the postindependence years was largely caused by the antinationalist sentiments of localities and regions and strong class distinctions; nationalism as a unifying force in the early years was thus severely restricted by the Latin American provincial loyalties.[30]

Economic nationalism arose in the 1890s, partly through the influence of men like Juan Bautista Justo, the founder of the Argentine Socialist Party.[31] The close association of the land-

28. Arthur P. Whitaker, *Nationalism in Latin America, Past and Present*, p. 10.

29. Ibid., p. 20.

30. John J. Johnson, ed., *Continuity and Change in Latin America*, p. 187.

31. Whitaker, *Nationalism in Latin America, Past and Present*, p. 21.

owner oligarchy with foreign enterprises centered in export activities brought the landowners under attack as collaborators in the exploitation of their own nations. Thus, it is difficult to distinguish nationalism in domestic politics from nationalism in international politics; the antiimperialist attacks were closely linked to attacks on the local oligarchy, who were called *vendepatristas*. An element of escalation in the rhetoric and politics of economic nationalism was introduced as the Latin American elites attempted to "refute the charge by proving themselves superpatriots and out-Hectoring the Hectors of populist nationalism."[32]

Nationalist sentiment had a distinct xenophobic quality at the turn of the century, when the hostility to foreign capitalists was blended with a hypersensitive cultural nationalism, as the United States emerged as the most powerful influence in the hemisphere. The publication of *Ariel* in 1900 by the Uruguayan writer José Enrique Rodó set the scene with the characterization of Ariel as the noble Latin American spirit and Caliban as the crass, materialistic North American. *Ariel* marked the beginning of Yankee-phobia.[33] The same theme was repeatedly evoked by Latin American intellectuals defending their culture against the encroachment of the United States. Jesús Semprúm wrote in 1918 of the "rough and obtuse Calibans, swollen by brutal appetites, the enemies of all idealisms, furiously enamored of the dollar, insatiable gulpers of whisky and sausages—swift, overwhelming, fierce, clownish."[34] But behind the vitriolic attacks on the United States was a reaction to their encounter with Western capitalism and the United States as the archetype of the Western industrial powers.[35] Hence, the *coloso del norte* became both admired and feared for its industrialization and power.

Economic nationalism was in full flower by 1910, and its anti-foreign-capital theme was prominent in the Mexican Revolution of 1910, the Uruguayan government of President José Batlle y Ordóñez, and in Juan Perón's declaration of Argentina's economic independence in 1947. In the twentieth century, Latin American nationalism became "much stronger, more diversified,

32. Arthur P. Whitaker and David C. Jordan, *Nationalism in Contemporary Latin America*, p. 182.

33. Gerhard Masur, *Nationalism in Latin America: Diversity and Unity*, p. 67.

34. Quoted in Donald M. Dozer, *Are We Good Neighbors?: Three Decades of Inter-American Relations, 1930–1960*, p. 4.

35. Masur, *Nationalism in Latin America: Diversity and Unity*, p. 70.

and more destructive. It became less nostalgic and benign and more dynamic, with a strong tinge of xenophobia."[36] As the depression struck in the 1930s, populist nationalism exerted its influence throughout the hemisphere. Led by members of the middle groups spawned by early efforts at industrialization, it sought to mobilize the support of the growing number of urban workers by concentrating on socioeconomic issues spiced with antiforeign attacks. The central government was called upon to actively intervene to promote industrialization, and its domestic power was asserted to be supreme, even over foreigners and foreign firms.

A new phase of nationalism developed as the middle sectors consolidated their position and took over large sections of the economy formerly in the hands of foreigners. The masses whom they had awakened as their allies against the entrenched oligarchies and foreigners demanded, as payment for their assistance, more tangible benefits in the form of higher wages, more jobs, and greater state services. The Latin American businessmen employed their influence to dissuade politicians from responding to the workers' demands. It is this resistance which is currently being attacked by the Latin American left and sympathetic elements within the military and the Church, who see the Latin American businessman as impeding socioeconomic progress. The purpose of the 1968 and 1969 military interventions in Peru and Bolivia, respectively, was nominally to overcome these and other obstacles to economic development and to fulfill the people's desire for basic reforms.

In 1967 Brazilian economist Roberto de Oliveira Campos attacked the "monopolistic nationalism" of some Latin American industrialists, who "seek to use nationalism as a device to preserve national monopolies and stave off foreign competition."[37] He strongly criticized "phantasmagoric nationalism," which rebels against a form of colonialism never evident in U.S.–Latin American relations, and its other variant, "opportunistic nationalism . . . through which unscrupulous politicians maneuver to divert the people's attention from the real cause of underdevelopment and seek solace from the frustrations of underdevelopment by transferring the guilt to foreign scape-

36. Whitaker and Jordan, *Nationalism in Contemporary Latin America*, p. 13.

37. Roberto de Oliveira Campos, *Reflections on Latin American Development*, p. 24.

goats."[38] These same sentiments were voiced by the respondents in the 1970 survey of the Council of the Americas.

In 1962 Salvador de Madariaga tried to explain to North Americans the nationalistic resentment of Latin Americans toward the United States. He argued that Latin American frustration, generated from feelings of neglect and powerlessness, became focused against the United States, which had become the "omnipresent, omniactive nation" in the Americas: "A Score of weak nations, poor in the midst of their natural riches, scattered over huge territories, heirs to a powerful and colourful past, but divided by nature and character, struggling to raise themselves to the status they think theirs by natural right, look with impatience, and at times with resentment, on the power, wealth and success of a *parvenu* nation which was still uncouth and rustic when they were already highly civilized."[39] In the following section, an overview of the history of U.S. relations with Latin America will provide a greater understanding of why these beliefs are still so tenaciously and passionately embraced in Latin America.

Shadow of the Colossus

Great Britain was the dominant power in the Western Hemisphere from the time of Latin America's independence movement until 1896. British interest in Latin America was centered on naval-military objectives—the possession of bases and fueling rights to insure British domination of the seas.[40] A boundary dispute between Venezuela and British Guiana led to the famous declaration of President Grover Cleveland's Secretary of State Richard Olney to Great Britain on July 20, 1895: "Today the United States is practically sovereign on this continent, and its fiat is law upon the subjects to which it confines its interposition. . . ."[41] The British, fortunately, did not accept the challenge which the United States was ill prepared to enforce, but their acquiescence in the dispute marked the beginning of the transition of the "United States replacing the British as the *caudillo* of the Western Hemisphere."[42] When the United

38. Ibid.

39. Salvador de Madariaga, *Latin America between the Eagle and the Bear*, p. 1.

40. Bailey, *Latin America in World Politics*, pp. 41–43.

41. Ibid., p. 44.

42. Ibid.

States acquired Cuba and Puerto Rico in the Spanish-American War of 1898, the British withdrew their fleet from the Caribbean and in 1903 dismantled their Caribbean bases. The separation of Panama from Colombia and its declaration of sovereignty was accomplished with the cooperation of the United States and was not opposed in any European capital. In 1904 the change was completed and American private capital began to flow into Latin America.

Although the Monroe Doctrine of 1823 has come to play such a central role in U.S.–Latin American relations, its proclamation had very little deterrent effect on the policies of the European powers. The Europeans "generally viewed it with annoyance and contempt."[43] Latin American countries seeking treaties with the United States to prevent intervention by European countries were rebuffed. The limited military strength of the United States inhibited U.S. protests over British actions in Central America and the Falkland Islands, and the French blockade of Buenos Aires and seizure of Veracruz in 1838. Spain called Secretary of State William Seward's bluff in 1861, when he protested the Spanish annexation of the Dominican Republic. Throughout the joint European expedition in Mexico and subsequent establishment and demise of the French-backed empire of Maximilian in the 1860s, the Monroe Doctrine was never mentioned by name in the diplomatic correspondence of the U.S. government.[44] Nor did reference to the Monroe Doctrine prove to be a barrier to European participation in the construction of an interoceanic canal.

The 1904 proclamation by President Theodore Roosevelt of the right of the United States to act as "an international police power" in the hemisphere was an attempt to justify the numerous interventions of the United States in Latin American affairs, often to protect private American financial interests. The following paragraphs indicate how vigorously the U.S. government employed its "big stick" in violation of Latin American sovereignty, under the guise of preventing European incursions: "In accordance with the Roosevelt Corollary, the United States took over the administration of the Dominican customhouses in 1904, to ensure payment of debts to European countries. In 1906, Cuba was intervened, under the formal terms of the Platt Amendment to the Cuban Independence Act. In 1907, the United States actively

43. Mecham, *Survey of United States–Latin American Relations*, p. 51.
44. Ibid., p. 61.

pressured for the adoption of a Central American treaty which it hoped would provide a tranquil environment for the Panama Canal it was already digging. American troops intervened in Panama itself in 1908, 1912, and 1918. In 1912, the United States established a virtual protectorate over Nicaragua, maintaining a sizable garrison of Marines. In 1914, American marines occupied Vera Cruz in an attempt to topple the government of Victoriano Huerta in Mexico. In 1916, General Pershing invaded Mexico in an unsuccessful effort to capture and punish the bandit-revolutionary Pancho Villa, who had sacked an American border town.

"Meanwhile, in 1915, in response to conditions of continuous chaos, the United States occupied Haiti, later signing a protectorate agreement. Having evacuated Cuba in 1909, American troops returned in 1916, leaving again in 1920. . . . In 1916, the Marines occupied the Dominican Republic, remaining until 1924. In 1926, Nicaragua was occupied. In 1923, another Central American treaty was signed with the prodding of the United States. . . ."[45] It is not difficult to understand why recollections of this period still scar Latin American memories and mar official and corporate relations of the United States.

Even though President Franklin Roosevelt subsequently announced the Good Neighbor policy with the signing of the nonintervention pledge of 1933, the specter of the military and political power of the United States being wielded to secure the interests of its businessmen in the area has continued to haunt the inter-American system. It is hard to forget the findings of a 1962 report to the Foreign Affairs Committee which listed over 100 instances when the U.S. president used military force in Latin America without the permission of Congress—and the chronology concluded with the year 1933. Thus, the actions of the U.S. government encouraged the anti-Yankee element of Latin American nationalism, fusing to it a passionate antipathy toward the extension of American investment in their countries. Francisco García Calderón, a Peruvian diplomat and writer, in a 1913 book bitterly declared: "Warnings, advice, distrust, invasion of capital, plans of financial hegemony—all these justify the anxiety of the southern peoples. . . . Neither irony nor grace nor scepticism, gifts of old civilizations, can make way against the plebeian brutality,

45. Bailey, *Latin America in World Politics*, p. 49.

the excessive optimism, the violent individualism of the [North American] people."[46]

Cuban patriot José Marti characterized the United States as the land "which proclaims its right by self-coronation to govern, by geographic morality, on the continent, and announces, through the mouths of its statesmen, in the press and in the pulpit, in the banquet hall and in congress, at the same time that it puts its hand on one island and tries to buy another, that all North America has to belong to it and that its imperial right from the isthmus on down has to be recognized."[47]

Campos called the Roosevelt Corollary "an extreme expression of the concept of patronizing imperialism."[48] Madariaga saw two dogmas in the Monroe Doctrine: "The dogma of the infallibility of the American President and the dogma of the immaculate conception of American foreign policy. . . ."[49] The feelings expressed by these Latin American intellectuals and statesmen were fervently shared by other segments of Latin American society.

The extreme actions of the United States to protect its perceived national interests provoked extreme retaliatory acts by Latin American governments. Although Latin Americans could not directly challenge the economic and political power of the United States, their response was not limited solely to fiery anti-Yankee speeches and articles. The highly visible presence of American firms provided an immediate target for the frustration and bitterness of Latin American nationalists. In the eyes of extreme nationalists, expropriation of American properties was the only suitable and forceful response that their governments could make to U.S. intervention and dominance. Increased taxes on foreign-owned enterprises, restrictions on foreign investment, and protective tariffs were simply means of tweaking the nose of the colossus of the North. Nationalization of U.S. interests was a defiance of the power of the United States; nationalization restored the wounded honor and pride of Latin Americans. The history of U.S. relations with Mexico, Cuba, Peru, and Chile manifests this pattern of events.

46. Francisco García Calderón, "Commercial and Cultural Intervention," p. 39.

47. Quoted in Robert N. Burr, *Our Troubled Hemisphere: Perspectives on United States–Latin American Relations*, p. 6.

48. Campos, *Reflections on Latin American Development*, p. 14.

49. Madariaga, *Latin America between the Eagle and the Bear*, p. 74.

EXPROPRIATION—THE ULTIMATE WEAPON OF NATIONALISTS

Latin American sensitivity and hostility toward foreign investment has always been most acute in the extractive industries and public utilities. Memories of past foreign interventions and the dubious terms and exploitative nature of many foreign concessions, often granted by venal regimes, have provided extreme nationalists with highly visible targets in their *gritos* to protect the national patrimony from the corrupt alliance between foreign capitalists and the *vendepatristas* of the old oligarchy. In prerevolutionary Mexico, foreigners dominated Mexico's mining, utilities, industry, and commerce.[50] After the Revolution of 1910 and the subsequent years of turbulence and violence, resentments grew concerning the role of foreign investment in controlling the fate of Mexico's future development. These nationalistic feelings were aggravated by memories of U.S. intercession in the Mexican Revolution, when President Woodrow Wilson ordered the navy to occupy Veracruz and General Pershing to pursue Pancho Villa into Mexico.

A vice-consul in Mexico during those stormy times recalls: "Some companies seemed to go out of their way to antagonize Mexicans. At times they gave the impression that they considered themselves above Mexican law. . . ."[51] The resentment of the arrogant and derisive attitudes of foreigners toward Mexican laws and institutions reached its peak in 1938, when President Lázaro Cárdenas expropriated American oil properties after a perceived affront to the nation's dignity during a dispute over the wage demands of oil workers. The greatest significance of the event was the "transcendental assertion of economic nationalism," when virtually all segments of Mexican society warmly applauded the action, including the Church and Mexican businessmen.[52] Cárdenas's emotional reply to U.S. claims that Mexicans would not be able to get the oil out of the ground reflected a definite emphasis on the psychological-satisfaction facet of economic nationalism: "If we cannot get it out, it will stay there. Then it will still be Mexican oil."[53] The positive value of these psychological rewards, which may appear to be detri-

50. Frank Brandenburg, *The Making of Modern Mexico*, p. 40.
51. William L. Beaulac, *A Diplomat Looks at Aid to Latin America*, p. 69.
52. Brandenburg, *Making of Modern Mexico*, p. 95.
53. Quoted in Nash, "Economic Nationalism in Mexico," p. 78.

mental to goals such as economic growth, was highlighted by one scholar: ". . . nationalism in the Mexican context played a motivational role akin to that which the Protestant ethic is alleged to have played in the development of the Atlantic community. It energized and gave purpose to the strivings of large numbers of Mexicans, and at the same time allowed them to forego immediate returns in favor of the larger end of *Mexicanidad*. . . . In the flow of history, the rapid nationalism came with the least economic opportunity, and the most pragmatic nationalism came with the greatest economic alternatives."[54]

Mexico has since acquired state ownership of the electrical power industry, railways, and telegraph systems, and the telephone system is almost totally government-owned. Mining laws require at least 51 per cent Mexican ownership, offering tax incentives to attract foreign investors. "Mexicanization" in other sectors of the economy is encouraged when investors apply for concessions; they must usually agree to make stock available to Mexican citizens. In 1966 new foreign investments in banking, finance, and insurance were severely restricted.

The economic presence of the United States was also pervasive in Cuba before the revolution. Americans owned 90 per cent of the telephones and utilities and 50 per cent of the railways and controlled 40 per cent of the sugar production (a decline from 70 per cent in 1928).[55] In 1960 the total U.S. investment in Cuba was $1.5 billion. Cuba's economic dependence was also reflected in 1957 trade patterns; Cuba exported 60 per cent of its products to the United States and 80 per cent of its imports were from the United States.[56] President John F. Kennedy acknowledged this situation and the political costs to the United States in 1963: "I believe there is no country in the world where economic colonialism, humiliations, and exploitation were worse than in Cuba in part owing to my country's policies during the Batista regime."[57] On a per capita basis, American investments in public utilities were over ten times larger in Cuba than in any other Latin American country. The visibility of these investments to consumers, the importance of utilities to economic development, and the

54. Ibid., p. 83.
55. Leland L. Johnson, "U.S. Business Interests in Cuba and the Rise of Castro," p. 443.
56. J. Wilner Sundelson, "A Business Perspective," p. 100.
57. Quoted in Ronald Steel, *Pax Americana*, p. 221.

Cuban telephone company's prior relationship with the dictator Fulgencio Batista were factors which compelled Fidel Castro to take action against the Cuban telephone company's proposed phone rate increase and to order the reduction of electricity rates shortly after he came to power.

The heavy American investment in the sugar industry meant that an eventual conflict would occur with Castro's agrarian reform program. But the refusal of American refineries to process Russian crude oil was the issue which led to the nationalization of the oil refineries. President Dwight Eisenhower responded by cutting the Cuban sugar quota. One month later Castro expropriated the telephone and electric utilities, oil marketing facilities, and all U.S.–owned sugar mills. What happened to foreign and Cuban private investments afterwards is well known. In March 1968 the small private businesses remaining in Cuba were confiscated. Now only limited agricultural production remains in the private sector of the Cuban economy.[58]

The nationalization of the International Petroleum Company (IPC), a subsidiary of Standard Oil of New Jersey, won praise for the unconstitutional military regime of General Juan Velasco Alvarado from both the left and the right. IPC had been the focal point of Peruvian national wrath for many years. The overthrown president, Fernando Belaúnde Terry, had failed to fulfill his 1964 campaign pledge that he would settle the long-simmering dispute within ninety days. General Velasco emotionally declared after the seizure: "The case of the International Petroleum Company is the problem of a company that has transgressed and offended our laws, usurped our rights by using all available means, and one that is determined to create conflict between two friendly governments."[59]

Goodwin has described a 1967 incident between IPC and the Peruvian government which influenced General Velasco's subsequent actions against the U.S. firm. It is an excellent example of the genesis of economic nationalism. In 1967 inflation forced the government to cut the value of the Peruvian sol by about half. IPC requested an increase in the government-regulated price for gasoline and was refused; immediately the company threatened

58. For full discussion of the 1968 intensification of the Cuban Revolution, see Carmelo Mesa-Lago, "The Revolutionary Offensive," pp. 22–29ff.

59. Richard Goodwin, "Letter from Peru," p. 43.

to stop importing the gasoline needed to make up the difference between the production of the country and its needs. The minister of war reacted by calling the general manager of IPC to a meeting and threatening to seize the IPC property if importation was halted. The company withdrew its threat and several months later was permitted to raise its prices. General Velasco had attended the meeting and was enraged that Peru was vulnerable to acts of a foreign company acting partly under the protection of a foreign government.

The Peruvian military regime also surprised the oligarchy and liberal critics by decreeing a sweeping agrarian reform. Democratically elected Belaúnde Terry had been unable to overcome the opposition of powerful landowners in the Peruvian Congress to enact his proposals for land reform. General Velasco's decree limited the size of the landholdings, encouraged formation of cooperatives, and expropriated foreign-held lands, including 25,000 acres of sugar plantation land and sugar mills owned by the American firm W. R. Grace and Company. The unusual occurrence of a military regime enacting a broad reform which had been encouraged by the United States but frustrated through the democratic process, drew an interesting response from officials. Assistant Secretary of State for Inter-American Affairs Charles Meyer, still negotiating on Peru's nationalization of IPC, frankly told the Foreign Affairs Committee: "I will be honest with all of you, and say, I don't know what position there is one can take, having been, as a partner in the Alliance for Progress, an exponent of agrarian reform, and redistribution of large estates among more people."[60]

The Christian Democratic regime of President Eduardo Frei, elected in 1964, embarked upon a "Chileanization" program in the copper industry under the slogan "Revolution in Liberty." The fact that copper accounts for about 80 per cent of Chile's foreign exchange earnings was a central factor. The large American-owned Kennecott Copper Corporation agreed to the Chileanization of its El Teniente mine, selling 51 per cent of its mining operations to the government and promising to reinvest in expansion of copper production. Anaconda, which obtained two-thirds of its copper from its Chilean operations, agreed to the Chilean government's purchase of 25 per cent of its new Exotica

60. U.S., Congress, House, Committee on Foreign Affairs, *Hearings, Foreign Assistance Act of 1969*, p. 1168.

mine.[61] The United States helped to finance the partnerships and expansion programs through Export-Import Bank loans and investment guaranties. Despite an agreement two years earlier, President Frei announced in his 1969 state-of-the-union message that the government intended to have a greater share in the ownership of the Anaconda copper mines.

In the ensuing negotiations, Anaconda was well aware of the pressures on Frei to nationalize the mines and the example of Peru's expropriation of IPC. On June 26 Anaconda accepted Chile's offer to "nationalize by agreement," in order to avert expropriation by legislation. The new agreement provided not only for Chileanization of Anaconda's operations, but also for government purchase of 51 per cent ownership by September 1, 1969, and an arrangement whereby Chile could buy the remaining shares anytime between 1973 and 1982.[62] While observing that the agreement might weaken prospects for new investments in Chile and Latin America, James Fowler of the Agency for International Development (AID) commented: "In the long run, U.S. investment in manufacturing and other mineral investment in Chile may actually be strengthened as the reduced role of investment by U.S. companies can no longer be used as a political irritant."[63]

Chile's Socialist President Salvador Allende won with an election platform which stated: "The central objective is to replace the present economic structure; ending the power of monopolistic national and foreign capital, . . . in order to begin the construction of socialism. . . ."[64] On December 21, 1970, President Allende proposed an amendment to the Chilean Constitution which declared that the state had "absolute, exclusive, inalien, and incontrovertible control" over all mineral rights in the country. In his announcement, Allende attacked the foreign-owned copper companies for their exploitation of the natural wealth of Chile: "Between 1930 and 1969, 3.7 billion dollars left our boundaries to increase even more the strength of firms which, on an international scale, control the copper deposits on five continents.

61. Eric N. Baklanoff, "U.S. Mineral Investments in a Nationalist Setting: Chile's Copper Mining Industry, 1944–1967," *Proceedings of the Council of Economics*, p. 249.

62. *New York Times*, June 27, 1969, p. 1.

63. U.S., Congress, House, Committee on Appropriations, *Hearings, Foreign Assistance and Related Agencies Appropriations for 1970*, pt. 2:1751.

64. *Washington Post*, January 3, 1971, p. B-1.

. . . I want to point out that 3.7 billion dollars is 40 per cent of Chile's total wealth, of the accumulated effort of Chileans over a period of 400 years. Roughly 40 per cent of that wealth left Chile between 1930 and 1969, and we cannot forget this fact."[65] Allende's proposed terms for nationalization authorized the Chilean comptroller general's office to determine the amount of compensation to the mining companies. Compensation would be in annual cash payments over a thirty-year period with a yearly interest rate of 3 per cent. U.S. firms were especially worried over a clause which would deduct the "excessive profits" of the years 1955–70 from the compensation payments.

In February 1971, the Chilean Senate approved the constitutional amendment, but accepted changes which offered greater flexibility on the period over which compensation was to be paid and raised the maximum interest rate to no less than 33 per cent per year. In September 1971, President Allende announced that $774 million in "excessive profits" would be deducted from compensation paid to U.S. copper companies with interests in nationalized Chilean mines. The deductions were based upon the amount of profits allegedly earned by the American firms above 10 per cent on their holdings since 1955. Anaconda placed the value of its Chilean investment at about $458 million and Kennecott at $140.7 million in its annual report for 1970. While the Chilean foreign minister subsequently stated that the companies would be charged for only 49 per cent of the "excess profits" taken during the period that the mines were jointly owned with the Chilean government, the comptroller general ruled in October 1971 that the American copper companies should receive no compensation for their nationalized holdings. The government of Chile also nationalized the holdings of Bethlehem Steel Corporation, "requisitioned" a Ford motor plant and used it to produce Fiats, and assumed management control of Chile's major telephone company, which is 70 per cent owned by International Telephone and Telegraph.

In conclusion, one can readily discern the genesis of Latin American economic nationalism in the emotional reaction to the dominance and interventionist role of the United States in the Western Hemisphere. While the Latin American hostility to foreign investment extends to European as well as U.S. capital,

65. *Prensa Latina*, December 23, 1970.

the growth of the colossus of the North overshadowed the fears and memories of the imperialist policies of the European powers. Fear of the political, economic, and military might of the United States, combined with a sense of cultural superiority and antipathy to the alleged materialistic values of the United States, gave rise to the "defensive" economic nationalism of the region.

Emotional or psychological motivations were often the foremost considerations of Latin American leaders, who recognized that rhetorical lambasts at the United States and its investors would bring popular acclaim and support from the general public, obviating or obscuring the need for fundamental reforms, new investment capital, and a rational allocation of resources for economic development. This situation will be more evident when the debate over the role of private enterprise in economic development is examined.

2. Private Enterprise

An Exotic Import

THE UNITED STATES has promoted private enterprise as the most dynamic agent of economic development, but this approach has encountered considerable resistance in Latin America. The image of capitalism is strongly colored by memories of the unsavory actions of earlier foreign investors, who resorted to political manipulation, bribery, and foreign intervention to amass profits at the expense of the host country. But these historic experiences with capitalism are not the only obstacle. The Latin American belief in the state as the major force in the economic life of the region, which dates back to the days of the Spanish empire, conflicts with the laissez-faire approach advocated by foreign investors. This chapter will discuss these historical experiences and cultural factors which diminish the appeal of capitalism and affect the attitudes of Latin American businessmen and society toward private enterprise.

THE FOREIGN CAPITALIST—A SHADY PAST

The image of private enterprise and capitalism held by Latin Americans today was created during the heyday of Dollar Diplomacy. Foreign investors are still remembered for their bribery and manipulation of local politics and the interventions of their governments to protect and expand private business interests in the hemisphere. In 1943, Uruguayan Alberto Zum Felde wrote in an essay: "Is it not proved that most of the 'revolutions,' frequent in this America, have been secretly promoted, financed and made use of by agents of foreign capitalism? Is it not equally proved that as many of the 'revolutions' had no other aim than to seize hold of the government in order to be able to negotiate from there with the big financial trusts which enabled illustrious statesmen to amass fat fortunes on the basis of the enslavement of the nation? Is it not a fact that the Chaco war, which bled Bolivia and Paraguay white for over two years, was secretly ruled by the rival interests of foreign oil companies?"[1] Germán Arciniegas attacked the corrupting effects of U.S. commercial activities in Latin America. He charged that American banks pressured the defenseless Latin American states into asking for loans, bribed the sons of presidents and government ministers, and encouraged the prostitution of the morality of these poor nations.[2] Madariaga highlighted some of the tricks employed by foreign investors during the era of "unscrupulous capitalism," such as watering capital and charging exorbitant prices for goods and services far exceeding their actual value.[3] The stormy years of the regime of Getulio Vargas in Brazil often found economic nationalism raging against foreign oil interests. Vargas fanned the flames of Brazilian nationalism in his alleged suicide note after his overthrow in 1954. His final words to his people placed the blame for his death on international economic and financial circles which had sought to thwart his efforts to obtain social liberty for all.[4]

An investigation by the U.S. Senate Finance Committee in 1932 confirmed many of the Latin American charges.[5] It was revealed that the lucrative commissions paid to investment bankers for floating South American securities often resulted in bribery, misrepresentation, and the draining of many Latin American treasuries of scarce and badly needed resources. One New York firm in the 1920s bribed the son of the Peruvian president-dictator in order to handle Peru's bond issues, while another firm

1. Quoted in Salvador de Madariaga, *Latin America between the Eagle and the Bear*, p. 7.
2. Angel del Rio, *The Clash and Attraction of Two Cultures*, p. 107.
3. Madariaga, *Latin America between the Eagle and the Bear*, p. 16.
4. DeLesseps Morrison, *Latin American Mission*, p. 216.
5. William P. Glade, *The Latin American Economies*, pp. 262–63.

paid the fee to the son-in-law of the Cuban president. Sometimes loans were floated but not utilized for the stated public project. Some U.S. bankers sought to increase their profits, even above the generous commissions and fees offered by Latin American governments, by deluding potential investors. A fictitious market would be created by bidding up the prices of the outstanding securities of a country before the issuance of new bonds.

The stigma of the past frustrates the current efforts of many U.S. firms to be good corporate citizens in their host country. Even though the American employer may offer higher wages and better working conditions than indigenous companies, the emotional issue of economic nationalism precludes a candid acknowledgment by public officials or public recognition of the "new" American businessman. One study found that Brazilian ultranationalist labor leaders would admit only privately the benefits of working for a North American firm over a local company. Brazilian employees of American companies feared being labeled an *entreguista,* one who would sacrifice the interests of his nation for personal gain, which carried an odious public stigma. A 1958 public opinion survey revealed that a sizable portion of the Brazilian population had a clear understanding of the meaning of *entreguismo.*[6]

Therefore, this early image of capitalism, based upon experiences reminiscent of the robber baron era in the United States, impedes the rational acceptance of private enterprise as a dynamic, constructive force in Latin America's struggle for economic development and social justice. While this may have been simply one historical period, the Latin American perception of American firms as exploiters and political manipulators continues to affect their attitudes toward U.S. investment. As suggested earlier, they have become "psychologically allergic" to the fear of foreign exploitation and domination.

The State—Friend, Not Foe

Colombia's former President Alberto Lleras Camargo observed after World War II that "the laissez-faire, free enterprise system has always been an exotic plant in Latin America, where the

6. Claude McMillan, "Industrial Leaders in Latin America," p. 39.

tradition of government control was rooted in three hundred years of Spanish and Portuguese rule."[7] In his excellent study *The Latin American Economies*, William Glade echoes that statement, rebutting the historians who interpreted the Spanish conquest as the work of individuals and private enterprise; he convincingly marshals facts to substantiate the early and sustained interventionist role of the state in Latin America's economic history.

The Spanish crown, watchful of any groups which might challenge its absolute power, was loath to allow its New World colonies to be organized by private monopolists, chartered companies, or recipients of feudal grants. While there were exceptions, they were closely supervised by representatives of the crown and the Church. Property rights were carefully prescribed, with the preeminent right of the crown establishing the basis for the twentieth-century doctrine of the social function of property: "Thus, in the concept of the *real hacienda*, the New World became the private estate of the crown in which private ownership was impossible without special dispensation. Even when the royal patrimony was alienated, the disposition of property rights seems not to have been absolute. Original title to minerals remained vested in the crown, as the royalty payments demanded of mine operators indicated. Property use was almost always legally subject to public regulation, and intermittent decrees suggest that, in theory at least, even land grants were conditional, and private property rights were contingent upon the crown's satisfaction that they were serving a public function."[8]

The Spanish did not follow mercantilistic policies toward their colonies to further the commercial and industrial development of the parent economy. Instead, Spanish actions were less specific and often contradictory, with the New World possessions benefiting primarily the royal treasury, the administrative system, and the clergy.[9] This was attributed to the Iberian disdain for manual labor and commerce. It was only after a change in dynasty that the French influence resulted in a more mercantilistic orientation toward the Spanish colonies. The state controlled access to commercial and trading opportunities, and in the private sector the influence of the state in the artisan guilds, *obrajes*, and

7. Arthur P. Whitaker and David C. Jordan, *Nationalism in Contemporary Latin America*, p. 191.

8. Glade, *Latin American Economies*, p. 58.

9. Ibid., p. 62.

consulados was overwhelming. The extensive interventionism of the state in manufacturing, according to Glade, stunted its growth and contributions to economic development. A key factor to note was that opportunities for material gain in the guilds and *obrajes* "depended less upon production and marketing efficiency than on the exercise of political influence to obtain more favorable regulatory treatment."[10]

Glade would challenge the conclusion of Stein and Stein that the colonial mining boom was "a classic example of private entrepreneurship in which miners, merchants, and the state collaborated and shared the returns."[11] Since the mining industry was a major source of revenue to the Spanish treasury, it was placed under close supervision and received extensive assistance from the crown. To stimulate mine production, the state supplied tools and instruments, technicians, loans, grants of funds, offers of aristocratic status, exemption from imprisonment for debt, tax and royalty reductions, and reduced prices for imported supplies. The mine operators were also subsidized through the *mita* system of coerced labor. However, the private mining sector continued to follow unsound business practices with poor financial and managerial organization, dissipated their profits by conspicuous consumption, and often resisted governmental efforts to introduce technological innovations. It was the public sector, Glade concludes, not private enterprise, which sought to modernize the mining industry.[12]

After independence, there was some experimentation with the political liberalism of Europe, but laissez-faire economic doctrines ran counter to the Iberian tradition of *dirigismo* and the demands of many economic groups for protection and support from the government; the *dirigismo* tradition—the state playing a central role in economic life of the nation—was maintained. Positivism in the latter part of the nineteenth century became almost the official ideology in some Latin American republics as a purported scientific approach to the organization of society and the state. Positivism, like liberalism, was predisposed toward capitalism by its defense of private property in Iberian law and tradition. Private wealth was viewed as necessary to promote

10. Ibid., p. 73.

11. Stanley J. Stein and Barbara H. Stein, *The Colonial Heritage of Latin America: Essays on Economic Dependence in Perspective*, p. 30.

12. Glade, *Latin American Economies*, pp. 74–76.

progress, and the accumulation of riches was seen as evidence of mental and moral superiority. But the positivists also saw the state as "an active agent of social change and as a principal ordering force in society," a belief which was contrary to the European liberal primacy of laissez-faire, but was a practical assessment of the weakness of domestic institutions.[13] State intervention continued to encourage and guide the private sector, and the foreign investment boom of 1850 to 1914 was promoted by concessions and subsidies from the state, liberal use of fiscal incentives, and heavy governmental borrowing abroad to pay for major projects. The Latin American governments often found it politically easier to grant generous concessions to foreigners, in return for their assistance in negotiating foreign loans, than to turn to the alternative policy of imposing taxes on the powerful landowners.[14]

Latin American industrial associations pressed for measures to protect them from foreign competition and assistance in the development of national manufacturing enterprises. Around 1914 the difficulties of the external sector, with its heavy reliance on foreign investment, fluctuating world prices for its exports, and new export competition, led to a reassessment of public policies. The desire to hasten the pace of economic development as a means of achieving greater economic independence became an overriding concern; the state was seen as the agent for this change by both conservatives and liberals: "The conservative preference for centralized and paternalistic government was linked with the liberal desire to promote social progress, while liberals and conservatives alike were often able to agree on the desire to foster industrialization and standardization of their economies."[15] Hence, the profound influence of the state in the economic affairs of Latin America has deep historical and cultural roots.

Frank Brandenburg's 1964 examination of Latin American private enterprise found that in all of the countries except Cuba, "the debate is not so much over whether ownership should be all private or all public as it is over what the proportions should be."[16] In the thirty largest companies in Argentina, Brazil, Chile, Col-

13. Ibid., p. 234.
14. Ibid., p. 372.
15. Ibid.
16. Frank Brandenburg, "The Development of Latin American Private Enterprise," Planning Pamphlet 121, p. 22.

ombia, Mexico, and Venezuela, the governments accounted for over 60 per cent of the total capital reserves. Only among medium- and small-sized companies did he find ownership to be overwhelmingly in private hands. Brandenburg noted the efforts to exclude foreigners, and often private enterprise in general, from the extractive industries and utilities; he speculated that Latin American leaders, many with southern European family backgrounds, may be adopting the southern European pattern of government ownership of public utilities. One might go one step further, then, and conclude that the interventionist role of the state was also understandable and normal in the light of Hispanic tradition.

Campos has explained why his fellow Latin Americans regard a high degree of involvement by the state in the economy as necessary, contrasting this view to the historic and ideological role of the state in the United States. Whereas economic growth was spontaneous in the United States, led by the aggressive entrepreneur of folklore, Latin American development has been demand-oriented, with government being pressured by the masses for increased living standards and consumption.[17] Others have elaborated on this historical comparison by pointing out that while the Latin American belief system perceived government as a friend and benefactor, the American tradition often regarded it as a natural enemy or a necessary evil ("eternal vigilance is the price of liberty"; "that government governs best which governs least").[18]

A Cultural Gulf

There were other cultural factors which impeded the development in Latin America of the capitalistic ethos that played such a major role in the history of the United States. One was the low status which the Iberian value system assigned to business or commercial success. The class structure favored land-owning, government employment, and church or military careers; business was very low on the Latin American social status scale. The political instability of the times, political intrigues which determined who would be favored by state protectionism or subsidies,

17. Roberto de Oliveira Campos, *Reflections on Latin American Development*, p. 8.

18. Whitaker and Jordan, *Nationalism in Contemporary Latin America*, p. 19.

and monetary disorders also inhibited the growth of a large Latin American entrepreneurial group.[19] Power-oriented behavior rather than achievement-oriented conduct was the road to riches and recognition, a fact that was reflected in the Latin American expression: "He who works has no time for making money."[20] This is in direct contrast to the belief of the Protestant ethic that hard work will be rewarded by material success, as Benjamin Franklin advised in *Poor Richard's Almanac:* "In short the way to wealth, if you desire it, is as plain as the way to the market. It depends chiefly on two words, industry and frugality."

Both Glade and Brandenburg dispute the notion that regional Catholicism diminished the incentives necessary for capitalism to thrive. Glade observes that many Catholic ethical precepts were ignored, the secularization of nineteenth-century Latin America did not provide a propitious environment for growth, and many European Catholic countries made greater advances than the Spanish possessions.[21] Brandenburg considers the major factors which retarded economic growth to be the restraints on entrepreneurship imposed by the primarily agricultural socioeconomic structure, authoritarian political regimes, and military dominance.[22] The emphasis on conspicuous consumption as a key to social mobility consumed scarce resources needed for entrepreneurial activities. The Latin American preference for tangible assets—land and buildings—likewise absorbed risk capital; the disdain for manual labor, inherited from the Spanish, also limited the number of new business endeavors.

The distrust and disparagement of profit weakened the major incentive of capitalism. However, the public cynicism toward profit reveals an ambivalence when the issue of national versus foreign profits is raised. The aforementioned 1958 survey in Brazil disclosed that while the public was accustomed to high profits, the exportation of profits by foreign investors became synonymous with exploitation in the minds of Brazilians from all levels of society: "They object to the exportation of profits *per se*."[23] This attitude is partly based on the belief that since it is taken for granted that Latin American businessmen seek high profits and

19. Glade, *Latin American Economies*, p. 207.
20. Ibid., p. 148.
21. Ibid., p. 85.
22. Brandenburg, "Development of Latin American Private Enterprise," p. 34.
23. McMillan, "Industrial Leaders in Latin America," p. 45.

avoid paying taxes, the more powerful and clever American firm has been even more successful in amassing a handsome profit at the expense of the public. The secrecy of foreign corporations concerning their foreign financial operations and profits is interpreted as substantiating the charge. The conclusion of a 1965 survey of the National Industrial Conference Board appears to reinforce this contention: ". . . more than 80 per cent of manufacturers surveyed earn money through exports, foreign licensing agreements or overseas manufacturing. About half have increased earnings from such sources in recent years. Yet few share the good news with their stockholders. Any reader of annual reports will find that vital information on foreign sales and earnings generally is lacking, buried in small print in footnotes or discussed in terms a layman cannot understand."[24]

There were times when the Latin American character and Hispanic culture were regarded by some intellectuals as the cause of the slow economic progress of the region, but even then, Latin Americans could fall back on *dignidad* to highlight their cultural advantages over the materialistic Yankees. Costa Rica's President José Figueres voiced this sentiment: "We have inherited all the defects of the Spanish character, but also some of its virtues. Our poverty does not lessen our pride. We have our dignity. . . ."[25]

THE LATIN AMERICAN BUSINESSMAN

Brandenburg found in his survey of 506 entrepreneurs that the majority of Latin American businessmen come from middle-class backgrounds. However, the insecure position of the middle groups within Latin America's social hierarchy fosters self-doubts often carried over to the Latin American middle manager. He shares these feelings of social insecurity in a system which emphasizes the eminent respectability of land ownership. Hence, he may see his roots in the soil and consider his business fatalistically, always seeing the possibility of returning to the land in case of failure. His political beliefs parallel those of other middle-class groups—professionals, intellectuals, civil servants, and labor leaders—but generally he does not participate as actively in politics. "On questions related to business and industry, his position

24. Quoted by Miguel S. Wionczek, "A Latin American View," p. 17.

25. Quoted in Gerhard Masur, *Nationalism in Latin America: Diversity and Unity*, p. 241.

can be summed up as follows: (1) He demands government protection from competition, particularly foreign. (2) He expects direct or indirect government subsidy. (3) He does not oppose government ownership or management of industry."[26] Many middle-class entrepreneurs receive their start by promoting economic nationalism to obtain an enterprise which was in the hands of foreigners and then rally nationalistic sentiment as protection against foreign competition. After they consolidate their position, they stress the need for private initiative, although continuing to support an interventionist public sector to protect domestic industrialization.[27]

Few of the Latin American entrepreneurs interviewed in Brandenburg's study oppose state development financing for private enterprise, especially for small business, although opinion is more divided regarding public financing for medium-sized and large industries.[28] Latin American governments consider such assistance to the private sector as a right and an obligation, justifying the use of public financing by the inability or unwillingness of private financial institutions to supply the Latin American business community with sufficient credit on reasonable terms and at modest interest rates. Brandenburg also noted that the average Latin American industrialist, despite his verbal defense of private enterprise, possesses many ideas in opposition to a free market economy. While they criticize foreign subsidies as monopolies which compete unfairly with local industry, there are numerous monopolies and oligopolies dominated by Latin American interests. "In fact, small and medium industrialists interviewed in Argentina, Brazil, Chile, and Mexico saw the twin specters of Castroism and government intervention as less immediate threats than extinction through local competition. Colombian and Venezuelan industrialists, in contrast, tended to subordinate the dangers of excessive competition to those of Castroism and potential government control."[29] Small businessmen are less tolerant of foreign investment than the larger firms—unless, of course, they are suppliers for foreign firms.

The family firm is still the prevalent form of private enterprise

26. McMillan, "Industrial Leaders in Latin America," p. 51.

27. Luis Ratinoff, "The New Urban Groups: The Middle Classes," p. 83.

28. Brandenburg, "Development of Latin American Private Enterprise," p. 70.

29. Ibid., p. 39.

in Latin America. In the unstable and complex political and economic environment of Latin America, the family enterprise offers security in business and commercial transactions. Relatives and friends often serve as the source of capital in the absence of capital markets, while the policy of placing kinsmen in governmental offices provides a form of political insurance against the vicissitudes of political life and public policy.[30] Having relatives in public posts is very important to a businessman: "the quest for economic advantage often had more of the character of petitionary activity before the favor-dispensing bureaucracy than that of bargaining activity by autonomous producers in a market, and political sanctions of deprivation and reward were frequently of much greater importance than market considerations."[31]

Albert Lauterbach's survey in the early 1960s of managerial attitudes toward economic development in ten Latin American countries observed that in the prevalent family firm, "management is intertwined with family matters and also with political affairs."[32] He found that management personnel policies are "strongly influenced by family status, political factors, personal acquaintance or recommendation by friends, and other noneconomic considerations."[33] But the family enterprise serves a very important psychological function, since it protects the Latin American businessman's individuality and uniqueness from being absorbed into a single group identity as in large American corporations.[34]

It is generally acknowledged that the Latin American businessman seeks a higher profit on his investment than his European or North American counterpart. The justification for this higher rate of return is that the unstable conditions in the hemisphere make his risk greater, while the weak local capital markets increase the interest rates on scarce capital for investment loans. Brandenburg found that in Colombia, Mexico, and Venezuela, large industrialists expected a return above 15 per cent; medium-sized entrepreneurs, above 25 per cent; and small industrialists, above 35 per cent. Regardless of size, industrialists in

30. Glade, *Latin American Economies*, p. 276.
31. Ibid., p. 147.
32. Albert Lauterbach, "Executive Training and Productivity: Managerial Views in Latin America," p. 358.
33. Ibid., p. 360.
34. Stanley M. Davis, "U.S. versus Latin America: Business and Culture," p. 91.

Argentina and Chile felt that they needed a return above 30 per cent, due to inflationary conditions. The rampant inflation in Brazil at the time of the study produced a profit expectance of over 60 per cent.[35] In cooperation with W. R. Grace & Company, he analyzed the true profits of fifty-one locally owned Latin American companies in five countries and concluded that inflation substantially reduced their true profits, no matter how they might appear to outside observers.[36]

The Latin American entrepreneur has not manifested a very venturesome spirit when it comes to risking his capital; Latin American management or ownership of enterprises does not reflect a spirit of entrepreneurship and innovation.[37] One study asked Latin American business leaders what personal attributes and characteristics they thought an entrepreneur should possess; only 3 per cent of the respondents in Argentina and Chile, and none in Colombia, mentioned the capacity for taking risks. The investigator explained that this was "a realistic assessment of the practical conditions of industrialization in Latin America."[38]

The different management approaches of Latin American and U.S. executives also reflect their respective cultures. Claude McMillan found that the Brazilian manager is less likely to involve middle-level management participation in decision making and is more suspicious of merit promotions and wages tied to production output. He is not as likely to emphasize training and upgrading as his American counterpart, since he considers the worker as having a fixed capacity to produce. His U.S. partner is sometimes critical of a Latin American tendency to hire an individual with questionable qualifications and then treat him as a

35. Brandenburg, "Development of Latin American Private Enterprise," p. 36.

36. The annual rate of takeout in profits and capital repatriation by U.S. firms from 1961 to 1968 was 12 to 15 per cent of the investment. However, as mentioned earlier, American companies are unwilling to publicize the amount of their profits from Latin American subsidiaries. The Bureau of Business Statistics of the Department of Commerce collects this data but will release only aggregate data. While the argument is advanced that disclosure of this information would harm the competitive position of a firm, fear that the amount of profit taken from a Latin American investment might become the focus of nationalist attacks is the more probable reason behind the reluctance of the business community to release profit figures. Respondents in the survey of the Council of the Americas demonstrated a similar reluctance to release these statistics.

37. Lauterbach, "Executive Training and Productivity: Managerial Views in Latin America," p. 377.

38. Fernando H. Cardoso, "The Industrial Elites," p. 111.

ward once he is on the payroll, in the manner of a *patron*, regardless of his performance or production needs. But a more serious misunderstanding relates to different perceptions of legal obligations: "To the American, the contract is a clear statement of the obligations and considerations of the contracting parties, and it is employed to minimize misunderstanding and to enforce compliance. Brazilian managers view the written contract more as an expression of intent at the same time the agreement was made; one whose applicability and value deteriorate with time. They are often appalled at the length and detail of the American's written contract proposal, but seldom object since they do not feel the written contract is to be taken too seriously."[39]

This same attitudinal difference is involved in many of the demands for divestiture of foreign ownership of concessions and enterprises granted and guaranteed by earlier regimes, or even (as in the case of Chile) by the same government under nationalist pressures. If, as one scholar has argued, most Latin American constitutions are only nominal constitutions, divorced from the reality of actual power relationships, is it not likely that contracts may also be perceived as statements of intent, subject to modifications as the environment and situation impose new demands upon the initial agreement?[40] While it is not an especially comforting thought for U.S. investors, this view may help to create a better understanding of the importance of political factors over economic or legal arrangements. Some of the advocates of divestiture base their arguments on such a premise.

A Skeptical Public

The Church has begun to question publicly the benefits and values of private enterprise in Latin America. At the 1968 Latin American Bishops Council (CELAM) in Medellín, Colombia, the clerics issued a statement which included a section titled, "International Tensions and External Neo-Colonialism." It was critical of the dependence of the area on external centers of power and pointed to the harmful effects of capital flight, profit remittances, and international indebtedness. The document denounced "imperialism of any ideological type, which may be exercised in Latin

39. McMillan, "Industrial Leaders in Latin America," p. 35.
40. J. Lloyd Mecham, "Latin American Constitutions: Nominal and Real," p. 965.

America in an indirect form and even with direct interventions."[41] The statement was hostile to both liberal capitalism and Marxism, since both systems "violate the dignity of the human person, since one has as pre-supposition the primacy of capital . . . in function of profit, while the other . . . in practice becomes a totalitarian concentration of power in the state."[42] They looked hopefully to the development of "communitarianism."

Peru's cardinal, Monsignor Juan Landazuri Ricketts, an early critic of the military regime, has come to support the expropriation of IPC, the agrarian reform, and the Velasco Doctrine, which states that key sectors of the economy should be under the control of nationals. Most significantly, he publicly repudiated the attack of the Peruvian National Society of Industrialists on the new Industrial Law as a violation of God-given property rights.[43] More revolutionary priests, like Colombia's Padre Camilo Torres, who was killed in 1966, have joined guerrilla forces against the injustices perpetuated by the existing regimes in countries like Guatemala and Brazil. The anticapitalist feelings of the Church and the military in Brazil were so strong that Roberto Campos, then a minister in the military government, organized secret meetings between churchmen, military officers, and businessmen in 1969 to reduce the hostility toward private enterprise. He told one meeting: "There is a spurious and unconscious alliance between the Church and the military in the belief that capitalism has not worked in Brazil and so it is time to move to another system. I would estimate that 60 per cent of you clergy and 40 per cent of you military are anti-capitalism. But you want capitalism without profits. You clergy want to subvert capitalism; you military want to purge it."[44]

A mid-1965 United States Information Agency (USIA) survey of public opinion in five major Latin American capitals disclosed that sizable minorities, averaging 35 per cent for the five cities, considered it a bad thing to have U.S. companies operating in their countries.[45] And even more unsettling for American investors was that majorities of those with opinions in three of the five

41. Quoted in Thomas G. Sanders, "The Church in Latin America," p. 296.

42. Ibid., p. 297.

43. George W. Grayson, Jr., "Peru's Military Populism," p. 76.

44. Quoted in Georgie A. Geyer, *New Latins*, p. 297.

45. United States Information Agency, Research and Reference Service, "Latin American Attitudes toward the Alliance for Progress and the Role of Private Investment."

cities favored expropriation of large companies owned by foreigners. Another disconcerting omen for private enterprise prospects in the hemisphere was that a clear majority in Santiago and large minorities in the other four cities favored government over private ownership of major industries. The 63 per cent support for government ownership in Santiago obviously meant that Frei's Chileanization program and Allende's nationalization of the copper industry have had the support of the general population. A comparison of survey results several years before in Rio de Janeiro had shown a definite trend of increased hostility to foreign investment; there was also a shift from divided opinion to a two-to-one sentiment in favor of expropriation. In all the 1965 surveys, the better-off respondents were more likely to favor private and foreign investment, while the poor favored government ownership of major industries and expropriation of large corporations owned by foreigners.

A seven-country survey by the USIA in 1967–68 revealed that anti-Americanism, while not a majority view among the respondents, was fanning the flames of economic nationalism after Che Guevara's death, the intervention in the Dominican Republic, and the relaxation toward the threat of the Soviet Union as memories of the 1962 missile crisis faded. However, nationalist sensitivity to economic exploitation, the visibility of private enterprise, and explicit anti-American and anti-business attitudes were peripheral then to the central issue of Latin American dissatisfaction with the slow pace of economic development: "Regarding economic matters, there is a marked shifting away from national economic problems to the questions of ownership of industry, viability of free enterprise and influence of foreign investments. Whereas in 1965 the people's main concerns were economic, not political; developmental not collectivistic; reform-oriented rather than ultra-nationalistic, by 1968 the general popular trend appears to suggest an emphasis on socialistic foreign investments and operations, a mental turning away from reform, the Church and the military as instruments of evolutionary change."[46]

Another study of Venezuelan undergraduate university students in 1964, and a follow-up survey when they were graduates in 1967, disclosed a mixed view of U.S. business and a more

46. Robert F. Delaney, "Latin American Opinion: Myth and Reality," p. 74.

critical appraisal of official U.S. policies. In 1964 these students "opted 54% for socialism, 9% for capitalism, 5% for communism and, curiously, 29% for an opinion described as 'an untried system.' "[47] The Venezuelan students equated "socialism with economic equality, equal opportunities and justice; state control of industry with state responsibility for social welfare," perceiving socialism as embracing more humanitarian values than capitalism.[48] When the same students were reinterviewed in 1967, significant attitude changes were recorded. Whereas in 1964, 54 per cent of the students preferred government ownership and 29 per cent private ownership, the 1967 survey found that the "bigness" of certain factories and the sensitive areas of extractive enterprises and public utilities were the issues where government ownership became the major policy preference. In addition, the survey indicated that while 54 per cent of the 1964 sample preferred socialism, by 1967 59 per cent of the same students opted for a "mixed economy," involving both state and private capital. There was also a decrease from 48 per cent to 31 per cent of the number of students who thought U.S. business was harmful to Latin America, although antagonism toward official U.S. policies remained high.

In summary, capitalism is not a popular concept in Latin America because of its association in earlier years with foreign investors who were engaged in bribery and manipulation of local politics to obtain great profits from the region, often aided by their governments. The present efforts of U.S. firms to blend into the environment and become good corporate citizens confront this historic remembrance, especially older companies whose records are not unblemished. Nationalist feelings are so acute that many local employees of American enterprises are afraid to affirm publicly the advantages of working for a U.S. company.

The state has always played a central role in the economic life of Latin America, as it has not in the United States. The Spanish crown, jealously protecting its New World possessions, closely controlled the activities of the private sector and dominated most areas of economic activity. Entrepreneurs were restrained and greatly dependent upon the state; political favors were often the key factor in the success of an enterprise. After independence, the state took the lead in fostering economic development and was

47. Ibid., p. 76.
48. Ibid., p. 75.

called upon by the private sector to assist local businesses through the granting of monopolies and protected markets.

Both the low status of the businessman on the Hispanic social scale and the disdain for manual labor and profit discouraged the development of a vigorous private sector. The drive for power had more importance than profit seeking, since through political influence a family firm could obtain special advantages. Thus political astuteness, not entrepreneurial ability, was the key to social mobility. The Latin American preference for tangible assets, high profits, and investments with a quick turnover reflected the way business had to be conducted in a turbulent political and economic environment. The family firm served as a form of security, both financially and psychologically, in the midst of such instability. Public attitudes toward private enterprise and foreign investment have shown an increasing hostility to the prominent role of foreign capital in their economies and a growing acceptance of nationalization as a solution.

Thus, many of the entreaties of U.S. officials to support the growth of private enterprise in the hemisphere land on fallow ground. Ideological warnings about the danger of the state exerting too great an influence in the economy are ignored by Latin Americans, long accustomed to the government playing a major role. Advocates of private enterprise must then seek to change the unsavory image of the capitalism of the past by demonstrating that foreign firms can be good citizens, sensitive to social and economic problems, and accommodate their policies to an environment where the state is considered the key actor in fulfilling the expectations of the people. It will not be an easy task.

3. The Costs of Foreign Investment

The Latin View

THE LATIN AMERICAN perception of the costs and benefits of foreign investment has been immensely influenced by the historic relationship and preeminence of the United States in the hemisphere. Again, the specter of political interference in their domestic affairs makes many Latin American decision makers fearful of the effects of admitting foreign investment. The ideas of the United Nations Economic Commission for Latin America (ECLA) provided hemispheric leaders with a theoretical approach to economic development which attributed much of the blame for the backwardness of the region to the industrialized countries and their investors.

This chapter will discuss the Latin American policy emphasis on retaining control over economic destiny, the alleged costs of foreign investment, and the recognized need for foreign capital under certain conditions. The preferred modes and channels for foreign investment will be examined, including import-substitution policies, local participation, and divestiture formulas.

ECLA—Latin America's Economic Gadfly

The formation of ECLA had a profound influence on economic development planning in the hemisphere. Under the leadership of Dr. Raul Prebisch, ECLA contributed a theoretical explanation for Latin America's adverse trade balance with the industrialized countries and presented a forceful argument for industrialization, stimulated through vigorous state activity. Therefore, any discussion of current Latin American attitudes and policies toward the role of foreign investment in economic development must be based on an understanding of the seminal ideas of ECLA in the post–World War II years.

The publications of ECLA challenged the prevailing theory of an international division of labor whereby the task of the periphery (the less-developed countries) "was that of producing food and raw materials for the great industrial centers."[1] The commission questioned the basic assumption that the benefits of technological progress would be widely distributed under such a system by lower prices or higher incomes; they noted that the industrialized center had accrued the bulk of the benefits of the increased productivity, a fact easily verified by comparing the standard of living of the masses in both areas and their respective abilities to accumulate capital. The reliance on the external sector—production for export—was shaken by the depression and World War II, which demonstrated the need for greater independence from the vagaries of foreign trade and stimulated the growth of domestic enterprise in Latin America. The economic cycles of the past had consistently placed Latin America at a disadvantage because of the low mobility of the factors of production, which resulted in rising prices for the manufactured import from the center countries while the prices of the primary product exports from the peripheries were steadily declining. Thus, Latin America found its demand for costly manufactured imports increasing while a deterioration in the terms of trade led to declining prices for its exports.

Industrialization was seen as a partial solution to this dilemma. Agricultural improvement was also important in the program for economic development, since increased agricultural productivity would create a labor surplus which only industry

1. United Nations, Economic Commission for Latin America, *Development Problems in Latin America*, p. 6.

could absorb productively.[2] One of the first objectives was the promotion of import-substitution industries. The domestic production of manufactured articles would reduce the expenditure of limited foreign exchange for imports from the center while simultaneously providing jobs and increasing national productivity. ECLA recognized a need for protectionism but rationalized the inefficiencies and costliness of such a policy. Hence, the charge that the prices of goods produced in a protected market might be higher than for the same imported product was dismissed, because "this conclusion does not take account of the fact that the productive factors employed in these industries could not be put to better use. It is therefore to the advantage of the economy to produce at relatively high cost rather than to leave productive factors lying idle or use them in ways that would adversely affect the terms of trade and, consequently, the capacity to import."[3] These nascent industries would also serve to diminish the vulnerability of a country to fluctuations in the world market. But while a reasonable degree of protectionism was required for industrialization of the periphery, ECLA sharply warned the industrialized countries against the adoption of protective economic policies which would endanger world trade stability.[4]

A related concept promoted by ECLA was the importance of state developmental planning, which ECLA was quick to point out did not necessarily imply the shackling of private enterprise. Two types of state intervention were envisioned: (a) the utilization of fiscal, monetary, and credit policies, domestic and foreign loans, and direct participation in investments to create an attractive environment for private enterprise; or (b) regulatory policies which would prescribe the areas and activities of private investment. Either approach would first require the formulation of investment targets to establish national priorities and the goals of economic development. Foreign capital was recognized as vital for economic growth because of the limited amount of domestic capital available and the undesirability of increasing national investment by forced savings through altering the current levels and patterns of consumption.[5]

2. Ibid., p. 21.
3. Ibid., p. 35.
4. Ibid., p. 57.
5. Ibid., pp. 64–65.

In 1954 ECLA expressed its concern over the small inflow of foreign capital into the region. The decline in portfolio loans in "social capital investment" after World War II was especially lamented, since the private bond market had played a major role in financing infrastructure projects deemed essential to attract private investment. This had serious consequences because the cost of interest paid on bond issues was viewed as far below the cost of profit remittances on direct foreign investment, which had comprised only one-third of the total investment of the region prior to the First World War. But, while the adverse balance-of-payments effect of foreign investment was worrisome, private investment could be accommodated if there was a significant increase in public loans at low rates of interest to offset the decline of the private bond market. ECLA accepted the Latin American tradition of restricting certain types of investment to the state, not on ideological grounds, but as a means to avoid future conflicts over the prices and policies of public utilities. Foreign capital would also be unwelcome when it sought to establish monopolies, or when the large size of the foreign enterprise would create internal tensions because of its disproportionate influence in domestic affairs. However, ECLA was skeptical about whether foreign capital would become interested in internal activities not associated with the traditional export sector. And, if foreign investment did increase dramatically, there would still be the attendant burden of service payments which would cost more than service payments on international loans. Discriminatory national policies against foreign capital, to protect local businessmen, would be minimized only if international credit and advanced technology were made available to the Latin American entrepreneur, thus obviating his fear of being at a competitive disadvantage vis-à-vis foreign investors.[6]

The analysis and policy recommendations of ECLA served as underpinnings for many Latin American governmental planners and the center / periphery theory was often employed by Latin politicians to levy the blame for the lack of socioeconomic progress on the industrialized center countries, particularly the United States. Needless to say, the ECLA theories were vigorously attacked by economists, businessmen, and government officials of the United States, whose rebuttals will be presented in the next chapter.

6. Ibid., p. 128.

THE FEAR-OF-DOMINATION SYNDROME

Latin Americans have often expressed their deep fear that private foreign investment would herald or symbolize the capitulation of their sovereignty to economic and political domination from abroad; this has already been discussed in relation to the rise of economic nationalism during the era of Dollar Diplomacy. But the size of the multinational firm of today, particularly in comparison to the economic resources and power of many Latin American republics, also makes them apprehensive over an "unequal struggle between a David nation and a Goliath industry."[7] An April 1970 statement by General Francisco Morales Bermudez, Peru's minister of economic affairs and finance, reflected this concern about possible external control over the economic destiny of a nation: "Development is motivated by a desire to reduce or limit dependence on exploitation by outside resources. . . ."[8]

The adverse political, economic, and psychological effects of foreign investment in sensitive sectors was highlighted in a June 13, 1969, speech by President Lleras Restrepo of Colombia. Mentioning the Cuban experience, President Lleras warned that beyond a certain point, foreign ownership or control of the means of production "tends to deform the personality of a nation and provokes therefore unpredictable reactions. No nation will accept indefinitely foreign domination of the commanding heights of its economy."[9] He added that unless present trends and attitudes change, private foreign investment will become a major source of friction and misunderstanding in the hemisphere. The theme of economic exploitation is inherent in the center / periphery theory of ECLA, where peripheral Latin America was to be perpetually relegated to a subordinate role of supplier of raw materials and primary products.

The foreign exploitation thesis has been applied mainly to the extractive industries. It is argued that the foreign entrepreneur enters the country by obtaining a lucrative mining concession under dubious circumstances, extracts the natural wealth of the nation with little linkage to the local economy and its de-

7. Salvador de Madariaga, *Latin America between the Eagle and the Bear*, p. 173.

8. Francisco Morales Bermudez, address at the third plenary session, eleventh meeting of the Board of Governors, Inter-American Development Bank, April 22, 1970.

9. Carlos Lleras Restrepo, address to the National Press Club, June 13, 1969.

velopment, garners exorbitant profits, and leaves the country with only "an empty hole" to show for the loss of its national patrimony. President Allende's attack on United States copper interests in Chile employed this argument: "In 1969, Anaconda earned 99 million dollars in profits on a world-wide scale. Of these profits 79 million dollars, that is to say 80 per cent, came from Chile. However, it invested only 16 per cent of the money in Chile that it invested on a world-wide scale. A 16 per cent investment yields 80 per cent of its profits. 'Caramba,' it is good business for the Anaconda Company to invest its money in Chile."[10] Allende's reference to Anaconda's extraction of $3.7 billion of Chile's natural wealth between 1930 and 1969 was mentioned earlier.

Table 3–1 would appear to support the Latin American charge that the extractive industries repatriate more capital than they invest in Latin America. During the period 1961–69, 93 per cent of the net profit remittances and fees inflow to the United States on U.S. direct investment in Latin America was derived from the mining and petroleum industries; 62 per cent of the total profit remittance was from petroleum investments alone. However, American investments in the manufacturing sector resulted in a net cumulative outflow of $224 million to Latin America during the same years, which would seem to reinforce the belief that manufacturing investments are less costly to the host country.

Latin Americans are skeptical of declarations by foreign governments and investors that foreign investment is apolitical. Instead, they recall past interventions by the U.S. and European governments on behalf of their businessmen. There is often the fear that the close relationship between Wall Street and Washington may lead to pressures for the admittance of private capital under favorable terms and protection of foreign investment at the expense of national policies. The restrictions on the U.S. foreign assistance program, particularly the hated Hickenlooper Amendment, are viewed as verification of the charge that foreign investment is accompanied by political interference in the domestic affairs of a nation.

This concern, based on historical experiences, reinforces the emphasis of the region on the juridical concept reflected in the Calvo Doctrine of the late nineteenth century.[11] The Argentine

10. *Prensa Latina*, December 23, 1970.

11. While I recognize that it is sometimes called the Calvo Clause, I have chosen to adopt the description used by the Department of State.

TABLE 3-1

U.S. Direct Investment in Latin American Republics and Other Western Hemisphere: Inflow and Outflow of Capital by Major Industry, 1961-69[a]
(in Millions of Dollars)

Year	New Direct Investment from U.S.					Income Received in U.S.					New Inflow to U.S.				
	Total[c]	Mining	Petroleum	Manu-facturing	Other	Total	Mining	Petroleum	Manu-facturing	Other	Total	Mining	Petroleum	Manu-facturing	Other
1961	219	32	63	78	46	824	198	438	75	113	605	166	375	-3	67
1962	29	-13	-67	133	-24	891	221	488	71	111	862	234	555	-62	135
1963	235	24	5	150	56	956	210	544	70	132	721	186	539	-80	76
1964	113	30	7	137	-61	1,011	245	531	98	137	898	215	524	-39	198
1965	271	43	-74	245	57	995	266	476	123	130	724	223	550	-122	73
1966	307	60	-37	160	125	1,113	327	499	147	140	806	267	536	-13	15
1967	296	71	-66	199	92	1,190	365	480	195	151	894	294	546	-4	59
1968	677	227	177	222	50	1,218	374	489	216	139	541	147	312	-6	89
1969[b]	344	-31	56	132	187	1,277	404	472	237	164	932	435	416	105	-23

Source: U.S., Department of Commerce, *Survey of Current Business*, October 1970, p. 38.

a. This compilation was the only available breakdown of revised figures by the headings and industries described.

b. Preliminary figures.

c. Totals are cited exactly as they appear in the Department of Commerce publication; slight discrepancies occur in some instances.

lawyer Carlos Calvo enunciated the doctrine that sovereignty is inviolable and under no circumstances can a foreign national call upon his own government to intercede on his behalf in juridical disputes within the host country. Such intervention, it was declared, would confer a privileged status on foreigners over nationals.[12] The Calvo Doctrine was invoked in 1964 by the Latin American delegates to the World Bank's meeting in Tokyo to consider the formation of an International Center for the Settlement of Investment Disputes. The Chilean governor, Felix Ruiz, voiced the "El No de Tokyo": "The new system that has been suggested would give the foreign investor, by virtue of the fact that he is a foreigner, the right to sue a sovereign state outside its national territory, dispensing with the courts of law. This provision is contrary to the accepted legal principle of our countries and, de facto, would confer a privilege on the foreign investor, placing nationals of the country concerned in a position of inferiority."[13] Ruiz was referring to the fact that the Calvo Doctrine has been incorporated into a number of Latin American constitutions as well as embraced as a juridical principle of the hemisphere.

Oswaldo Sunkel of the University of Chile, formerly associated with ECLA, concluded from his examination of Latin American development programs "that self-determination, independence and a reduction in foreign dependence are among the fundamental objectives."[14] This is manifested in their economic policies for development and industrialization and in their political pronouncements against absorption into another culture as a dependent country (*país sucursal*). Campos discussed economic nationalism in Latin America with the Joint Economic Committee in 1969, and explained it in terms of a "fear-of-domination syndrome . . . that prompts governments to absorb, control, or foreclose certain sectors, preempting them for national command. This fear is directed against too large a foreign preponderance in certain industries, stifling the growth of local entrepreneurship, or against globalist decisionmaking by large multinational concerns, that make decisions on production and marketing from an

12. J. Lloyd Mecham, *A Survey of United States–Latin American Relations*, pp. 94–95.

13. International Bank for Reconstruction and Development, press release no. 57, excerpt from the statement by Felix Ruiz (Tokyo, September 9, 1964).

14. Oswaldo Sunkel, "National Development Policy and External Dependence in Latin America," p. 25.

international viewpoint, disregarding local priorities. Or finally, against the extra-territorial principle which leads U.S. corporations abroad to conform to Washington directives and not to host countries' policies in relation to exports, profit remittances, and capital repatriation."[15]

The fear-of-domination syndrome is very evident in the structural theory of dependency, which attributes the underdevelopment and political dependence of the region to the growth of international capitalism. This approach rejects the arguments that foreign private investment and the presence of a national capitalist class will accelerate economic growth or enhance the sovereignty of the peripheral nations. Proponents of the dependency thesis charge that the creation of international and internal structures by the world expansion of capitalism "deepens and aggravates the fundamental problems" of the Latin American peoples.[16] The capitalism being urged upon the poor countries is thus considered not to be the independent variety which spurred the economic growth of the United States, England, and Japan, but a "dependent form of capitalism, embedded within the world capitalist system as a whole."[17]

The Latin American countries are economically and politically dependent upon the developed capitalist countries for export markets, economic assistance, bilateral and international loans, capital, and technology. The gap between the rich and poor nations and the elites and masses in the developing countries continues to grow. The development that does occur benefits only a small segment of the population, while labor is "superexploited." Dependent capitalism thus produces "backwardness, misery, and social marginalization."[18]

Structural reform of these internal and external relations is considered the foremost concern of the region.[19] Major land reform would reduce one of the major impediments to economic development and a redistribution of income would diminish the power of the privileged classes. However, these critics differ over

15. U.S., Congress, Joint Economic Committee, *Hearings*, *A Foreign Economic Policy for the 1970's*, pt. 1:93.

16. Theotonio Dos Santos, "The Structure of Dependence," p. 231.

17. Thomas E. Weisskopf, "Capitalism, Underdevelopment and the Future of the Poor Countries," p. 9.

18. Dos Santos, "Structure of Dependence," p. 235.

19. Celso Furtado, *Economic Development of Latin America: A Survey from Colonial Times to the Cuban Revolution*, p. 255.

how power should be wrested from the foreign-oriented and traditional elites who would vigorously oppose structural reforms to eliminate the severe income inequality.[20]

All of these views agree on one basic point: the necessity of enhancing Latin America's political and economic independence against the intrusion of foreign governments and capital. Again, it is the Latin American perception that the introduction of American investment will infringe upon Latin American sovereignty that generates the cautious and sometimes hostile attitude toward the American businessman.

A Balance-of-Payments Drain?

Latin Americans also question the desirability of foreign private investment on economic grounds. It is often charged that the various costs of direct foreign investment are too high and thus impede the progress of economic development. In June 1970, at the panel of foreign private investment in Medellín, Colombia, the chairman of the Inter-American Committee of the Alliance for Progress (CIAP), Carlos Sanz de Santamaría, opened the discussion by identifying three "fundamental questions" relating to three areas of potential conflict: (a) Are the costs of present modes of foreign private investment too high in terms of the magnitude of the transfers that they entail? (b) Does it restrain the growth of Latin American enterprise and diminish its rate of growth? (c) Is it compatible with the attainment of national development goals?[21]

One of the most controversial issues is the question of the balance-of-payments cost of foreign investment. ECLA raised this point in its analysis of the long-range expense of profit remittances from foreign enterprises compared to the allegedly "cheaper" service costs of receiving capital through portfolio investments or

20. For an overview of this economic theory see Ziad Keilany, "Structuralism in Latin America: A Radical Approach to Modernization" (unpublished manuscript). The debate is continued in Francisco C. Weffort, "Notas sobre la 'teoría de la dependencia': ¿Teoría de clase o ideología nacional?" pp. 355–60, and Fernando Henrique Cardoso, "¿'Teoría de la dependencia' o análisis concreto de situaciones de dependencia?" pp. 360–65. A very sophisticated theoretical analysis of the subordinate position of peripheral nations to center nations is presented in John Galtung, "A Structural Theory of Imperialism," *Journal of Peace Research*, pp. 81–117. His discussion of imperialism, which is defined in terms of a condition of disharmony of interest between center and peripheral countries, is applied to both capitalist and socialist center nations.

21. Alliance for Progress weekly newsletter, June 22, 1970.

by low-interest international loans. But the argument now hinges on comparisons between the amount of new direct foreign investment flowing into the region and the total outflow of foreign capital in the form of profit remittances and licensing, management, and engineering fees. A 1969 Organization of American States (OAS) paper offered instructions to Latin Americans for the calculation of the balance-of-payments impact of foreign investment: ". . . it is essential that foreign private enterprise promote the development of exports, or the substitution of imports, particularly at the regional or subregional level. . . .

"To this end it is necessary, on the one hand, to know the real increase in foreign currency holdings resulting from such expanded exports or the real savings in foreign currency effected through the substitution of imports, and, on the other hand, to deduct the transfers of foreign currency abroad made by foreign investors as amortizations and profits. On the basis of the difference thus established it will be possible to determine accurately the efficacy of such contributions to the balance of payments.

"Thus, there are foreign investments which do not help the balance of payments of a country, but, on the contrary, aggravate the trend toward imbalance. This does not mean that such investments have not increased the product of a given country. . . .

"In such cases it will be necessary to compare the value of the technological contributions of such foreign investments with the net cost of the foreign exchange that they represent."[22] This formula for calculating the balance-of-payments effect has been widely accepted in the region, much to the chagrin of foreign investors.

On the surface at least, a 1969 report by the Foreign Affairs Subcommittee on Inter-American Affairs would seem to substantiate the Latin American fears. The subcommittee found that during the 1961–68 period of the Alliance for Progress, "the net private capital outflow to the United States amounted to approximately 4 billion dollars."[23] Although the subcommittee acknowledged that most of the outflow represented income on investments made prior to 1961, the report declared: "Whatever their

22. Organization of American States, Inter-American Economic and Social Council, "The Role of Foreign Private Investment in the Development of Latin America," p. 3.

23. U.S., Congress, House, Committee on Foreign Affairs, *Report*, *New Directions for the 1970's: Toward a Strategy of Inter-American Development*, p. 8.

TABLE 3-2

U.S. Direct Private Investment in Latin America, 1961-69
(in Millions of Dollars)

Year	Reinvested Earnings	New Direct Investment from U.S.	Income Received in U.S.	Net Inflow to U.S.[a]
1961	255	173	730	557
1962	268	-32	761	793
1963	173	69	801	732
1964	216	143	895	752
1965	306	176	869	693
1966	302	190	965	775
1967	181	184	1,022	838
1968	358	677	1,218	541
1969[b]	376	345	1,277	932[c]

Source: U.S., Department of Commerce, *Survey of Current Business*, October 1970 and preceding issues.

a. The positive numbers in this column represent the alleged balance-of-payments drain on the Latin American economies.

b. Department of Commerce preliminary figures.

c. The jump in the inflow of capital to the U.S. in 1969 resulted from the involuntary sales of majority interests in 2 mining companies to the Chilean government and the sale of a public utility company to the Peruvian government.

particular cause, private capital outflows and Latin America's continuing adverse balance of trade with the United States have cut into resources which otherwise may have been available for financial development and socially desirable reforms."[24] Table 3–2 shows the net flow of capital from U.S. direct private investment for 1961–69, based on Department of Commerce figures. It lends support for the Latin American charge that there has been a net drain of dollars to the detriment of the Latin American balance of payments—if one accepts ECLA's narrow formula for calculating the costs of foreign investment.

24. Ibid.

The arguments of foreign investors which emphasize the other advantages which accrue to the host country through foreign private investment are rejected by Latin American nationalists who embrace a simpler and politically more attractive explanation for the slow pace of economic development. The Latin American balance-of-payments claim thus has the political merits of reinforcing the historic antipathy toward foreign capital, coalescing diverse groups through the emotional rallying cry of economic nationalism, and offering a convenient rationale—and often scapegoat—for the unfulfilled expectations of the masses for social and economic improvements. Thus, the widely held belief that foreign investment is costly to the local economy influences the public statements and actions of Latin American officials.

Foreign Investment as Development Agent

Latin Americans also question the value of foreign investment as an input into the developmental process. Memories of the former enclave pattern of investment, when foreign investors were solely interested in production for export and sought isolation from the turbulence and needs of the surrounding environment, still persist in the minds of some Latin American decision makers. They feel that foreign enterprises, whose decisions are made in Wall Street board rooms, are most concerned with utilizing their subsidiary as part of a worldwide marketing system than in contributing to local development goals. Therefore, the processing of many products might be done by the parent company and the local subsidiary operated only as a source of primary products.[25] In other instances, international markets might be reserved for the main offices or subsidiaries in other countries.[26] It is additionally charged that foreign investors might wish to establish enterprises in nonvital sectors, thus absorbing scarce local resources of manpower and capital and perhaps displacing actual or potential national entrepreneurs who had the requisite capital and skills to meet these secondary needs. This argument is advanced by many Latin American entrepreneurs, who seek state protection for their smaller and usually less efficient enterprises.

25. Sunkel, "National Development Policy and External Dependence in Latin America," p. 37.

26. Roberto Campos and Aldo Ferrer, "Foreign Investment and Latin American Economic Development," Organization of American States, Inter-American Economic and Social Council, p. 13.

Felipe Pazos, a member of the OAS Committee of Nine, has warned of one major problem concerning foreign investment as a development agent: "The main weakness of direct investment as a development agent is a consequence of the complete character of its contribution. As it brings enterprise, management and technology to the country, it may inhibit the emergence and formation of local personnel and local institutions to perform these essential functions. In so far [sic] as this happens, foreign investment does not help the country to advance towards self-sustaining development. But on the other hand, direct investment strengthens existing local enterprises and encourages the creation of new ones through its expanding effects on income, through its training of local personnel, through its direct purchases of parts, intermediate goods, raw materials and services from local enterprises . . . and / or its provision of cheaper and more abundant supplies of inputs to local enterprises. . . ."[27] His ambivalence toward foreign investment and concern about its impact on local enterprises are shared by other Latin American elites.

Latin American leaders feel that private investment flows are not and cannot be adequate to meet the capital requirements for development of a viable economic infrastructure of roads, public utilities, and an educated, healthy work force. As ECLA stated, profits in some of these areas are too small to attract private enterprise, and foreign investments in other fields create political tensions. Instead, more economic assistance and better trade relations with the industrialized countries are sought. The Latin American foreign ministers in the May 1969 Consensus of Viña del Mar agreed "that private foreign investment should not be considered assistance, nor should it be computed as part of financial cooperation for development."[28] This topic will subsequently be explored in an analysis of the role of private enterprise in the foreign assistance program of the United States.

The North American model, which postulates that private enterprise is the most efficient mobilizer of resources, is increasingly being challenged. Gabriel Valdés, Chile's foreign minister, told the American Chamber of Commerce in Santiago on July 18, 1969: "You Americans keep telling us to develop private

27. Felipe Pazos, "The Role of International Movements of Private Capital in Promoting Development," p. 196.

28. U.S., Department of State, translation of "Consensus reached at the CECLA Ministerial Meeting at Viña Del Mar," May 29, 1969.

capitalism as you did and saying that we will arrive at the same position. But your nineteenth-century ideals can't be ours today. The pressures for change are too strong."[29] Colombia's Alberto Lleras Camargo was critical of the emphasis in U.S. policy on the private entrepreneur under laissez-faire conditions as the key element of development: "Our people were invited, one might say with impertinence, to realize similar great achievements, when all the conditions in the world had changed. . . ."[30]

The skeptical attitude toward the contributions of capitalism did not reflect a bias for communism; instead, a nationalist position was often announced. Peru's General Bermudez declared: "Neither the short sightedness and impositions of capitalism nor the impositions and arbitrariness of communism will lead to a balance in world politics; neither the one nor the other will assure the economic independence of developing countries."[31] It is interesting to observe, however, that Japan's rigid restrictions on foreign capital have been considered as a model by some Peruvian planners.[32] A 1969 paper written for the Latin American Economic and Social Council also discussed Japan's treatment of foreign investment, although it recognized that most Latin American countries were behind Japan's level of industrialization in the postwar years.[33]

From Import Substitution to Export Promotion

As discussed earlier, import substitution through industrialization was one of the earliest goals of the ECLA theorists. The perceived advantage of import substitution, even with national protection of inefficient manufacturers, was that it would relieve the burden of foreign exchange by cutting imports from abroad to meet local demands. But some major weaknesses in this approach have come under attack in recent years. One study pointed out how the development of light industry in the first phase of industrialization permitted sizable savings of foreign exchange and had

29. Excerpts from the address of Gabriel Valdés Subercaseaux were translated and sent to member companies of the Council for Latin America in a memo from Enno Hobbing, August 12, 1969.

30. Quoted in Harvey S. Perloff, *Alliance for Progress*, p. 12.

31. Bermudez, address of April 22, 1970.

32. Esteban Ferrer, "Peru: The General as Revolutionary," p. 43.

33. Organization of American States, "Role of Foreign Private Investment in the Development of Latin America," p. 16.

a backward linkage to stimulate other activities requiring relatively simple technology and low capital density.[34] But problems developed when Latin American countries began to develop basic industries such as metals and metallurgy, chemicals, and paper, which required inputs of complex processed semimanufactures and materials produced in other basic industries, large amounts of capital, a high level of technology, and large-scale plants. The foreign exchange savings diminished as many products were made for the local market by light industry, while the input demands for heavy industry increased because the local economy did not have the capacity to produce the input of capital and technology which was required. Thus, the backward linkage of this phase of industrialization proceeded slowly.

Latin American policy makers responded to this situation by protecting these infant industries and their inefficient scale of operation; this raised the costs of inputs and equipment for the rest of industry, making the final price of their finished products uncompetitive in the world market, which reduced the likelihood of exports to redress their balance-of-payments problem. It is revealing to note that more than 90 per cent of Latin American exports are still related to traditional export activities. Foreign capital, it is charged, has thus "reenforced the trend toward insulated, compartmentalized industrialization" by producing for local markets (which was what the ECLA planners emphasized) rather than for world trade.[35] Thus, import-substitution policies have made the Latin American economies more dependent upon costly imports, more vulnerable in their balance of payments, and more unstable in their economies.[36]

The solution most of these critics propose is that foreign investment be admitted and regulated to ensure that it contributes to export-oriented production. If foreign investment promotes manufactured exports, it will "enable Latin America to participate in the process of international economic interdependence fundamentally related to world trade in manufacturing; help to eliminate the domestic bottlenecks by raising the export ration, reconstituting international reserves and strengthening the

34. Campos and Ferrer, "Foreign Investment and Latin American Economic Development," p. 3.

35. Ibid.

36. Sunkel, "National Development Policy and External Dependence in Latin America," p. 37.

capacity for transferring external debt service abroad; and, finally, facilitate the specialization of Latin American industrial production by encouraging greater efficiency, broader manufacturing development, and a more rapid expansion rate."[37] The Consensus of Viña del Mar expressed this attitude in its call for general preferences in favor of semimanufactured and manufactured goods from the less-developed countries and elimination of U.S. import restrictions on semimanufactured and manufactured products of importance to Latin America.[38] Latin American anger and dismay at President Nixon's New Economic Policy with the import surcharge will be discussed later.

Nationalist Restraints on Foreign Capital

The cautious recognition of the need for private foreign investment has led to the adoption of Latin American policies which seek to obtain capital in a manner consistent with national development goals and at a diminishing political and economic cost to the host nation. In 1969 President Lleras Restrepo of Colombia called for such a policy: "It is necessary to formulate a new policy regarding private foreign capital. This type of investment must be mutually beneficial. It must effectively contribute needed additional capital resources. It must transfer technological and administrative knowledge. It should pioneer in new activities rather than taking over existing investments. Local managers and technicians must be encouraged, or if necessary trained as eventual replacements for foreign personnel."[39] The Consensus of Viña del Mar also called for such an approach. Brazil's minister of finance, Antonio Delfim Netto, in a 1969 address to the Council for Latin America, emphasized that each nation must retain control of economic decisions. His government would prefer investments which enlarged exports or provided import substitution through new technology; local participation was also viewed as important to bolster domestic industry.[40]

These new national economic policies seek to prescribe or restrict the role of foreign private capital in sensitive sectors, such

37. Campos and Ferrer, "Foreign Investment and Latin American Economic Development," p. 4.
38. "Consensus of Viña del Mar," May 1969.
39. Lleras Restrepo, address of June 13, 1969.
40. Antonio Delfim Netto, Council for Latin America Report 6, p. 13.

as public utilities, and in fields which are critical to the foreign exchange of the nation, as with the copper industry in Chile. These "commanding heights" are deemed of crucial importance to the sovereign power of a nation; the introduction of foreign capital in these sectors undercuts the authority of the government, unless accompanied by programs which provide for the eventual transfer of ownership of all or part of the equity holdings of foreign investors to domestic governmental or private control. Peru's Velasco Doctrine, articulated by President Velasco on April 6, 1970, stipulated this objective: "The state should guarantee the legitimate rights of foreign investors to receive profits from their investment. From this point of view, foreign investment in Latin America should be channeled through mixed companies or private companies subject to a fixed time limit for reversion to the state once the total amount of the investment and an acceptable amount of profits have been recovered. In this way, foreign capital would have its capital and profits guaranteed, but all companies with foreign participation would progressively become nationally owned companies with decisive state participation. This, we think, would be a way of making the interests of our country compatible with the interests of those who want to invest in Latin America."[41] Peru's new industrial law set priorities for industrial development, with basic industries having the highest priority. Incentives would be offered to attract foreign investment in the emphasized fields, although it is believed that the first-priority industries would eventually become owned by the state.[42]

The Latin American demands for local participation in the management and ownership of foreign enterprises, whether formally described as Mexicanization or Chileanization, are derived from obvious concerns over the perceived costs of foreign private investment. Pressures may be exerted by a variety of methods on foreign enterprises to open participation to nationals. Renault was the winner, in bidding among ten companies from seven countries, of a Colombian government contract to participate in the establishment and operation of an automobile assembly plant; the contract stipulated at least 50 per cent Colombian participation in the venture. The agreement reached with Renault specified 70 per cent government partici-

41. Quoted in Ferrer, "Peru: The General as Revolutionary," p. 41.
42. George W. Grayson, Jr., "Peru's Military Populism," p. 74.

pation in the motor plant and 50 per cent in the assembly plant.[43] It was reported that Ford and General Motors disqualified themselves by failing to submit bids which accepted the 50 per cent stipulation. The government then began negotiations for a truck assembly plant with the same stipulation in the contract; this time Ford and General Motors did not object to the 50 per cent requirement.[44] Although there is no Colombian statutory requirement for local participation in foreign enterprises, administrative decisions on new bids for mineral exploration rights require Colombian participation. Negotiations over a nickel development venture involve the question of state participation. The U.S. Embassy in Bogotá is well aware of this trend; its September 1969 economic report stressed the emphasis on "national interest" and "mutual" benefit of the Colombian government and the private investor.[45]

Venezuela is not expected to renew its oil concessions when they expire in 1983. Already a new system of "service contracts" has been introduced which offers shorter terms for exploration and exploitation than the old concessions, and the state retains the right to 80 per cent of the explored blocks of land. Service contracts are seen by the Venezuelan government as an instrument to give the State Petroleum Corporation (CVP) operating experience so that it will be prepared to take over the oil concessions when they begin to expire in 1983.[46] In May 1969 Ecuador and Colombia also negotiated more favorable agreements with U.S. oil companies.

Regional Integration for Whom?

Another major concern of Latin American regimes is that foreign investors might gain the bulk of the benefits from economic development and regional integration because of their greater skills, capital, and capability to expand on a regional basis. This worry has affected the progress toward economic integration in the Latin American Free Trade Association and the Central American Common Market. A 1969 CIAP paper stated: ". . . one of the most

43. Colombian-American Chamber of Commerce newsletter, July 16, 1969.
44. *New York Times*, July 12, 1969, p. 47.
45. U.S., Department of State, "Economic Trends Report," unpublished, September 17, 1969, pp. 6–7.
46. U.S., Department of State, "Petroleum: Service Contracts," unpublished, October 10, 1969.

serious obstacles to the creation of the Latin American Common Market is the fear—which we consider justified—that private foreign investors will avail themselves intensively of the broad industrial prospects that such a market offers."[47] This wary attitude was reflected in a survey of Latin American governments and businessmen by ECLA and the OAS in 1961, which prompted the study to recommend consideration of a common policy toward foreign private investment.[48]

The disadvantage of national firms vis-à-vis multinational corporations in the setting of regional integration plans has been explained by their "lack of external connections and familiarity with the markets in the various countries," as well as the inherent competitive weakness due to their limited resources and experience solely within protected markets.[49] The director of regional economic policy of the State Department told the Foreign Affairs Committee in 1969 that the Latin Americans' "fear that the foreigner will 'skim the cream' off the integrated market may have been one factor inhibiting progress in integration."[50] This attitude has been very evident in the debate over the foreign investment restrictions of the Andean Common Market.

In October 1970 the junta of the Andean Common Market proposed a common policy toward private foreign investment. Some of the major points were: majority ownership (51 per cent equity) would be sold to local nationals within fifteen years, a regulation which would apply to all new and existing investments; new foreign investments in the extractive industries would be sharply limited; and new foreign investments in banking and insurance would be prohibited. The junta also suggested new regulations on profit remittances, declared that foreign patent holders could not restrict local licenses, and prohibited takeovers of national firms. The Colombians and Ecuadorians were not pleased with the proposed regulations, although the ideas did reflect the national policies of Peru, Bolivia, and Chile. Pressures were placed on Colombia to seek modification of the guidelines or

47. Organization of American States, "Role of Foreign Private Investment in the Development of Latin America," p. 6.

48. Quoted by Miguel S. Wionczek, "A Latin American View," p. 25.

49. Campos and Ferrer, "Foreign Investment and Latin American Economic Development," p. 19.

50. U.S., Congress, House, Committee on Foreign Affairs, *Hearings*, *New Directions for the 1970's: Toward a Strategy of Inter-American Development*, p. 227.

withdraw from the Andean Pact, and according to one source, the resistance of Colombia led to agreement on a modified Foreign Private Investment Code in December 1970.[51]

The code is less restrictive than the original junta draft, particularly in its distinctions between existing and new foreign investment. New foreign investments in basic services industries such as public utilities, banking, insurance, transportation, and heavy industry will be forbidden. Existing foreign banks, transportation, communication, and marketing companies will be required to divest themselves of 80 per cent (in the junta draft, 60 per cent) of their shares to national investors. The final code exempts existing firms in the basic industries and public service industries from the earlier divestiture requirements, provided they forego the benefits of the Andean Pact trade liberalization measures. Foreign companies were given fifteen years in Colombia, Chile, and Peru to comply with the new provisions, and twenty years in Bolivia and Ecuador. It is important to note that the Committee of the Cartagena Agreement declared: "One of the fundamental objectives of the common regime must be the strengthening of national companies in order to enable them to participate actively in the subregional market. . . ."[52] The importance of access to modern technology and managerial innovations was recognized in the code.

CONFLICT AT THE CONFERENCE TABLE

Several recent international conferences on direct foreign investment highlighted the gulf between the thinking of the United States and other foreign investors on the one hand, and Latin American governments and businessmen on the other. At the February 1970 Caracas conference of the Special Committee of the InterAmerican Economic and Social Council, the United States sponsored a statement which emphasized the usefulness of foreign enterprise, while Latin American delegates favored the policy declaration of the Consensus of Viña del Mar with its emphasis on joint ventures. Neither President Nixon's message to the conference nor the address of Assistant Secretary of State Meyer mentioned the touchy issue of the role of private enter-

51. *The Economist*, January 9, 1971, p. 78.

52. Unofficial translation of Decision 24 of the Committee of the Cartagena Agreement during sessions of December 14–31, 1970, Lima, Peru, p. 2.

prise, although the president did take the occasion to announce that his 1971 budget request earmarked $30 million to develop local securities markets and commissions in Latin America. Prime Minister Eric E. Williams of Trinidad and Tobago, who chaired the conference, temperately addressed the issue from the Latin American viewpoint: "Should we not recognize that we envelop in the simple term 'private foreign investment' a large package of services? Why not unscramble the package into its constituent elements and separate those services which the large international firm has to offer the developing countries of Latin America from those activities which the peoples and governments of the host countries feel that they, as sovereign countries, ought to exercise? Why not distinguish between ownership and control of property on the one hand, and management and technology on the other?"[53] It is important to note that no agreement was reached at the conference on this question of the role of private foreign enterprise.

The Medellín Conference in June 1970 issued a memorandum which was praised by the Council of the Americas as being "so realistically judicious about the terms of such investment that it may well be regarded as an intellectual and consensual breakthrough for development in the Hemisphere."[54] Several delegates were quoted as saying that the Medellín Memorandum made the Consensus of Viña del Mar obsolete. However, it should be pointed out that there were governmental representatives present from only seven Latin American countries, with Peru and Chile conspicuously absent. The U.S. investors were obviously pleased with the references to the business sectors as the "most dynamic forces" of the advanced countries, the need for Latin American countries to develop closer relationships with these forces, and the calls for firm rules of the game and improvement of the investment climate. However, missing from the memorandum were statements on some of the more controversial issues, which appear to have been skirted; for example, the balance-of-payments effects of foreign private investment were said to require further study. The possibility of conflict between multinational firms and host countries over the external locus of decision making, desire for local participation, and

53. *Christian Science Monitor*, December 7, 1970, p. 3.
54. Council of the Americas, "The Business Sectors Constitute the Most Dynamic Forces."

take-overs of domestic companies by foreign interests were discussed, but no clear consensus emerged.

The January 1971 Rome Conference on foreign private investment was warmly applauded by some U.S. business representatives because of its increased understanding of the prerequisites of foreign investment, while other observers offered a more critical evaluation. The main topics of the conference were the operations of the multinational corporation and the Foreign Private Investment Code of the Andean Common Market, and discussions of both questions emphasized the transfer of technology, perhaps the most generally acknowledged benefit of foreign investment.[55] The Latin Americans were especially disturbed over the tendency of the multinational firm to transcend national boundaries. The more sanguine appraisals of the Rome Conference as a bench mark toward creating rapport on the vital role of foreign capital overlooked the fact that the Latin American representatives were largely from the financial and industrial elite, who are not necessarily attuned to the thinking of the Latin American political decision makers or public opinion in the region.

In summary, the sensitivity of Latin Americans to the economic and political prominence of the United States in the hemisphere has led to a reappraisal of the advantages of foreign investment. ECLA's analysis of the adverse trade position of the less-developed periphery countries vis-à-vis the industrialized center stressed the increasing dependence of the periphery, which could only be overcome through industrialization and import-substitution policies. Foreign investment was considered more costly than capital received through portfolio investments or international assistance.

Fear of economic dominance and political interference in their domestic affairs has always concerned Latin Americans. The nineteenth-century Calvo Doctrine was an assertion of the right of sovereign nations to adjudicate all disputes within its borders; it is still invoked to deny the right of foreign investors to appeal to

55. The following statement illustrates the Latin American recognition of the need for technology: "A new era of international investment has dawned, in which the predominant characteristic is the exploitation of technology, as opposed to the previous one, which was frequently abusive, characterized by exploitation of the natural resources of the country" (Organization of American States, "Role of Foreign Private Investment in the Development of Latin America," p. 4).

their governments for intervention in investment conflicts. Key sectors of the economy, because of their political sensitivity and importance to the foreign exchange of the nation, are coming under greater regulation.

The balance-of-payments cost of foreign investment is an especially controversial question. Latin Americans are prone to calculate the effects of foreign capital by simply comparing the inflow of new capital to the outflow of profit remittances and fees, ignoring the impact on the productivity, employment, and tax revenues of the nation. It is politically more appealing to reaffirm the popular belief that foreign investment has been and is exploitive. Foreign investment is also criticized for impeding the development of the local private sector and demonstrating a lack of concern for local development goals.

The transfer of technology is viewed as the greatest benefit that foreign investment can introduce, but the mode of foreign investment has come under scrutiny by Latin American leaders who wish to ensure that foreign subsidiaries will not be operated to the disadvantage of the host country. Thus, greater emphasis is being placed on whether a firm contributes to the exports of the host country and develops local sources of supply. Local participation is considered one means of protecting the interests of the country, and in some cases, divestiture is proposed. National and regional restrictions on foreign capital are designed to prevent the more sophisticated U.S. firms from garnering the bulk of the benefits from economic development and regional integration.

The basic thrust of recent Latin American economic policies is to assert independence from foreign influence. Large foreign holdings, dominating critical sectors of the economy, are deemed a threat to the development of the nation and a challenge to its sovereignty. Foreign capital is desired, but under conditions which ensure the host country that there will be a transfer of technology and know-how, a diminishing presence in certain fields, and a positive contribution to the trade balance of the nation.

Mexican economist Victor Urquidi has pinpointed the cause of the difficulty of formulating a rational long-term policy toward foreign investment in the ambivalence and defensive attitudes of Latin American policy makers: "Short-term economic or political expediency usually overrides serious attempts to evaluate the role of foreign private capital and lay new foundations for its collaboration in economic development. . . ."[56] His evaluation is very perceptive of the psychological and political obstacles which economic nationalism has erected to a mutually beneficial relationship between foreign investment and Latin American development goals.

56. Victor Urquidi, "The Implications of Foreign Investment in Latin America," p. 112.

4. The Benefits of Foreign Investment

View from the States

THE EMPHASIS in official and private U.S. circles on the role of private enterprise in economic development is based on ideological, political, economic, and security arguments. Raymond Vernon has outlined, from the viewpoint of U.S. policy, the major economic and political advantages of private investment to the less-developed countries and to the United States.[1] The ideological tenor of the United States' perception of the contributions which private enterprise brings to a developing country was reflected in a 1964 congressional report: "Private investment is an effective instrument making for political stability: (a) by supporting the rise and vitality of a solid, articulate middle class made up of managers, property owners, and small capitalists; and (b) by providing a bulwark in support of individual freedom against the rise of arbitrary power, an ever present risk under a 'controlled economy.'

"Private investment is an effective instrument promoting economic growth and economic stability: (a) by decentralizing decision making, rewarding risk taking, and diffusing losses; and

1. Raymond Vernon, "The Political Economy of Private International Investment," pp. 266–70.

(b) by its efficiency in making use of the initiative of millions of persons, households, and business firms as centers for bringing together the always limited resources of know-how, manpower, and property to achieve maximum output of wanted goods and services."[2]

This chapter focuses on the perception of the benefits of foreign investment for developing countries, as viewed from the perspective of the United States. The arguments advanced by American officials and businessmen in defense of the role of foreign investment in economic development are often in direct conflict with the Latin American perception of the costs of foreign capital. Each side selectively chooses its data, and the respective conclusions often reflect the ideological and political attitudes of each position, rather than objective assessments of the advantages and disadvantages of foreign investment as a development agent. This clash highlights the important role of psychological factors in Latin American economic nationalism and in the American response to this phenomenon.

Pattern of U.S. Hemispheric Investment

The United States overtook Britain as the major source of new foreign private investment in Latin America during the period 1915–30; after World War II, the total value of U.S. direct investment in the region surpassed British holdings. But whereas British investment was often in the form of Latin American bonds and securities, American investors felt safer with equity investments, particularly after an unfortunate experience with portfolio investments in the 1920s. At the conclusion of World War II, 43 per cent of all U.S. overseas investment was in Latin America. However, by 1969 American investors had turned to Europe and other areas, and Latin America's share of U.S. direct investment was only 19 per cent of the world total. Europe appeared to offer a more stable investment climate than Latin America, especially after Fidel Castro came to power (see Table 4–1). The postwar investment boom in Latin America was centered primarily in the extractive industries; in 1959, 53 per cent of U.S. direct investment was in petroleum, mining, and smelting (see Table 4–2).

The nature of American investment in the hemisphere has

2. U.S., Congress, Joint Economic Committee, *Report, Private Investment in Latin America*, p. 3.

been dramatically altered by the rising force of economic nationalism. Investments in the politically sensitive public utilities field have dropped from 20 per cent in 1950 to 5 per cent in 1969 of the total U.S. investment in Latin America, while American investment in the extractive industry has declined slightly relative to other economic activities during the same period. The most significant shift has been in the manufacturing sector, where U.S. investment has almost doubled in the last

TABLE 4-1

Net Growth of U.S. Direct Investments, Selected Years, 1929-69
(in Billions of Dollars)

Years	1929 ($)	1946 ($)	1950 ($)	1959 ($)	1969 ($)
Total investment	7.5	7.2	11.8	29.7	70.8
Areas					
Canada	2.0	2.5	3.6	10.2	21.1
Latin America[a]	3.5	3.1	4.6	9.0	13.8
Europe	1.4	1.0	1.7	5.3	21.6
Middle East and Africa	.1	.2	1.0	2.0	4.8
Other Areas	.5	.4	.9	3.2	9.5
Industries					
Manufacturing	1.8	2.4	3.8	9.7	29.5
Petroleum	1.1	1.4	3.4	10.4	20.0
Mining and smelting	1.2	.8	1.1	2.9	5.6
Public utilities	1.6	1.3	1.4	2.4	2.7
Other industries	1.8	1.3	2.1	4.3	13.0

Source: U.S., Department of Commerce, *U.S. Business Investments in Foreign Countries*, 1960, and *Survey of Current Business*, October 1970.

a. Including European dependencies in the Western Hemisphere.

TABLE 4-2

U.S. Direct Investments in Latin America by Major Industries, Selected Years, 1929-69[a]
(in Millions of Dollars)

Year	Total ($)	Mining and Smelting ($)	Petroleum ($)	Manu-facturing ($)	Public Utilities ($)	Trade ($)	Other ($)
1929	3,519	732	617	231	887	119	933
1936	2,847	708	453	192	937	100	457
1943	2,798	405	618	325	875	143	433
1950	4,576	666	1,303	781	942	245	640
1959	8,990	1,416	3,312	1,426	1,150	687	998
1961[a]	8,255	1,105	3,247	1,655	664	763	732
1964	10,205	1,354	3,590	2,507	615	1,036	1,103
1969	13,811	1,922	3,722	4,347	695	1,406	1,720

Source: U.S., Department of Commerce, *U.S. Business Investments in Foreign Countries*, 1960; *Survey of Current Business*, October 1970; and "United States Direct Investments in the Latin American Republics, by Country and Major Industries, at Year End 1955-57."

a. Includes European dependencies in Western Hemisphere, with the exception of 1961, which presents the revised figures for the Latin American republics only, excluding the $954 million invested in the European dependencies.

twenty years. It is important also to note the selective pattern of American investment in the region (see Table 4–3). In 1969, 62 per cent of the total investment in the Latin American republics was concentrated in four countries—Mexico, Argentina, Brazil, and Venezuela. Venezuela benefited most from the postwar boom because of the flow of American capital into its petroleum industry. During the 1950s, Latin American leaders pointed to the concentration of American investment in just a few countries and the imbalance in the extractive sector as minimizing the contribution of foreign investment to the economic development of the region.

The Cuban Revolution had a deep impact on American investors; between 1959 and 1964, there was only an 8 per cent increase in U.S. investment in the hemisphere. However, after the Cuban missile crisis and the failure of the *fidelistas* to topple other governments, American investment surged ahead, increasing 31 per cent from 1964 to 1969. The confidence of American investors in Brazil was restored after the military coup of 1964. Rampant inflation and nationalist attacks on foreign capital during the administrations of Jânio Quadros and Joãs Goulart brought a decline in the level of American investment, but between 1964 and 1969 it increased 64 per cent because of the investment climate the generals had imposed. In 1969, 68 per cent of U.S. investment in Brazil and Mexico and 63 per cent in Argentina was in the manufacturing sector; petroleum investments were still important in Venezuela, but they had declined from the levels reached in the 1950s.

The Balance-of-Payments Issue—Betwixt and Between

U.S. officials and businessmen have reacted sharply to the Latin American charge that foreign investment represents a costly drain to their local economies. The thrust of the American rebuttal is that the Latin American formula for calculating the balance-of-payments effect of foreign capital is too narrow and thus ignores many of the other contributions of foreign investment to economic development in the hemisphere. There have been two major studies of the effects of U.S. investment in Latin America, one by the Department of Commerce in 1957 and another by the Council of the Americas in 1970; each presented data to support the contention of the United States that the total contribution of U.S.

TABLE 4-3

U.S. Direct Investments in Latin America by Country, Selected Years, 1929-69
(in Millions of Dollars)

Country and Area	1929 ($)	1936 ($)	1943 ($)	1950 ($)	1959 ($)	1961 ($)	1964 ($)	1969 ($)
Total, Latin American Republics	3,463	2,803	2,725	4,444	8,487	7,585	8,119	11,665
Mexico	682	480	286	415	759	830	1,034	1,631
Cuba	919	666	526	642	955	..[a]	..[a]	..[a]
Panama	29	27	110	58	328	486	659	1,071
Other Central America[b]	206	121	173	255	350	..[c]	..[c]	630
Argentina	332	348	380	356	361	660	882	1,244
Brazil	194	194	233	644	839	1,006	997	1,633
Chile	423	484	328	540	729	735	789	846
Colombia	124	108	117	193	399	425	508	684
Peru	124	96	71	145	427	436	464	704
Venezuela	233	186	373	993	2,808	3,007	2,786	2,668
Other countries	197	93	124	203	262	..[c]	..[c]	554
Total, Western Hemisphere dependencies	57	44	78	131	772	954	1,311	2,144

Source: U.S., Department of Commerce, *U.S. Business Investments in Foreign Countries*, 1960; *Survey of Current Business*, October 1970; and "United States Direct Investments in the Latin American Republics, by Country and Major Industries, at Year End 1955-57."

a. The Claims of U.S. investors for property losses in Cuba total an estimated $1.5 billion.

b. Includes Costa Rica, El Salvador, Guatemala, Honduras, and Nicaragua.

c. Complete data not available.

investment to the economic development of the region can only be evaluated by examining statistics for export promotion, import substitution, tax revenues, local employment and training, transfer of technology, and local expenditures.

During the 1946–58 period, the repatriation of income by U.S. firms exceeded new capital inflow and reinvested earnings by \$1.3 million; the extractive sector alone withdrew \$1.87 billion, while manufacturing had a net inflow of U.S. dollars into the hemisphere.[3] American firms produced \$2.1 billion of exports for the region in 1955—30 per cent of all Latin American exports—and production for import substitution netted the region \$3.7 billion in 1955. The Latin American subsidiaries and operations employed 616,000 Latin American employees and paid over \$4 billion in 1955 for wages and salaries, taxes, and local materials, services, and equipment. Export earnings generated sufficient foreign exchange to pay for all imports and income remitted to the United States by the companies and provided a \$900 million foreign exchange surplus to the countries in the region in 1955.

The Council for Latin America commissioned Herbert May, a former State Department official, to analyze the contributions of U.S. private investment to Latin America's growth. May concluded in his report to the council that "the *net* positive contribution of U.S. investment to Latin America's balance-of-payments during 1965 to 1968 was about 8.55 billion dollars annually."[4] He termed the ECLA charge of a balance-of-payments drain a "logical fallacy." Such a calculation ignored, he argued, U.S. expenditures in 1966 of about \$2,455 million for wages and salaries, almost \$6,200 million for materials, supplies, and services, and tax revenues of \$1,613 million—approximately 14.7 per cent of the total tax revenues of the region. His data provided a partial rebuttal to the Latin American charge that extractive firms exploited the host country, since in 1957 U.S. petroleum affiliates paid 60 per cent of the total expenditure by all U.S. affiliates for Latin American taxes; however, by 1966 the figure had dropped to 47 per cent, still a significant share of hemispheric tax revenues (see Table 4–4). May also found that of the approximately 475,000 people em-

3. U.S., Department of Commerce, Office of Business Economics, *U.S. Investments in the Latin American Economy.*

4. Council for Latin America, "The Effects of United States and Other Foreign Investment in Latin America," report by Herbert K. May, p. 1.

ployed by U.S. manufacturing affiliates in 1966, only about 7.5 per cent of the managerial staff were North Americans. The net figure of $8.55 billion included a savings in foreign exchange of $4.79 billion a year through import substitution.

The Council of the Americas has acknowledged that if one employs the Latin American formula of measuring the impact of

TABLE 4-4

Current Expenditures by All U.S. Affiliated in 1957 and 1966[a] for Wages and Salaries; Materials, Supplies and Services; and Taxes[b] (in Millions of Dollars)

Type of Expenditure by Industry	1957 ($)	1966 ($)
Wages and Salaries		
Manufacturing affiliates	354	1,147
Petroleum affiliates	413	500
Mining and smelting affiliates	179	222
Other nonmanufacturing affiliates	356	584
Total, all affiliates	1,302	2,453
Materials, Supplies, and Services		
Manufacturing affiliates	1,458	3,940
Petroleum affiliates	1,186	1,432
Mining and smelting affiliates	317	392
Other nonmanufacturing affiliates	267	438
Total, all affiliates	3,228	6,202
Taxes		
Manufacturing affiliates	149	464
Petroleum affiliates	635	769
Other nonmanufacturing affiliates	265	380
Total, all affiliates	1,049	1,613

Source: Council for Latin America, "The Effects of United States and Other Foreign Investment in Latin America," May Report.

a. Estimate figures.

b. The 1960 report of the U.S. Department of Commerce, *U.S. Business Investments in Foreign Countries*, did not break down tax-payments separately by mining and smelting affiliates.

foreign investment, there has been a greater annual remittance of U.S. capital than inflow of new American investment into the region (see Table 3–2). However, the council defended the U.S. investor by pointing to the benefits derived from U.S. investment and argued that the inflow of U.S. official bilateral assistance during the Alliance for Progress more than compensated for the net outflow of private capital.[5] Between 1961 and 1968 there was an outflow from the region of $3,835 million in American private capital, while there was a net inflow of U.S. foreign assistance of $5,202 million, which provided a net positive flow of funds to Latin America of $1,367 million. This argument is surprising since the differences of opinion within the organization have prevented the Council of the Americas from testifying in support of the U.S. foreign assistance program.

The Department of State has also sought to rebut the Latin American charge of exploitation by declaring that a simple comparison between "*annual* inflows versus outflows is both misleading and inappropriate . . ."; a more valid comparison would require an analysis of the annual remittances versus the cumulative or book value of the total U.S. private investment of the hemisphere.[6] The State Department provided Congress with a table of U.S. direct investment and repatriated profits from 1961 to 1967 which revealed an annual remittance by U.S. companies of less than 10 per cent of the total value per year.[7]

The controversy over the costs of foreign investment compelled Assistant Secretary Meyer to tell the sixth meeting of the Inter-American Economic and Social Council on June 20, 1969: "It is said that private investment results in a net outflow of resources from the recipient country. To me this is like trying to capture a moving situation with a still camera. Investment cannot be considered simply as an accounting procedure in which the direct inflow of new investment is measured against the direct outflow of remittances. What must be considered is the overall contribution in terms of increased production, added employment, new exports created, and imports replaced. In short, it is the continuing effect on economic activity and welfare and not the

5. Council for Latin America, "Are We Taking More Out of Latin America than We Are Putting In?" Report 5.

6. U.S., Congress, House, Committee on Foreign Affairs, *Hearings, Foreign Assistance Act of 1969*, p. 1173.

7. Ibid., p. 1174.

short term and partial effect on the balance of payments in a fixed period that is the true measure of the contribution of investment."[8] He appeared to be replying to many of the points in the Consensus of Viña del Mar. James R. Fowler, deputy coordinator of the Alliance for Progress, attacked the Prebisch center / periphery theory before a House committee in 1969, as "interesting and ingenious, but economically unfounded."[9] He attributed the persistence and popularity of the ECLA thesis to its emotional appeal in the less-developed countries and to the incompleteness of statistics for the encompassed period to prove or disprove the theory of exploitation by the industrialized countries.

The question of the balance-of-payments effect of private foreign investment has been of great interest to the Treasury Department and to American economists. One tool they employ to determine balance-of-payments payback is "recoupment periods," which "purport to measure how long it takes for a single investment outflow to produce an equal and opposite cumulative stream of balance-of-payments receipt. The number of years recognized is typically calculated by dividing the dollar investment outlay by the sum of the incremental annual balance of payment inflows attributable to the specific outlay."[10] One study found the following average payback periods: world total—8.1 years; Canada—10.2 years; Latin America—9.7 years; Western Europe—6.5 years; and other parts of the world—6.6 years.[11] Sharp debate has arisen in the United States over the methods of calculation and whether there should be short recoupment periods of one to three years.[12]

President Lyndon B. Johnson, after attempting voluntary restraints, established a mandatory foreign direct investment program on January 1, 1968, to improve the U.S. balance-of-payments position, which was adversely affected by the Vietnam War. The new Office of Foreign Direct Investments was charged with the

8. U.S., Department of State, *The Department of State Bulletin* 61 (July 14, 1969):9–10.

9. U.S., Congress, House, Committee on Appropriations, *Hearings, Foreign Assistance and Related Agencies Appropriations for 1970*, pt. 2:1743.

10. F. Michael Adler, "The High Cost of Foreign Investment Restraints," p. 74.

11. Ibid., p. 81.

12. G. C. Hufbauer and F. Michael Adler, "Foreign Investment Restraints: Objective—Removal," p. 38.

responsibility of reducing foreign direct investment by $1 billion in 1968. The less-developed countries were favored by allowing direct investments of 110 per cent of the direct investment of a firm during the base years 1965–66. These controls were not well received by the international business community, which sought their early elimination. Businessmen argued that the program reduced needed U.S. investments in the less-developed countries, a charge which Don Cadle, the acting director of the Office of Foreign Direct Investments, vigorously denied.[13] The 1969 hearings to terminate the foreign direct investment controls brought forth many statements from U.S. investors defending their positive contributions to the U.S. balance of payments. It must be remembered, of course, that some of these figures represent global investments, not simply investments in Latin America or the less-developed countries generally.

A vice-president of Minnesota Mining and Manufacturing Company stated: "In the past several years, amounts received from overseas operations have exceeded capital funds sent overseas by about 100 million dollars annually."[14] A spokesman for International Telephone and Telegraph Corporation (ITT) declared that ITT, based on its 1968 performance, was repatriating at the rate of $1 billion every ten years, and this figure would probably double in the next ten years.[15] The president of Kennecott Copper Corporation, Frank R. Milliken, speaking for the U.S. mining industry, said: "If we compute balance-of-payments flows in a meaningful and realistic way, taking into account royalties, licenses, fees, interest, and similar returns, as well as the capital flows which are encompassed within the control program, we find that in the 8-year period immediately preceding the January 1, 1968 regulations (that is 1960–1967) the net contribution of the mining industry was $2.113 billion."[16] He pointed out that the investment controls were designed primarily to stem the outflow to Europe, but the mining industry had only 1.3 per cent of its entire overseas investments there. The book value for the mining industry in Latin America was $1.218 billion in 1967, which was 34.3 per cent of the entire book value. Thus, the

13. U.S., Congress, House, Committee on Foreign Affairs, *Hearings, Foreign Direct Investment Controls*, p. 221.
14. Ibid., p. 306.
15. Ibid., p. 312.
16. Ibid., p. 176.

investment of the mining industry was concentrated in areas consistent with the U.S. policy objectives of encouraging economic development in the less-developed countries.

The United Fruit Company, well known in Central America and throughout the hemisphere, testified that its repatriated earnings from operations in the less-developed countries increased from $12 million in 1965 to approximately $25 million in 1968. In addition, almost 50 per cent of the expenditures of the company were for the import of U.S. materials, supplies, and equipment.[17] The spokesman also stated that United Fruit Company employed 44,000 people, paid taxes of $18 million in 1968, and maintained hospitals, schools, and health programs. In 1970 the president of CPC International, Inc., defended the contribution of the multinational corporation to the U.S. economy before the Joint Economic Committee. He emphasized that American direct foreign investment had made a positive balance-of-payments contribution in 1969 of about $4.6 billion.[18]

During the hearings on foreign investment controls and the multinational corporation, American foreign investors were compelled to present evidence that their overseas holdings helped to reduce the U.S. balance-of-payments deficit. While their testimony may have allayed the concerns of Congress and the Treasury Department, the figures they cited—which highlighted the repatriation of U.S. profits exceeding the outflow of new foreign investment—could prove supportive of the ECLA contention of a balance-of-payments drain on the Latin American economies. Statements which emphasized expenditures for the purchase of U.S. materials and equipment could also be attacked by nationalists who would prefer to see the development of local sources of supply. Therefore, the U.S. foreign investor finds himself criticized no matter which way he turns; the American labor movement and governmental officials see an adverse impact on the U.S. economy from foreign investment, while Latin American nationalists view the repatriation of U.S. capital as a manifestation of exploitation.

Assistant Secretary of the Treasury John Petty, in August 1970, aptly expressed the paradox of the entire debate over the balance-of-payments effects of foreign investment: "I find it hard

17. Ibid., p. 87.

18. U.S., Congress, Joint Economic Committee, *Hearings*, *A Foreign Economic Policy for the 1970's*, pt. 4:767.

to understand how such investment can simultaneously be harmful to both economies, the United States and those abroad."[19] However, he loyally termed the Latin American calculation of profits as a return flow of capital as "both misleading and inappropriate."[20] When the issue is so complex, with so many conflicting interpretations on such a sensitive matter, it is no wonder that the politically simple and emotionally satisfying answer is often seized upon in the hemispheric debate.

Profitability and Defensive Investment

The issue is complicated further by the question of what level of profits can be considered reasonable for foreign investment. May's report disputed Latin American assertions that American companies were exploiting the area through exorbitant profits. He found that while the average rate of return of all U.S. investments in Latin America was between 11.9 per cent and 13.3 per cent during the period 1960–68, the returns from the extractive industries were "substantially higher" than the general average and those for manufacturing investments and in other categories "were substantially lower than the general average."[21] However, he pointed out that the return on manufacturing investments in all other regions of the world, with the exception of Canada, were substantially higher than the U.S. return of 10.4 per cent on its Latin American investments during 1960–68 (see Tables 4–5 and 4–6). He compared his figures on the rate of return on U.S. direct investment in Latin America vis-à-vis other parts of the world to the profitability of British direct investments in the hemisphere and concluded that British direct investment in Latin America also reflected lower rates of return than available investment opportunities elsewhere. These facts would appear to bolster arguments that Latin America must offer greater inducements and a hospitable investment climate to attract foreign investment during a period of capital scarcity and excellent alternative investment opportunities—at least for manufacturing enterprises.

But the advantage of foreign private investment to the

19. John R. Petty, "The U.S.–Latin American Trade and Payments Relationship," p. 94.

20. Ibid., p. 93.

21. Council for Latin America, *Effects of Foreign Investment in Latin America*, May Report, p. 21.

TABLE 4-5

Annual Rates of Return on U.S. Direct Investments in Manufacturing in Latin America and Other Regions of the World, 1960-68[a]

Year	Latin America (%)	Canada (%)	Europe (%)	Africa (%)	Middle and Far East (%)	Oceania (%)
1960	11.2	8.7	16.7	15.8	4.8	19.9
1961	10.1	7.5	14.0	16.1	17.5	13.4
1962	10.4	9.0	11.7	28.3	15.6	19.7
1963	8.8	10.2	12.5	30.0	14.7	18.6
1964	11.1	9.8	14.2	24.4	19.3	17.3
1965	11.6	9.8	13.0	18.7	19.1	13.9
1966	11.4	9.2	11.2	14.7	16.2	12.7
1967	8.0	8.0	9.5	13.8	18.7	12.5
1968[b]	11.4	8.3	10.6	11.4	20.2	11.5

Source: Council for Latin America, "The Effects of United States and Other Foreign Investment in Latin America," May Report, p. 66.

a. The percentages represent the ratios of total earnings in each year (including reinvested earnings) to the total outstanding investment in manufacturing at the end of the previous year.

b. Preliminary figures.

economy of the United States is more involved than simple profitability calculations. For example, it has been asserted that every dollar invested abroad generates forty-two cents in U.S. exports, which, in a less-developed area like Latin America, means the sale of equipment, materials, and supplies.[22] It is this situation which has led several observers to declare that U.S. direct investment in the less-developed countries has had a more favorable effect on the balance of payments of the United States than U.S. investment in the developed countries.[23] Others point

22. Quoted by an official of United Fruit Company, House Committee on Foreign Affairs, *Hearings*, *Foreign Direct Investment Controls*, p. 88.

23. Charles D. Hyson and Dale R. Weigel, "Investment in the LDCs: The Unresolved Debate," p. 40.

TABLE 4-6

Annual Rate of Return on U.S. Direct Investments in Latin America by Principal Industry Categories, 1960-68[a]

	Rate of Earnings				
Year	Total (%)	Manu-facturing (%)	Petroleum (%)	Mining and Smelting (%)	Other Industry (%)
1960	12.2	11.2	11.7	15.8	11.4
1961	12.4	10.1	14.9	15.4	8.9
1962	13.1	10.4	15.1	17.9	9.7
1963	11.9	8.8	14.6	17.2	7.7
1964	12.7	11.1	15.0	20.0	7.4
1965	13.0	11.6	14.5	21.5	8.4
1966	13.3	11.4	14.4	25.2	8.2
1967	12.2	8.0	15.3	26.1	6.6
1968[b]	13.2	11.4	15.4	23.0	7.7

Source: Council for Latin America, "The Effects of United States and Other Foreign Investment in Latin America," May Report, p. 63.

a. The percentages represent the ratios of total earnings in each year (including reinvested earnings) to the total outstanding investment in each industry category at the end of the previous year.

b. Preliminary figures.

out that the large multinational firm garners a higher yield than other foreign competitors because of better management skills and the advantage of international scale.[24] Thus, Latin American entrepreneurs are not the only ones concerned over the competitive advantage of the large U.S. corporation; European and Japanese firms are also worried.

But profit maximization is not the principal motivation behind foreign private investment. Prospects for new markets or protection of existing markets is more likely to influence the overseas investment of American firms. A 1952 Department of

24. Adler, "The High Cost of Foreign Investment Restraints," p. 70.

Commerce survey showed that 38 per cent of the companies studied had invested abroad in order to avoid losing their overseas markets.[25] In a 1959 examination of seventy-two U.S. firms, increased profits were the avowed motive for foreign investment of only twenty companies and the sole motive of only eight firms.[26] A survey by McGraw-Hill in 1960 reported that 48 per cent of the corporate respondents cited prospects for new markets as the most important factor in a foreign investment decision, 20 per cent said higher profits, and only 6 per cent mentioned the lower cost of foreign labor.[27] Thus, the first decision of a U.S. firm to export its product leads to a situation where, because of this desire to expand or protect its foreign market from discriminatory regulations, the corporate decision is made to invest abroad. One writer expressed this idea in the following proposition: "Exports should perhaps properly be viewed as the natural forerunners of U.S. direct foreign investment. Rather than foreign investment displacing exports we should think of exports as leading to investment abroad."[28] Therefore, the commonly held view that foreign investments are made on the basis of systematic scanning of the world for profitable opportunities is inaccurate. Neoclassical economic theory does not recognize that investment decisions are not made solely on the basis of profit maximization, because of the uncertainty of the key variables which determine profit; maintenance of sales and exports take on greater importance. This factor has caused some individuals to question the effectiveness of current U.S. programs to encourage private investment in the less-developed countries by reducing risks and increasing profits through tax concessions.[29] The above considerations are the basis of the theory of "defensive investment."

The 1970 hearings on foreign economic policy and multinational corporations reflected this thinking. The statements of U.S. corporate leaders, defending themselves against labor charges that American jobs were being exported abroad, clearly indicate the primacy of the concept of defensive investment. Eldridge Haynes, chairman and president of Business International, Inc.,

25. Quoted by Raymond F. Mikesell, "Promoting United States Private Investment Abroad," Planning Pamphlet 101, p. 30.

26. Jack N. Behrman, "Foreign Associates and Their Financing," pp. 88–89.

27. Ibid., p. 89.

28. Adler, "High Cost of Foreign Investment Restraints," p. 77.

29. Hyson and Weigel, "Investment in the LDCs: The Unresolved Debate," p. 37.

told the Joint Economic Committee: "*I know of no company, not a single company, that has invested abroad in productive facilities when there was a reasonable chance of winning a significant share of the market by exporting* [sic]."[30] He declared it false to say that direct investment exported jobs since it actually stimulated domestic U.S. economic activity by the increased exports of machinery and inflow of capital into the United States from royalties, fees, interest, and dividends. The chairman of the board and president of Charles Pfizer and Company, John J. Powers, described the reason for the growth of sales and production operations overseas as stemming primarily from the need to compete in markets where the host governments required local production by restricting or heavily taxing the import of finished goods or basic materials. He concluded: "It is not then a question of exporting jobs or of export substitution. The fact is unless investments are made, the market would be lost and the flow of exports dried up."[31]

The growth potential of Latin American markets is an important factor in the expansion of U.S. investments in the hemisphere, as a vice-president of Celanese Fibers Group Company has indicated. While mass markets exist at the present time, larger markets will exist in the future as the population increases, development occurs, and the level of individual consumption is raised.[32] However, as regional integration programs progress, the markets will expand and Latin American governments will be provided with increased bargaining leverage over the modes and conditions for foreign investment; they will be pressured to enact such restrictions by local businessmen who fear foreign competition.

The Council Speaks Out

The policy statements of the Council of the Americas highlight the conflicting viewpoints between U.S. investors and Latin American governments and businessmen. In addition to the argument mentioned earlier concerning the net positive flow of combined U.S. private and public investment in Latin America,

30. U.S., Congress, Joint Economic Committee, *Hearings*, *A Foreign Economic Policy for the 1970's*, pt. 1:93.
31. Ibid., p. 131.
32. F. D. Uno, "The Latin American Investment Climate," p. 13.

the council criticized the Latin American balance-of-payments charge by explaining that any successful investment over the long run will realize profits plus capital recovery in excess of the original investment: "However, the degree to which remittances exceed inflows during any arbitrary time period will depend on the investment opportunities available within the country concerned, and on the relative attractiveness of alternative investment opportunities elsewhere."[33] Hence, part of the responsibility for any capital outflow must be assumed by the Latin Americans if they fail to provide a favorable investment climate.

The council acknowledged that the total remittances on U.S. investment in Latin America exceeded new capital inflow during the 1959–67 period, but attributed this to the oil industry in Venezuela. It had made two large investments of over $1 billion between 1946–49 and 1955–57, and the substantial disinvestment after 1958 was because of the lack of reinvestment opportunities in several Latin American countries and investor uncertainty after the Cuban Revolution. However, the popularity of the ECLA balance-of-payments argument in Latin America undoubtedly encouraged the chairman of the council, David Rockefeller, to urge council members in December 1968 to undertake at least one export promotion project to increase Latin American exchange earnings, perhaps equal to the volume of their profit remittances.[34]

The council has described the conditions which are imperative for U.S. private investment to make an optimal contribution to Latin American socioeconomic development:

1. Clear and liberal definition of areas that private enterprise, local or foreign, can enter.
2. No rigid requirements imposing joint ventures or stock distribution or time limits on existence of an enterprise undertaken by a foreign investor.
3. Fiscal, monetary, or exchange incentives could be used to attract private investment.
4. Profit and other remittances should be free of any restrictions.

33. Council for Latin America, "The Role of Private U.S. Investment in Latin American Economic Development," Report 5, October 1969, p. 2.

34. Quoted in Jerome Levinson and Juan de Onís, *The Alliance that Lost Its Way*, p. 143.

5. Creation of a multi-lateral system of insurance against expropriation and other noncommercial risks with Latin American participation.
6. Reinvestment of profits could be encouraged by incentive and even changed thusly into depressed geographic areas or activities.
7. A reasonable degree of political and economic and financial stability.[35]

Hobbing, the staff director of the council, told the Foreign Affairs Committee in 1969 that the establishment of firm rules of the game by Latin American governments was of highest priority in the eyes of the business community in Latin America: "Even the demonstration of what foreign investment has contributed or can contribute is probably secondary to some agreement on the rules of the game. . . ."[36]

The consensus of the council was that Latin American policy makers had to be made to realize the imperative of constant rules of the game: "A business can live with adverse rules but it has to know what they are and it has to know that there is not going to be a capricious change."[37] The sensitivity to foreign investment was heightened by the large role of Latin American governments in their economies, which restricted the growth of a vigorous domestic private sector and made the presence of foreign capital appear disproportionately large. One solution, which Hobbing suggested, would be for Latin American governments to divest themselves of some of their state-owned enterprises, thus permitting the expansion of the private sector.[38]

The U.S. business community strongly objected to the Latin American trend toward state enterprises. State enterprises absorbed revenues needed for investment in infrastructure and social improvements and, by limiting the areas of private foreign enterprise, they reduced the total available capital in a country and limited the opportunity to acquire new technological and managerial inputs from foreign investments. The ideological argument was advanced that inefficient state enterprises, unguided by the capitalistic tools of profit and competition, would waste the

35. Council for Latin America, Report 5, October 1969, p. 7.

36. U.S., Congress, House, Committee on Foreign Affairs, *Hearings*, *New Directions for the 1970's: Toward a Strategy of Inter-American Development*, p. 387.

37. Ibid., p. 386.

38. Ibid., p. 378.

sorely needed scarce resources of skilled labor and local capital, while national pride and bureaucratic interests would prevent abandonment of bankrupt or inefficient state enterprises. Managerial and technological improvements would be difficult to adopt, because in state-owned enterprises "the drive for greater efficiency usually has a lower priority than the retention of political appointments and over-employment."[39]

The council defended the take-over of local firms in Latin America by foreign investors; such actions were considered in the national interest of the host country, since foreign investors would save the local firm from bankruptcy and improve its efficiency through the introduction of new managerial and technological techniques. Foreign take-overs would also bolster the efforts of the host country toward export expansion and import substitution, reduce the prices of the product to its customers, increase the employment of nationals, and expand the level of production. The introduction of foreign capital would, in addition, free local capital for new investment.[40]

The executive vice-president of the council, Henry R. Geylin, in testimony before the Foreign Affairs Committee said that the anti-Americanism manifested in the region existed only in a small sector of society. He declared that "anti-American feeling is fostered usually through fear of encroachment in the national private sector."[41] Latin American businessmen generated anti-American sentiment as a defense against the threat of competition. "They are not used to the idea that they have to compete in the market. This is the basic difference between our concept of private enterprise and Latin America's concept of private enterprise. . . ." He commented that the Latin American labor force would rather work for a U.S. corporation than a national firm, and "the people are either indifferent to or don't believe in the threat of economic domination."[42]

The council advocated a flexible governmental policy on joint ventures, underscoring that they were viable only when they "are realistically based on each partner's effective contribution."[43] The position of the council was that rigid equity requirements for

39. Council for Latin America, Report 5, October 1969, p. 6.

40. Ibid., p. 5.

41. House Committee on Foreign Affairs, *Hearings*, *New Directions for the 1970's*, p. 387.

42. Ibid.

43. Council for Latin America, Report 5, October 1969, p. 4.

enterprises with heavy capital requirements or complex technology were counterproductive, since they could discourage needed new investment. The use of scarce local capital for joint ventures also had the disadvantage of limiting its productive input, since it would only replace capital which foreigners would have been willing to invest. The council viewed the demand for joint ventures rather cynically: "Latin Americans only want to take equity positions in prosperous and promising U.S. ventures in their countries. . . ."[44] Another problem concerned the world marketing arrangements of the parent company: "Where local equity does not serve the functioning of internationally-oriented management, it serves neither the interests of the U.S. company, nor ultimately, of the host country. . . ."[45] Geylin colorfully summed up the position of the council in 1969: "We have found that forced joint ventures are not good. Basically what you look around for is a nice love affair where there is a happy marriage but a shotgun wedding usually winds up in acrimonious divorce."[46]

The council attacked the fade-out, or divestment, formula for foreign investment as an "unworkable and unrealistic proposal. Foreign investors do not invest to go out of business."[47] Future uncertainties about fiscal and monetary policies, technology, and the nature of the market preclude a prudent investor from entering into such an agreement; foreign companies, it was argued, presently have the necessary flexibility to adapt to these changes and wait longer than expected for recovery of their investments, while foreign governments would be unlikely to grant them terms generous enough to meet the unexpected circumstances. Divestiture was viewed as contrary to the development goals of the less-developed countries because scarce local capital would be used to purchase existing investments rather than to engage in new productive investment, and the foreign investor would be unlikely to seek new investment or agree in the divestiture contract to reinvest in the host country. The council warned that as the "take-over deadline approaches, a foreign investor would probably be reluctant to inject new technology and managerial skills or undertake to expand export markets, perhaps at the expense of

44. Council for Latin America, "The Matter of Joint Ventures," Report 5, November 1969.

45. Ibid.

46. House Committee on Foreign Affairs, *Hearings*, *New Directions for the 1970's*, p. 377.

47. Council for Latin America, Report 5, October 1969, p. 3.

subsidiaries in other countries where he can maintain ownership."[48]

In conclusion, U.S. investors and government officials emphatically reject the ECLA charge that foreign investment creates a balance-of-payments drain on the Latin American economies. They point out that the Prebisch theory examines only the annual flow of capital and ignores the other contributions of foreign investment to the host country: tax revenues, employment, increased production, and import substitution. However, the lack of available statistics for the earlier years makes it difficult either to refute or prove the center / periphery argument that the industrialized countries exploited the less-developed countries. Studies are cited as evidence of the positive impact of U.S. direct investment in the hemisphere, but the cold facts confront an emotional climate and a different formula for the calculation of the effects of foreign investment. The paradox is that U.S. investors are compelled to defend themselves both against American critics who feel that foreign investment is detrimental to the U.S. economy, and against Latin American nationalists who see the excess of profit remittances over the inflow of new investment as a manifestation of economic exploitation.

Studies have indicated that U.S. investment in Latin America has not been as profitable as alternative investment opportunities in other parts of the world; this supports an emphasis by the business community on inducements and a favorable investment climate. However, U.S. investment in Latin America is accompanied by the export of U.S. goods and services, which stimulate domestic production and benefit the U.S. balance of payments. The corporate decision to export a product often leads to the decision to invest abroad as a means to expand or protect the overseas market. Therefore, despite the growing Latin American restrictions on foreign investment, the market of the hemisphere will continue to attract foreign investors who are sensitive to domestic and foreign competition and wish to maintain their present market or take advantage of integration efforts and the economic growth potential of the region.

Joint ventures are seen by many foreign investors as a means to overcome political objections to foreign capital, but a key factor is the choice of a competent partner. Some critics question whether joint ventures reduce nationalist attacks and fear that the

48. Ibid.

parent company will favor wholly owned subsidiaries over joint ventures. As the initial benefits of a foreign investment to the host country cease to be spectacular, pressures mount for the divestment of the enterprise to local ownership. Some U.S. economists propose fade-out formulas whereby the foreign investor is allowed to obtain a profit on his investment but agrees to divest over an agreed-upon number of years; the suggestions usually encourage a continued relationship with minority equity to ensure the flow of new technology. It appears unlikely, however, that Congress will agree to fund international agencies to finance the divestment of U.S. investments in the hemisphere.[49]

The Council of the Americas rebutted the Latin American balance-of-payments charge and commissioned a study to demonstrate the contributions of U.S. foreign investment to the economic development of Latin America. Members have been urged to promote export production as a means to ease the burden of profit remittances. Council spokesmen stress the need for firm rules of the game, so that the investor can know what is expected of him. Latin American businessmen, who fear competition, have been identified as the source of much of the agitation against foreign investment. Policy statements have strongly opposed state-owned enterprises in the hemisphere and defended the take-over of local companies by U.S. firms. The council opposes rigid equity requirements for joint ventures and is concerned over the problems they create for worldwide marketing arrangements. Fade-out formulas are deemed unworkable and unrealistic; they would frighten away potential investors and discourage the input of new technology into enterprises scheduled for divestiture.

49. Albert O. Hirschman proposed the creation of an Inter-American Development Corporation in his provocative monograph, *How to Divest in Latin America, and Why*, p. 12ff. Raul Prebisch suggested that a subsidiary of the Inter-American Development Bank could assist in the transfer of shares in foreign enterprises to Latin American private enterprise (see *Change and Development: Latin America's Great Task*, report submitted to the Inter-American Development Bank, p. 158). Senator Jacob Javits issued a clear warning about divestment programs sponsored by U.S.-financed international institutions in an address to the American Management Association in New York on February 1, 1971: "I am aware that there is some discussion that the Inter-American Development Bank or possibly some other international institutions develop a program whereby bank funds would be used to further the disinvestment programs. It is my view that such programs would have politically explosive implications in the U.S. Congress that could be detrimental to any international institution proposing such a program."

5. Foreign Aid or Private Initiative?

THE CONFLICTING VIEWPOINTS on the benefits of private enterprise in the economic development process were particularly manifest in the U.S. foreign assistance programs in the post–World War II years. Latin Americans constantly pressed the U.S. government for economic assistance, looking enviously at the flow of American dollars to Europe under the Marshall Plan. Washington's response throughout most of the Truman and Eisenhower administrations was to shunt aside these requests for increased governmental aid with statements referring to the adequacy of current Export-Import Bank loans for "sound projects" and the availability of U.S. private capital if a favorable investment climate in Latin America was created. Since private enterprise was seen as the most effective means to foster economic development, the Latin American republics were advised to concentrate their efforts on creating the conditions and inducements necessary to attract domestic and foreign capital. This issue was raised at almost every Inter-American conference in the postwar period. The question of economic assistance was debated at the Inter-American meetings in Mexico City in 1945, Rio de Janeiro in 1947, Bogotá in 1948, Washington, D.C., in 1951,

Caracas in 1954, Rio de Janeiro in 1954, and Buenos Aires in 1957.[1]

This chapter will present the official American view of the role that private enterprise was to play in U.S. foreign assistance programs during the Truman and Eisenhower administrations. The perception of American policy makers that private capital was the key catalyst for economic growth influenced attitudes toward Latin American requests for "softer" loans and greater amounts of aid. The ideological faith in private initiative, based on the economic development of the United States, overlooked the different conditions and attitudes toward private enterprise in Latin America. These American perceptions were eventually shaken, not by economic arguments, but by two events—Vice-President Nixon's stormy Latin American trip and the rise of Fidel Castro.

Point Four for Development

In Mexico City in 1945, the Inter-American Conference on Problems of War and Peace adopted the Economic Charter of the Americas, which acknowledged the central role of private businessmen in the development of the hemisphere. Latin Americans agreed to the charter, according to one source, because it appeared to endorse the policy of import substitution.[2] The charter urged Latin Americans to encourage private enterprise and included specific guaranties for foreign entrepreneurs, including a section titled "Elimination of Excesses of Economic Nationalism." In September 1947 Secretary of State George C. Marshall told the delegates at the Inter-American Conference for the Maintenance of Continental Peace and Security, in Quitandinha, Brazil, that the long-term economic development of Latin America required "a type of collaboration in which a much greater role falls to private citizens and groups than is the case in a program designed to aid European countries to recover from the destruction of war."[3]

The most vigorous promoter of U.S. private investment in Latin America was President Truman's secretary of commerce,

1. Edwin Lieuwen, *U.S. Policy in Latin America*, p. 112.

2. J. Warren Nystrom and Nathan A. Haverstock, *The Alliance for Progress*, p. 26.

3. Quoted in Donald M. Dozer, *Are We Good Neighbors?: Three Decades of Inter-American Relations, 1930–1960*, p. 242.

Averell Harriman. He advanced a program which sought treaties of friendship, commerce, and navigation to ensure the equitable treatment of U.S. private investments; foreign governments would provide prompt, adequate, and effective compensation in the event of expropriation, convertibility of the currency of their country, and fair levels for profit remittances. Harriman was behind the adoption of the Economic Agreement of Bogotá at the Ninth International Conference of American States in 1948, which encouraged this same goal, but through collective action. The Economic Agreement was signed by several delegations but with reservations on the articles referring to private investment; only three governments—Costa Rica, Panama, and Honduras—ratified the agreement, Honduras with reservations.[4]

The policy of the U.S. delegation expressed in 1948 at the conference was maintained throughout most of the 1950s: "There was and is a strong feeling in a number of other American republics that their economic development should be carried forward and given its principal impetus, not by private initiative as it is known in the U.S., but through government development corporations financed by foreign and local government capital, or, at the most, mixed government and private financing, with a considerable degree of governmental influence and control in planning and operations. . . . The United States delegation took the position that we strongly favored sound economic development, that we believed that private capital, whether domestic or foreign, would have to be counted upon and should be allowed to do the main part of the job, that only through private capital channels could an adequate volume of foreign capital be furnished, and that the United States Government itself had no interest or desire to force private American capital into any country where it was not welcomed."[5]

President Truman's Point Four Program called for technical assistance for the underdeveloped areas as well as expansion of the investment guaranty program. The Economic Cooperation Act of 1948 had established a guaranty program for convertibility of American corporate earnings in countries participating in the Economic Recovery Program, which thereby excluded the nonparticipating Latin American countries. In his inaugural address on January 20, 1949, President Truman declared: "With the coop-

4. Ibid., p. 244.
5. Quoted in Harvey S. Perloff, *Alliance for Progress*, p. 12.

eration of business, private capital, agriculture, and labor in this country, this program can greatly increase the industrial activity in other nations and can raise substantially their standards of living.

"Such new economic developments must be devised and controlled to benefit the peoples of the areas in which they are established. Guarantees to the investor must be balanced by guarantees in the interest of the people whose resources and whose labor go into these developments.

"The old imperialism—exploitation for foreign profit—has no place in our plans. What we envisage is a program of development based on the concepts of democratic fair dealing."[6] Thus, Truman's Fair Deal approach would be extended to the undeveloped countries.

In his testimony before the Foreign Affairs Committee on September 27, 1949, Undersecretary of State James E. Webb explained the two parts of the Point Four Program. U.S. cooperation with the underdeveloped areas would enhance U.S. national security, strengthen the United Nations, and foster democratic governments, since "democracy is most secure where economic conditions are sound."[7] But the "practical economic benefits" to the United States were also highlighted. The flow of investment capital would provide dollars for the purchase of American capital goods and equipment, stimulate increased trade, and permit the development of sources of basic minerals and raw materials important to the developed countries. He emphasized that Point Four was an expanded and coordinated approach to the stimulating of technological exchange and capital investment.[8]

While the program sought to increase the flow of private capital, the administration recognized that public loans would be necessary for such projects as public utilities, transportation, and communications; such funding would come from the International Bank and, in some cases, the Export-Import Bank. The Truman administration planned to expand existing facilities for informing U.S. businessmen of investment opportunities in underdeveloped areas and to minimize risks which were particular to foreign investments. They proposed to intensify the efforts

6. Quoted in *Partners in Progress*, report to the president, March 1951, p. 92.
7. U.S., Department of State, *The Department of State Bulletin* 21 (October 10, 1949):550.
8. Ibid., p. 551.

to secure treaties which safeguarded the interests of foreign investors and requested that the Export-Import Bank be authorized to guarantee the American investor against the risk of being unable to convert his earnings into dollars. Private investors would bring both needed capital and technological know-how to these areas, but they were counseled to follow the "same standards of conduct which enlightened business is following here at home."[9] Secretary Webb felt that it was necessary to point out to the committee that the modest program was not charity: "It is an enlightened, businesslike attempt to solve one of the most crucial problems with which our world is confronted."[10] But the investment guaranty program was unable to garner the support of either Congress or the American business community. Business organizations felt that the responsibility for creating the conditions to attract foreign investment rested upon the Latin Americans themselves and that the guaranty program would only weaken their incentive to make the necessary changes to stimulate foreign capital.[11] The State Department negotiated four treaties to reduce the risks to U.S. investors, but only the treaty with Nicaragua was subsequently ratified into law.[12]

Advisory committees informed President Truman of the need for both private investment and governmental assistance to further the economic development of the Third World. In 1950 the administration received the Report to the President on Foreign Economic Policies, which saw private investment as having a major role to play in economic development through the transfer of technological and managerial skills: "There should be a constant reevaluation of the role which it can play, and the need for public investment correspondingly adjusted."[13] Investment treaties and guaranties against nonconvertibility and expropriation were to be sought and the possibility of promoting private investment in the less-developed countries through tax incentives explored. But, most significantly, the Gordon Grey Report highlighted the limitation of private capital in the development of

9. Ibid., p. 552.

10. Ibid.

11. Dozer, *Are We Good Neighbors?: Three Decades of Inter-American Relations, 1930–1960*, p. 246.

12. J. Lloyd Mecham, *A Survey of United States–Latin American Relations*, p. 191.

13. *Report to the President on Foreign Economic Policies*, November 10, 1950, p. 61.

the economic infrastructure of the less-developed countries: "It must be frankly recognized that private investment cannot be expected to solve the problem of financing development alone."[14] Hence, this important developmental need had to be met through official U.S. lending.

The International Development Advisory Board, chaired by Nelson Rockefeller, was directed by President Truman to examine the proposals of the Grey Report concerning the underdeveloped areas and the objectives and policies of the Point Four Program. The 1951 *Partners in Progress* study concluded: "It is the considered judgment of the Advisory Board that neither government nor private groups, nor international agencies, nor national agencies can do the job of international economic development *alone*. Each has its proper role and a highly important role. It is not a question of government versus private effort or of international versus national effort. The task of the Overseas Economic Administrator is to hitch all the horses into a single team."[15] Some of the recommendations affected private enterprise: adoption of tax credits on income from investment in underdeveloped areas, negotiation of commercial treaties, Export-Import Bank underwriting on the transfer risk on foreign investment, and creation of an International Finance Corporation as an affiliate of the International Bank to stimulate private enterprise. They also proposed the appointment of an experienced businessman as an assistant administrator to the overseas economic administrator with the responsibility to work with private enterprise to facilitate the employment of private initiative and capital in foreign economic development programs.

The strongest efforts of the Truman administration to promote U.S. foreign investment in the underdeveloped areas occurred in late 1952.[16] The administration pointed to the increased flow of new American investment into Latin America in the post-war years as proof of the success of its efforts. However, almost 30 per cent of this total was petroleum investments by U.S. firms, induced less by government policies than by the high profit returns in Latin America, "which rose from 20.4% in

14. Ibid., p. 63.
15. *Partners in Progress*, p. 25.
16. For details of comprehensive program, see Dozer, *Are We Good Neighbors?: Three Decades of Inter-American Relations, 1930–1960*, pp. 246–47.

1945 to 28.4% in 1948 and which represented the highest rate of return for any major category of investment."[17]

The Gospel of Private Enterprise

During the Eisenhower administration the promotion of U.S. investment abroad was elevated by some officials to the ecclesiastical mission of fostering the "gospel of private enterprise." The major challenge faced by the new administration was the perceived leftward course of the regime of Col. Jacobo Arbenz, elected president of Guatemala in 1951. The inclusion of Communists in his government and a land reform program which expropriated some lands owned by the United Fruit Company quickly put the United States and Guatemala on a collision course.

On October 14, 1953, Assistant Secretary of State for Inter-American Affairs John M. Cabot indignantly rejected the objections of the Guatemalan government to the intercession of the United States on behalf of the United Fruit Company. Cabot took the occasion to denounce Latin American attacks on U.S. investors as part of a global Communist offensive: "In Latin America they are seeking through a tremendous campaign of calumny to destroy our prestige, to weaken our economy and that of our sister Republics by vicious attacks on our private companies operating in Latin America. Not a few honest people have been misled to a greater or lesser degree by this campaign. Recognizing a few words of truth in a lengthy Communist diatribe, irritated with the United States by the frustration we all face in this ever narrowing world, they unwittingly lend aid and comfort to their mortal enemies."[18] The United States, Cabot declared, recognized Latin America's desire to develop its economy with the help of U.S. economic assistance, but it was neither politically feasible nor economically possible at that time. Instead, U.S. assistance would be channeled through trade and private capital.

Secretary Cabot recognized that no matter what benefits foreign investment might bring, extreme nationalists would still label it exploitation and imperialism; however, he acknowledged that such abuses had occurred in the past. Cabot also realized that

17. Ibid., p. 247.
18. U.S., Department of State, *Our Foreign Policy in Latin America*, p. 6.

private capital would not be eager to invest in roads, public housing, railways, and utilities. Therefore, U.S. policy must be that "private enterprise should be encouraged in every possible way but that it cannot do the entire job of helping develop our sister Republics."[19] He pointed to statements by President Eisenhower that the United States would not try to force its economic system on others, and encouraged understanding if Latin Americans sought to construct their infrastructure through governmental rather than private efforts. "The fact is that, by cooperation with other governments to provide basic facilities, we shall strengthen the system of private enterprise in our sister Republics. . . ."[20] This attitude of tolerance toward state enterprises in Latin America was not endorsed by everyone in the Eisenhower administration.

President Eisenhower recommended the establishment of a Commission of Foreign Economic Policy early in his administration. In January 1954 the so-called Randall Report was presented to the president. The report declared that U.S. foreign economic policy should rely "upon the incentives of the free enterprise system, the stimulating effects of competition, and the stabilizing influence of free markets."[21] It recommended termination of all grant aid unless it contributed to U.S. security; if aid was deemed necessary but was unavailable from private or international sources, loans rather than grants should be utilized. But contrary to the more circumspect view on the role of private capital in economic development evident in the Grey and Rockefeller reports, the Randall commission declared: "The United States government should make clear that primary reliance must be placed on private investment to undertake the job of assisting in economic development abroad. It should point out that the United States resources for public loans are limited and inadequate in relation to total investment needs, and that public lending or other forms of public financing will not be a substitute for private investment."[22] One member of the commission, David McDonald, questioned the emphasis on private investment: "We should not make a fetish of our opposition to public foreign lending. . . ."[23] The commission highlighted the posi-

19. Ibid.
20. Ibid., p. 11.
21. *Report to the President and to the Congress*, Commission on Foreign Economic Policy, January 23, 1954, p. 2.
22. Ibid., p. 18.
23. Ibid., p. 26.

tive effect of sound American foreign investments on U.S. trade, economic activities, and employment, as well as the fact that by strengthening the free world economy, such investment would relieve the burdens of military aid. In a minority report, two other dissenters argued that foreign economic policy should be considered primarily on the basis of its effect on the U.S. economy; though they agreed with the commission's emphasis on foreign private investment, they opposed the recommendations for a guaranty program, which "would merely encourage rather than discourage the danger of confiscation of foreign investments by socialistically inclined governments."[24]

President Eisenhower adopted many of the Randall commission's recommendations. He included in the administration's tax bill provisions to implement a 14 per cent tax reduction on income from foreign investment; pledged continued use of treaties to establish rules to ensure the fair treatment of foreign investment; requested that Congress broaden the guaranty program to protect American investors against losses caused by war, revolution, and insurrection; and subscribed to the commission's view that grant assistance should be terminated whenever feasible. The president outlined the four major points of his program quite simply:

> Aid—which we want to curtail,
> Investment—which we wish to encourage,
> Convertibility—which we wish to facilitate, and
> Trade—which we wish to expand.[25]

These principles were closely followed throughout most of his administration.

The U.S. representative to the Inter-American Economic and Social Council, Mervin L. Bohan, in a statement on May 20, 1954, referred to the economic growth of the United States in the nineteenth century as an achievement of private enterprise: "Indeed, our continued experience during the present century has only confirmed in our minds that *the way of economic life which goes by the name of private enterprise is the sound and true gospel. . .*"[26] (italics added). He explained that the reluctance of

24. *Minority Report*, report to the president, January 1954, p. 5.

25. U.S., President, *Public Papers of the Presidents of the United States*, Dwight D. Eisenhower, 1954, p. 363.

26. U.S., Department of State, *The Department of State Bulletin* 30 (June 7, 1954):876.

the United States to participate in programs under which governments engaged directly or indirectly in industries which supplant private efforts was related to the fact that state enterprises were vulnerable to pressures which made them less likely to be profitable, efficient, or competitive. While urging a reassessment by Latin American governments of the role of foreign capital and initiative in their economic development, he acknowledged that "the U.S. can just as profitably examine and more clearly define certain of its policies in the foreign economic field."[27]

Secretary of State John Foster Dulles made strenuous efforts in 1954, at the Tenth Inter-American Conference in Caracas, to obtain a joint declaration that a Communist-dominated regime in the hemisphere represented a threat to inter-American security under the Rio de Janeiro Treaty of 1947; subsequently the Latin Americans were able to bargain successfully for another hemispheric economic conference. In November the Inter-American Economic and Social Council met in Quitandinha, Brazil. Raul Prebisch was instrumental in forming a Committee of Experts to prepare a report for the conference which stressed both international assistance and Latin American self-help. The Report of the Experts was quickly dismissed by U.S. Secretary of the Treasury George Humphrey, who espoused the familiar refrain that only private enterprise could do the job; he called upon the Latin Americans to improve the investment climate through controlling inflation and maintaining reasonable exchange rates.[28]

On January 10, 1955, the president reiterated his policy proposals of the previous year. The self-interest of the United States required such a foreign economic policy because it would strengthen American allies, lessen political instability and the threat of Communist subversion, and benefit the economy and standard of living of the United States through increased world trade. The administration recommended congressional approval of U.S. membership in the International Finance Corporation (IFC) of the International Bank, which would be charged with the task of bolstering the private sector in the less-developed countries. The major reservation expressed by the Eisenhower administration concerned a provision to have the IFC participate in ownership and management through equity financing; this

27. Ibid., p. 877.

28. Jerome Levinson and Juan de Onís, *The Alliance that Lost Its Way*, p. 41.

was viewed as contrary to the basic concept of private enterprise.[29]

Henry F. Holland, Eisenhower's assistant secretary for inter-American affairs in 1955, shared the strong sentiment of others in the administration against aiding Latin American government-run enterprises, and as Milton Eisenhower attested, vowed to prevent any American loans to the Mexican government's Pemex petroleum industry.[30] Holland's reasoning was simple: "We strongly believe that except in special circumstances our Government should stay out of the field of business. . . . Our experience has convinced us that as a rule government-run enterprises are not as strong and do not make as great a contribution to the national economy as do their counterparts operated by private citizens."[31] The contribution of the United States to Latin American economic progress, it was asserted, should be through increased trade, foreign investment, and dissemination of technical information. Holland thought that the most effective aid would be to help private enterprise in the hemisphere, and he spoke highly of "the businessmen of the Americas" who had the "sense of social responsibility that is the finest development of twentieth century private enterprise."[32] The creation of the requisite conditions to attract private capital would be the best action Latin American governments could undertake to further economic progress. These views led Holland to rebuff Latin American proposals for an Inter-American Development Bank (IDB) to finance projects which he felt could be funded by private capital: "Governmental investment, we believe, should supplement and never displace private investment."[33]

This theme was echoed over and over in Latin American diplomatic ears whenever requests were made for long-term, low-interest loans. At the Buenos Aires Inter-American Economic Conference in 1957, the new secretary of the treasury, Robert D. Anderson, reiterated the same argument: "History has demonstrated the vital role of the competitive enterprise system in the economic life of our hemisphere. Just as true leadership is best in

29. *Expanding Private Investment for Free World Economic Growth*, special report to the president, April 1959, p. 23.

30. Milton Eisenhower, *The Wine is Bitter*, p. 158.

31. U.S., Department of State, *Objectives of U.S. Foreign Policy in Latin America*, p. 13.

32. Ibid., p. 7.

33. Ibid., p. 31.

a climate of political freedom, so in the economic field the system of competitive enterprise promises the most in the satisfaction of man's material needs. This system produces most of what people want most."[34] Anderson felt that the need was to utilize fully existing sources of financial assistance, rather than to establish another financial institution such as the Inter-American Development Bank. Vice-President Nixon was repeating the same theme just months before his memorable Latin American trip. He phrased the issue in terms of meeting the Communist economic challenge, which would be defeated if the United States based its policies on one fundamental principle: "The recognition that the most productive source of economic progress is private rather than government enterprise."[35] Governmental assistance was viewed as crisis capital, to be boldly used whenever it had an opportunity "to strengthen free economies against the shoddy temptations of Communist trade or the menace of Communist subversion. . . ."[36] But, Nixon maintained, only private capital could meet the investment needs of the underdeveloped areas.

However, voices of dissent within the Eisenhower administration began to be raised against the U.S. opposition to the Inter-American Development Bank. The president appointed his brother, Milton Eisenhower, as his personal representative to visit Latin America in 1953. His subsequent visits, conversion to support of an Inter-American Development Bank, and wrangles with more orthodox minds within the administration are described in his book *The Wine Is Bitter,* which relates how he, Undersecretary Douglas Dillon, and Assistant Secretary Roy Rubottom became increasingly concerned over social injustice in Latin America and the need for new U.S. policies. Milton Eisenhower participated from September 1956 to May 1957 in preparatory meetings of hemispheric presidential representatives; during these talks the Latin Americans again broached the question of an Inter-American Development Bank for financing investments to overcome social problems. Although he argued privately with State Department and Treasury officials, he was unable to change the historic position of the United States; the final document omitted the IDB proposal. As he sadly recalled, "I

34. Levinson and de Onís, *Alliance that Lost Its Way*, p. 43.

35. U.S., Department of State, *The Department of State Bulletin* 37 (November 4, 1957):704.

36. Ibid., p. 705.

had no choice but to support United States policy or resign."[37] He received assurance, however, that the Inter-American Development Bank proposal would be considered again, and in August 1957 the United States did agree to study the possibility of U.S. funding.

Milton Eisenhower discussed in his book how his own vocal support of private enterprise in the hemisphere changed as he recognized that private enterprise in Latin America often is "an opportunity for the privileged rich to get richer—at the expense of the underprivileged."[38] He spoke warmly of the modern actions of American investment in Latin America, but acknowledged that the spotted historical record is still widely remembered. He warned U.S. businessmen against advocating an approach to economic development which exclusively relies on private enterprise with the underlying assumption that the Latin American private sector is the same as in the United States: "We must recognize the vast differences between enlightened capitalism and capitalized feudalism, between a system that merits militant labor support and one that leads to labor discontent and often bitter opposition, between a practical economic democracy and an entrenched economic plutocracy."[39] Milton Eisenhower also felt that it was advisable for the ownership of public utilities to be in local hands, preferably private hands, to avoid a major source of political friction.[40]

The complacency of the Eisenhower administration toward the hemisphere, with its pat formula of private investment for economic development, was rudely and profoundly shaken by the violence which greeted Vice-President Nixon on his goodwill trip to Latin America in April and May 1958. The tumultuous demonstrations against the Latin American policies of the administration caused an immediate reevaluation of many of its traditional answers; President Eisenhower quickly sent his brother on another trip to Central America. Shortly after Vice-President Nixon's trip, President Juscelino Kubitschek of Brazil sent President Eisenhower his analysis of the problems of Latin America which had brought about Nixon's reception, and in subsequent talks with State Department officials, he suggested a grandiose

37. Eisenhower, *The Wine Is Bitter*, p. 207.
38. Ibid., p. 158.
39. Ibid., p. 68.
40. Ibid., p. 135.

program of economic development which became Operation Pan America; a regional conference was planned to consider the proposal. Before the informal meeting of foreign ministers in Washington in September 1958, the Eisenhower administration announced that it would consider the establishment of the Inter-American Development Bank. The meeting authorized the drafting of the agreement to create the bank, which was signed on April 8, 1959. The conference also established an OAS special committee, called the Committee of Twenty-One, to plan the hemispheric program for economic and social cooperation.

But even these policy shifts and the victory of Fidel Castro in January 1959 did not completely change the emphasis of the administration on private enterprise. President Eisenhower's budget message on January 17, 1959, again stressed the benefits of private investment which would accrue to developing countries if they would improve their investment opportunities. In April 1959, a report prepared under the direction of Richard Straus for the Department of State was released, titled *Expanding Private Investment for World Growth.* The Straus Report did not claim that private foreign investment was a panacea for economic backwardness, but it did stress that foreign investment brought benefits which did not accompany governmental assistance. The factors which impeded private enterprise were seen as also delaying economic development. One emphasis in the report was that foreign assistance should help to develop local private enterprise, and U.S. firms could assist through personnel training and involvement in community social problems. The report recommended tax incentives for U.S. foreign investment in less-developed countries and extension of the guaranty program to cover losses from revolution, insurrection, or civil strife.

Undersecretary of State Dillon referred to the tax incentive recommendations of the Straus Report on June 2, 1959. Although he mentioned in his speech the "gospel of private enterprise," it was in a different context: "Partnership arrangements with local businessmen are especially useful in spreading the gospel of private enterprise. I am glad to see that our business leaders are more and more coming to realize and accept the importance of this principle of local partnership."[41] American businessmen were urged to be sympathetic to local efforts to achieve economic

41. U.S., Department of State, *The Department of State Bulletin* 40 (June 22, 1959):910.

growth, since the best way to encourage a favorable investment climate was to demonstrate to the host country the social and economic contributions of private enterprise.

In early 1960 President Eisenhower made another trip to South America. Part of his message concerned the primacy of private foreign investment for economic development. In an address to the Chilean Congress, he discussed the global competition for foreign capital and its scarcity; he stated that foreign capital "will flow only to those areas where it is actively sought, welcomed, and treated fairly."[42] But this note of caution was followed by a new viewpoint: "More and more it seeks the partnership of local capital and local experience."[43] In his book *Waging Peace,* President Eisenhower mentioned his personal talks with Latin American leaders: "In private conversations with the four Presidents I visited, I reminded them of the fact that if Latin America is to progress, it must attract increased private investment from overseas, a flow that is certain to dry up unless foreign investors believe that Castroism is to be repudiated by the nations of the Latin American continent. . . . Unhappily not one of the four felt able, for local political reasons, to assert an all-out opposition to the Castro movement. No one would admit that the happenings in Cuba were helping to block his country's economic advance, because of the reluctance of investors to come into any nation where they fear expropriation."[44]

In August 1960 Eisenhower recommended a new program for socioeconomic development in Latin America. Feeling the pressures of social unrest in Latin America and the danger of Castro's influence spreading throughout the region, Congress quickly authorized an appropriation of $500 million to establish a special hemispheric social development fund. On September 12, 1960, the Act of Bogotá was formalized; the signatories pledged cooperation to solve economic and social problems of the region. Ambassador William Beaulac later recalled that the slight attention to the role of private investment in the Act of Bogotá disturbed some American delegates: "Representatives of many of the Latin American governments had no stomach for strengthening the role

42. U.S., Department of State, *Strengthening Friendship and Trust among the American Republics: President Eisenhower's Visit to Brazil, Argentina, Chile, and Uruguay, February–March, 1960,* p. 14.

43. Ibid.

44. Dwight D. Eisenhower, *Waging Peace,* p. 532.

of private capital, particularly foreign capital, and the United States representatives were more interested in dimming Castro's prospects in Latin America. Social improvement tomorrow seemed to them to offer the best hope of containing Castroism."[45] The historic tension in the respective positions was still very much in evidence.

The Neglected Neighbor

Campos has described the policies of the post-World War II period as guided by the "peninsular school of thought." The European peninsula had the greatest geopolitical priority because of the Soviet threat, so the United States concentrated its resources there. Since U.S. economic resources were limited, the needs of the underdeveloped countries were to be met, as far as possible, by private capital. Campos felt that the United States employed its foreign aid as an "ideological bactericide" to prevent contamination by communist ideology. This policy placed Latin America in a residual position, which he called the period of the "perilous lull."[46] The pattern of U.S. foreign investment and economic and military assistance during these years would appear to support his caustic appraisal.

In the preceding chapter, it was shown that while U.S. direct investment in Latin America did increase from $3.1 billion in 1946 to approximately $9.2 billion in 1961, Latin America's share of U.S. foreign investment declined vis-à-vis other areas of the world. In 1959, 53 per cent of U.S. direct investment in the hemisphere was concentrated in the extractive sector, particularly in the petroleum industry in Venezuela. Table 5–1 reveals the slow but steady increase in U.S. governmental loans and grants to Latin America between 1946 and 1961, totaling approximately $4.8 billion over this period, excluding military assistance. It should be noted, however, that 61 per cent of the total economic aid consisted of long-term "hard" loans from the Export-Import Bank. Loans and grants under the military assistance program during the postwar years totaled $419 million, 8 per cent of all economic and military aid. The changing policy toward grants versus loans over these years can also be observed; whereas in

45. William L. Beaulac, *A Diplomat Looks at Aid to Latin America*, p. 22.

46. Roberto de Oliveira Campos, *Reflections on Latin American Development*, pp. 15–18.

TABLE 5-1

Total U.S. Loans and Grants to Latin America, Fiscal Years 1946-61: Net Obligations and Loan Authorizations (in Millions of Dollars)

Program	Postwar Relief Period 1946-48 ($)	Marshall Plan Period 1949-52 ($)	Mutual Security Act Period 1953-57 ($)	1958 ($)	1959 ($)	1960 ($)	1961 ($)	Total 1946-61 ($)
AID and predecessor agencies, total	..	19.5	245.6	87.9	123.0	105.0	253.8	834.8
Social Progress Trust Fund	..	..	..	..	..	..	..	..
Food for Freedom (Public Law 480)	..	0.1	305.2	63.2	33.3	44.4	145.6	591.8
Export-Import Bank (long-term loans)	170.7	495.9	1,117.3	191.3	411.1	105.3	449.9	2,941.5
Other U.S. economic programs (includes Inter-American Development Bank)	99.0	78.2	107.0	11.8	8.9	86.5	1.9	393.3
Total economic programs	269.7	593.7	1,775.1	354.2	576.3	341.2	851.2	4,761.4
Total military assistance program	..	0.2	151.8	47.9	54.0	53.7	111.4	419.0
Total economic and military[a]	269.7	593.9	1,926.9	402.1	630.3	395.0	962.6	5,180.5
Loans	196.3	496.3	1,356.2	242.7	488.5	174.5	696.3	3,650.8
Grants	73.4	97.6	570.7	159.4	141.8	220.5	266.3	1,529.7

Source: Figures presented by the Agency for International Development, U.S. Congress, House, *Hearings*, *New Directions for the 1970s*, pp. 12-13.

a. Expressed in loans and grants, last two lines of table.

the 1946–52 period, grants comprised only 19 per cent of U.S. economic and military aid to Latin America, in 1960 56 per cent of American assistance consisted of grants to the Latin American governments.

In summary, both the Truman and Eisenhower administrations viewed private enterprise as the key to economic development. Latin American requests for financial assistance from the United States met with little success; instead, they were urged to improve the investment climate in their countries as the best means to attract private capital. The prevailing American ideology and the priority of rebuilding Europe combined to deny Latin America the necessary public funds to deal with its economic and social problems. The historic role played by private enterprise in the economic growth of the United States, a deep antipathy to governmental involvement in economic affairs, and the natural desire to expand American investments and trade—all contributed to the lengthy gestation of the Inter-American Development Bank. It took the shock of events to change the thinking of the American government—not profoundly or lastingly, but as an expedient to contend with the rising specter of *fidelismo* in the hemisphere. To Latin Americans, this period marked a shift in the attitude of the United States from being a Good Neighbor to being an Unconcerned Neighbor.

6. Alliance for Progress

The Forgotten Businessman

JOHN F. KENNEDY first mentioned his idea of an *Alianza para el Progreso* in a campaign speech in Tampa, Florida, in October 1960. His new approach to Latin America stressed the need for an "Alliance for Progress" to strengthen the forces of democracy and improve the opportunities of all persons in the hemisphere through social and economic progress.[1] The same speech mentioned the need to stimulate private investment and encourage American investors "to immerse themselves in the life of the country . . . through mixing capital with local capital, training local inhabitants for skilled jobs, and making maximum use of local labor."[2] In his book, *The Strategy of Peace*, the presidential candidate called for individual tax treaties as one means to induce a greater flow of private capital into Latin America. However, he cautioned: "Latin Americans do want to use American capital within their own political and economic framework. They resent our insisting upon a larger role for their private enterprise, which cannot cope with many of their problems, or a larger role for our private investors, who have limited their inten-

1. Jerome Levinson and Juan de Onís, *The Alliance that Lost Its Way*, p. 52.
2. Arthur M. Schlesinger, Jr., *A Thousand Days*, p. 184.

tions almost entirely to extractive industries and to only five countries (Brazil, Cuba, Mexico, Venezuela, and Chile)."[3] He demonstrated a concern for the character and concentration of previous U.S. investment in the region and an awareness of the Latin American ambivalence toward private enterprise.

This chapter will discuss the formulation of the Alliance for Progress and its apparent neglect of the role of private enterprise in the economic development of the hemisphere. The matter of perception is involved in the belief of the business community that they were excluded from participating in the Alliance; statements and efforts of the Kennedy administration to encourage the flow of private capital were skeptically received by U.S. investors. These questions arise: Were the statements in accord with the policies of the administration, and could the Kennedy administration—or any other administration—allay the fears of U.S. businessmen still reeling from the costly Cuban expropriations of American property?

Retreat from the Gospel of Private Enterprise

Upon his election in November 1960, Kennedy appointed a task force on Latin America headed by Adolf Berle, Jr., an experienced diplomat and former assistant secretary of state for inter-American affairs. The members first met at the Harvard Club in November 1960, and their report was delivered to the president-elect on December 19, 1960; it embodied many of the principles incorporated into the Alliance for Progress. The Harvard Clearing House Report assigned to the private sector an important role in the economic development of Latin America under the Alliance, but recognized the Latin American prejudice against foreign investment.[4] The task force also advised that the United States should give greater emphasis to indigenous capital and end its doctrinaire opposition to loans for state enterprise. The report called upon the president to make clear to Latin Americans that private enterprise "is not the determining principle or sole objective of American policy."[5]

Kennedy solicited the ideas of the Venezuelan ambassador in Washington, José Antonio Mayobre, for a major speech on Latin

3. John F. Kennedy, *The Strategy of Peace*, p. 139.
4. William L. Beaulac, *A Diplomat Looks at Aid to Latin America*, p. 47.
5. Schlesinger, *A Thousand Days*, p. 185.

American policy. Mayobre invited nine prominent Latin American economists, including Raul Prebisch, Felipe Pazos, and Felipe Herrera, to assist him in preparing a frank memorandum on the Latin American position. The memorandum, while acknowledging the necessity of self-help, called for long-term economic assistance, a socioeconomic program which would stir the masses of Latin America, and warned of the resistance of the traditional oligarchy to such fundamental reforms.[6] They also stressed that the local entrepreneur must be assisted to overcome his hostility to foreign competition and warned the administration that the Alliance would be doomed if it were seen as an entering wedge for American private investment.[7] The demands for change were seen as too strong to wait for private enterprise to bring about the necessary structural changes, so vigorous state action would be required. Their view received a nod of agreement from White House aide Arthur Schlesinger, who was sent on a fact-finding mission to Latin America in February. Schlesinger has described the emphasis of the Eisenhower administration on private enterprise for economic development as a theory of "immaculate private conception," conveniently ignoring the partisan fact that the same policy was embraced by the Truman administration.[8] He felt that such a theory and policy ignored the early history of the United States, when the government played a major role in the building of turnpikes, canals, harbors, railroads, and schools. President Kennedy unveiled his new Latin American policy to the Latin American diplomatic corps on March 13, 1961.[9] He called for a ministerial meeting of the Inter-American Economic and Social Council of the OAS to develop a cooperative program to fulfill the objectives of a new Alliance for Progress.

The August 1961 Punta del Este Conference gave birth to the Alliance for Progress. U.S. businessmen were not included in the conference until shortly before it began, and then only as observers, not members of the American delegation.[10] A group of businessmen and bankers offered to establish a permanent private enterprise committee to work with the International Development Bank and to assist in the planning for the role of private foreign

6. Levinson and de Onís, *Alliance that Lost Its Way*, pp. 56–58.
7. Ibid., p. 141.
8. Schlesinger, *A Thousand Days*, p. 166.
9. Harvey S. Perloff, *Alliance for Progress*, p. 21.
10. For a list of the members of the U.S. delegation, see *The Department of State Bulletin* 45 (August 21, 1961):318.

investment in national development plans, but their offer was not accepted. They felt that the target figure of the Alliance—$300 million of U.S. direct investment per year—was unrealistic, considering the investor's fear of Castroism.[11] More will be said later about their feelings of being shunted aside by the New Frontiersmen. The U.S. business community and some Latin American businessmen were disturbed by the only passing references to private enterprise in the Alliance documents. The Kennedy administration appeared to have accepted the ECLA thesis of development and the approach of the Mayobre Memorandum to foreign investment, and seemed to desire a clean break from the earlier adherence to the "gospel of private enterprise." The "Declaration to the Peoples of America" contained only one comforting reference to the goal of utilizing the capabilities of the private sector: "To stimulate private enterprise in order to encourage the development of Latin American countries at a rate which will help them to provide jobs for their growing populations, to eliminate unemployment, and to take their place among the modern industrial countries of the world."[12]

Businessmen were not especially reassured by the Charter of Punta del Este. The private sector was mentioned regarding the desire to accelerate the pace of industrialization, but the wording did not indicate a recognition that foreign investment might help the domestic efforts. There were other references to the role of the private sector in assisting economic and social development and its role in the self-help emphasis in national development programs.[13] However, there was no mention of the most salient worry of U.S. businessmen after Castro's actions—protection against unwarranted and uncompensated nationalization of foreign property. Needless to say, the imposed low profile of U.S. foreign investment in the Alliance for Progress was bitterly resented.

President Kennedy had acted before the Punta del Este Conference to put his own mark on the foreign assistance program of the United States. In his March 22, 1961, foreign aid message to Congress, he declared that the foreign aid program in the 1960s must have as its fundamental task the demonstration that

11. Levinson and de Onís, *Alliance that Lost Its Way*, p. 71.

12. Pan American Union and the Agency for International Development, *Alianza para el Progreso: The Record of Punta del Este*, documents from the special meeting of the Inter-American Economic and Social Council, p. 2.

13. Ibid.

economic growth and political democracy can develop "hand in hand," rather than the negative goal of fighting Communism.[14] He proposed a new unified administration for the aid program, country planning, and special attention to countries relying on self-help. But, he declared: "The instrument of primary emphasis —the single most important tool—will be long-term development loans at low or no rate of interest, repayable in dollars, and designed to promote growth in those less-developed nations which have a real chance for ultimate self-reliance but which lack the ability to service loans from normal lending institutions."[15] The shift from the earlier emphasis on private foreign investment as the engine of economic development was explained in the Summary Presentation of the Foreign Assistance Act, which argued that large volumes of private capital would flow into the less-developed countries only when economic development was well under way.[16] However, President Kennedy did not ignore the importance of foreign investment; he called for the use of loan and investment guaranties for private enterprise.

The administration clarified its approach on the role of private investment in economic development during the 1962 hearings on the Foreign Assistance Act. Richard Goodwin, the newly appointed assistant secretary for inter-American affairs, explained how the entire focus of the Alliance was to create the conditions for increased foreign investment in Latin America: ". . . our whole program is trying to strike at the basic condition which has caused both capital flight and this tremendous decrease of private investment in Latin America by trying to keep the conditions of political stability which make it possible for a company to go in without fear of expropriations stemming from political considerations.

"That is the aim of our whole policy in Latin America, military, economic, political, the whole range of policies, and we intend to create also the economic progress which among its other consequences, will increase consuming power, demand, the possibilities and potential for private investment, as it has in Europe and elsewhere where there has been economic growth."[17] Fowler

14. U.S., President, *Public Papers of the Presidents of the United States*, John F. Kennedy, 1961, p. 205.

15. Ibid., p. 209.

16. Raymond F. Mikesell, ed., *U.S. Private and Foreign Investment*, p. 579.

17. U.S., Congress, House, Committee on Foreign Affairs, *Hearings, Foreign Assistance Act of 1962*, p. 277.

Hamilton, administrator for the new Agency for International Development, told the Foreign Affairs Committee that an Office of Finance and Private Enterprise was being established to encourage private enterprise and "insure adherence to sound standards for development lending."[18] Theodore Moscoso, U.S. coordinator for the Alliance, stressed that a goal of the program was "the development of homegrown, democratic-minded private enterprise as the basis for a dynamic economy and the protection and stimulation of U.S. and other foreign investment which contributes critically to the growth of these countries."[19] Moscoso also expressed concern over the Latin American businessman's lack of social awareness, which could result in socialistic economies if the United States did not reenforce Latin American private enterprise.

Secretary of State Dean Rusk expressed to the National Business Advisory Council in mid-October the desire of the administration to see "American business expand substantially its role in modernizing the economies of the less developed countries."[20] He mentioned the creation of a new Office for International Business below the undersecretary of state to provide additional help to American businessmen. The United States recognized the right of sovereign states to expropriate private property, but, Rusk explained to the businessmen, such actions had an adverse effect on other private investment which was needed to supplement limited public funds: "We consider it extremely unwise for developing nations to alienate foreign investors, thereby stunting economic growth."[21] He reassured them that the government would intercede when there was harassment or "economically unjustified expropriation."[22] However, the primary responsibility to avoid political risks rested with each firm and its flexible consideration of the feelings of the host country. In typical New Frontier style, he urged them forward: "The risks are there; the long-term opportunities are there. The developing nations represent a classic challenge to American private enterprise."[23]

18. Ibid., p. 4.
19. Ibid., p. 391.
20. U.S., Department of State, *The Department of State Bulletin* 47 (November 5, 1962):687; an address made on behalf of Secretary Rusk by William C. Foster.
21. Ibid.
22. Ibid.
23. Ibid., p. 688.

FAILURE OF THE ALLIANCE INVESTMENT TARGET

The first annual review of the Alliance for Progress, in October 1962, indicated that the low profile of private foreign investment in the charter was matched by a low response from foreign investors. The chairman of the U.S. delegation, Treasury Secretary Douglas Dillon, told the delegates in Mexico City that "private enterprise has not always been made to feel that it is truly a part of the Alliance."[24] At the ministerial meeting, the final assessment of the first year of Alliance operations concluded: "The flow of foreign private capital to Latin America has diminished and there is strong evidence of substantial capital flight from Latin America. Taking into account the limitations to the availability of public funds, it is clear that the objectives of the Alliance cannot be achieved without the full participation of the private sector and adequate measures must be taken to assure maximum contribution to growth by the private sector."[25] In the future, individual governments should make available to the private sector "incentives to strengthen the important role it is destined to play in economic and social growth of Latin America under the Alliance."[26] The same discouraging evaluation of the flow of private investment into Latin America was made by Assistant Secretary for Inter-American Affairs Edwin Martin on December 4, 1962. He observed that in the first year of the Alliance, U.S. investors took out more capital than they introduced, contrary to the Alliance target of $300 million from private foreign investment (see Table 3–2).

The grumblings of American investors surfaced during the May 1962 hearings before a subcommittee of the Joint Economic Committee. Rodman C. Rockefeller, vice-president and director of International Basic Economy Corporation, perhaps best summarized the dissatisfaction of the business community: "If the private sector is going to be counted on for a major contribution to the Alliance for Progress, it is going to have to be taken into the Alliance on the basis of equality, and included in the planning programs at every level of development.

24. U.S., Congress, Senate, Committee on Foreign Relations, *Hearings, Foreign Assistance Act of 1963*, p. 446.

25. U.S., Department of State, *The Department of State Bulletin* 47 (December 10, 1962):899.

26. Ibid., p. 901.

"Only on this basis will we be able to overcome the fears of the private sector that it is the forgotten man of the Alliance for Progress."[27] A vice-president of W. R. Grace and Company voiced the doubts of businessmen after the Punta del Este Conference about whether U.S. private capital was to play a role in the Alliance; he was not completely convinced in the following months of any administration enthusiasm for new private capital.[28] A high Sears, Roebuck and Company official stated that participation of the private sector appeared to be absent from government planning or discussions.[29]

According to presidential aide Theodore Sorensen, President Kennedy was upset by the cuts in his foreign aid program by the chairman of the Appropriations Subcommittee, Otto Passman, a longtime foe of foreign aid "giveaways." As a calculated risk, Kennedy appointed a conservative panel under General Lucius Clay to review his 1963 AID request. The report from the Committee to Strengthen the Security of the Free World was presented to the president in March 1963. The ideological mission of foreign assistance and private enterprise was spelled out: "Latin America must be encouraged to see its essential choice between totalitarian, inefficient, state-controlled economies and societies on the one hand and an economically freer system on the other."[30] U.S. aid should not be used to establish government-owned enterprises which competed with existing private endeavors. Instead, the United States should help Latin America to realize the benefits of private enterprise and create the conditions to attract foreign capital.

The Department of Commerce mobilized support for greater emphasis on the private sector in the Alliance by appointing a Commerce Committee for the Alliance for Progress. The Commerce Committee, headed by Peter Grace, decided that the reluctance of foreign investors stemmed from the political and social ferment in the region, Castroism, the Brazilian expropriations, and the popularity of socialist solutions. A very fundamental rethinking would have to take place to insure that "the philosophy of economic liberty and equal opportunity . . . is brought to bear *in*

27. U.S., Congress, Joint Economic Committee, *Hearings, Economic Policies and Programs in South America*, p. 63.

28. Ibid., p. 76.

29. Ibid., p. 78.

30. *The Scope and Distribution of United States Military and Economic Assistance Programs*, report to the president, March 1963, p. 12.

every aspect of economic, social and political life in Latin America."[31] While governmental loans and grants had their place, the greater potential and effectiveness of private capital would have the greatest long-term impact on economic growth. Other familiar refrains to Latin American ears were also expressed by the Commerce Committee, including the need for a "hospitable climate" for foreign investment. But despite the emphasis on private initiative, U.S. governmental support was sought by the business community, since profits were proportionally small and risks great. They argued for generous tax incentives, tax sparing, and expansion of PL 480 loans from 25 per cent to 50 per cent to the private sector. The committee recognized the political sensitivity of public utilities and suggested management contracts funded by AID.

Wooing the Private Sector

President Kennedy's foreign aid message of April 2, 1963, declared that the "primary new initiative in this year's program relates to our increased efforts to encourage the investment of private capital in the underdeveloped countries."[32] American ambassadors and missions would be more vigorous in urging the full use of the private sector, improving the investment climate, and gaining full acceptance of the investment guaranty program. His strong endorsement of the private sector's role warmed the business community, although not much was said about his support for joint ventures: "Economic and social growth cannot be accomplished by government alone. The effective participation of an enlightened U.S. businessman, *especially in partnership with private interests in the developing country*, brings not only his investment but his technological and managerial skills into the process of development. His successful participation in turn helps create that climate of confidence which is so critical in attracting and holding vital external and internal capital" (italics added).[33] The president incorporated into his legislative program the recommendation by the Commerce Committee of a tax credit for a trial period to stimulate new investment in the less-developed countries.

31. *Proposals to Improve the Flow of U.S. Private Investment to Latin America*, report to the president, March 1963, p. 5.
32. Presidential Papers of John F. Kennedy, 1963, p. 299.
33. Ibid., p. 300.

Administration witnesses were asked to respond to many of the ideas and recommendations of the Clay Report. Secretary Rusk's answer to the recommendation that no U.S. assistance be given to state-owned enterprises which competed with private enterprise was to declare that current policies shared that attitude. However, he added, there might be cases which required increased productivity, when a government enterprise was the quickest way to mobilize capital from the country itself.[34] AID administrator David E. Bell told the Foreign Affairs Committee that AID shared the belief that development would move forward most rapidly under the stimulus of private enterprise. But, he cautioned, there were unique historical and cultural differences which might lead to different development approaches in other countries.[35] Bell also advised the committee that the United States stressed self-help measures, one of which was an improved attitude toward the private sector. Both Rusk and Bell were queried about the low level of new investment in Latin America; Rusk foresaw an upturn in U.S. direct private investment in the hemisphere in 1963, while Bell identified what he felt was the major reason for the sluggishness of the private sector—the Cuban expropriation of American investments. The nationalization of approximately $1.5 billion in American holdings, according to investor claims, had obviously shaken the business community to its core.

Moscoso felt that U.S. efforts on behalf of private enterprise had not received adequate publicity,[36] and dismissed estimates of Latin American capital flight as "gross exaggerations"; his sources indicated that it had averaged less than $300 million annually during the previous decade.[37] Another AID official testified that the entire foreign assistance program was oriented toward the creation of an investment climate conducive to private enterprise. To implement this, AID had "issued instructions to every embassy and every mission, together with the Commerce Department, and the political side of the State Department," requesting a report of all promising specific business opportunities which could be brought to the attention of potential U.S. investors.[38]

34. U.S., Congress, House, Committee on Foreign Affairs, *Hearings, Foreign Assistance Act of 1963*, p. 23.

35. Ibid., p. 113.

36. Ibid., p. 854.

37. It is estimated by others that $10–12 billion of Latin American capital is abroad today (Juan Cameron, "Threatening Weather in Latin America," p. 208).

38. House Committee on Foreign Affairs, *Hearings, Foreign Assistance Act of 1963*, p. 453.

The new outlook of the administration was appreciated by Emilio G. Collado of Standard Oil Company of New Jersey.[39] He looked with favor at Treasury Secretary Dillon's remarks in Mexico City, the Clay Report, and the foreign aid message of the president. He and his colleagues were no doubt pleased with Undersecretary of State Averell Harriman's speech on the occasion of the second annual review of the Alliance on November 13, 1963; Harriman had stressed the need to stimulate both the public and private sectors on a pragmatic, not ideological, basis.[40] In an address on May 16, 1963, T. Graydon Upton, executive vice-president of the Inter-American Development Bank, declared that many businessmen felt they were the stepchildren of the Alliance. Upton then tried to explain how the situation had arisen: "In the first year of the Alliance it appears that insufficient emphasis was put on this element. Perhaps the Administration felt that "harping" on the virtues of private investment had been such a U.S. practice in the dialogue with Latin America during the decade of the fifties that emphasis should be placed on public loans; in part there may have been a feeling that private capital would do its part automatically if public funds were injected at the rates proposed and accompanied by the improved social climate that was foreseen as a result of the Alliance. Whatever the motivation for this under-emphasis of the private sector in the early days of the Alliance, it has now become quite clear that the participation of the private sector, both domestic and foreign, has been very seriously lagging."[41]

However, the debate over whether the Alliance had initially snubbed the private sector continued. John D. J. Moore, vice-president of W. R. Grace and Company and chairman of the U.S. Inter-American Council, a predecessor of the Council of the Americas, criticized the "very pointed exclusion" of the business community from the Punta del Este conference in 1961: "There were no business people there and it was principally through the efforts of two countries, Argentina and Peru, that the private enterprise language got into that charter at all."[42] A 1964 report

39. Senate Committee on Foreign Relations, *Hearings, Foreign Assistance Act of 1963*, p. 446.

40. U.S., Department of State, *The Department of State Bulletin* 49 (December 16, 1963):941.

41. T. Graydon Upton, address to the Forum of the Americas, unpublished (May 16, 1967).

42. U.S., Congress, Joint Economic Committee, *Hearings, Private Investment in Latin America*, p. 9.

from a subcommittee of the Joint Economic Committee agreed with the business community's version of their exclusion. It was painfully clear to businessmen and their congressional supporters that private enterprise was not allotted a central role in the Alliance for Progress, such as it had been accorded in prior administrations in the formulation of Latin American policies.

Lincoln Gordon, who had participated in the creation of the Alliance, dismissed as "simply wrong" the charge that the Alliance reflected a bias against private enterprise: "I imagine that the allegations of antibusiness bias were based on the emphasis in the Charter of Punta del Este on national economic planning, on social objectives, and on the need for reform. But none of these are incompatible with a strong private enterprise system."[43] A large amount of government-to-government aid was needed, according to Gordon, to build the economic and social infrastructure necessary for the development of Latin American private enterprise. Latin Americans, however, did not share Gordon's assessment of the important role of private enterprise in the Alliance. In 1965 Mexican economist Victor Urquidi wrote: "Direct foreign investment is in a sense secondary and complementary, and not the primary object of policy under the Alliance."[44] In a *Foreign Affairs* article in October 1963, Colombia's former President Camargo saw the Act of Bogotá and the Alliance as signaling a shift from the emphasis on private capital to a "conviction that such collaboration ought to come mainly from public funds."[45] It is no wonder that businessmen were alarmed by the new approach, which seemed to move the foreign investor from the driver's seat to the rear of the new vehicle for economic development in the hemisphere.

As Table 6–1 indicates, there was a significant increase in the level of U.S. governmental assistance to Latin America after 1960. From 1946 to 1960 U.S. aid to Latin America was only 7 per cent of the total American economic assistance program, but in the first year of the Alliance Latin America received 25 per cent of the total U.S. economic assistance. Total American economic aid jumped from $341 million in 1960 to over $1 billion in fiscal year 1962. It is

43. U.S., Department of State, *The Department of State Bulletin* 55 (July 4, 1966):18.

44. Victor Urquidi, "The Implications of Foreign Investment in Latin America," p. 112.

45. Alberto Lleras Camargo, "The Alliance for Progress: Aims, Distortions, and Obstacles," p. 470.

TABLE 6-1

Total U.S. Loans and Grants to Latin America, Fiscal Years 1962-70; Net Obligations and Loan Authorizations (in Millions of Dollars)

Program	Foreign Assistance Act Period									Total
	1962 ($)	1963 ($)	1964 ($)	1965 ($)	1966 ($)	1967 ($)	1968 ($)	1969 ($)	1970 ($)	1962-70 ($)
AID and predecessor agencies, total	478.7[a]	542.1	602.9	523.0	638.3	557.0	496.9	290.4	377.7	4,507.0
Social Progress Trust Fund	226.0	127.3	42.3	101.1	23.8	5.0	4.8	1.5	2.9	534.7
Food for Peace (Public Law 480)	126.4	165.1	287.3	96.4	142.5	62.1	201.3	112.8	152.6	1,346.5
Export-Import Bank (long-term loans)[b]	60.4	60.7	166.1	144.8	127.7	464.4	293.8	275.9	186.5	1,780.3
Other U.S. economic programs (includes Inter-American Development Bank)	120.2	79.1	82.9	283.7	287.9	281.2	331.2	327.1	321.1	2,114.4
Total economic programs	951.3	913.6	1,015.4	1,004.2	1,092.5	905.3	1,034.5	731.8	854.3	8,502.9
Total military assistance program	132.8	82.3	75.9	67.3	82.0	76.5	99.2	67.0	57.2	740.2
Total economic and military	1,144.5	1,056.6	1,257.4	1,216.3	1,302.2	1,446.2	1,427.5	1,074.7	1,098.0	11,023.4

Source: U.S., Department of State, Office of Statistics and Reports, Agency for International Development, *U.S. Overseas Loans and Grants and Assistance from International Organizations, Obligations and Loan Authorizations, July 1, 1945-June 30, 1970*, p. 31.

a. Includes $100 million loan for Chilean Reconstruction and Rehabilitation.

b. Excludes refunding of $533.9 million, as follows (in millions): FY (fiscal year) 1961, 292.2 for Brazil; FY 1963, 65.3 for Argentina and 2.6 for Costa Rica; FY 1964, 85.6 for Brazil; FY 1965, 6.6 for Brazil and 40.0 for Chile; FY 1966, 15.4 for Argentina and 2.5 for Costa Rica; and FY 1967, 23.8 for Bolivia.

noteworthy that while 61 per cent of U.S. economic aid during the period 1946–61 was from the Export-Import Bank, these long-term loans for "sound" projects comprised only 6 per cent of U.S. economic assistance in the first two years of the Alliance. Also, approximately 40 per cent of the total economic and military aid came from government grants, not loans. Therefore, the Alliance did indeed represent a significant shift from the policies and attitudes of the 1950s. The Kennedy administration responded to the requests for substantial economic assistance, in the form of soft loans and grants, to facilitate social and economic development in the hemisphere. The flow of foreign private capital into the region lagged far behind the infusion of public funds, largely because of the insecurity of the U.S. investor in the wake of the Cuban Revolution.

In conclusion, the Alliance for Progress appears to have been forged with the conscious desire to depart from previous U.S. policies toward Latin America. The rise of Castro and his popularity in the hemisphere demanded that the Alliance focus on the social and economic problems of the region which contributed to the growing restlessness. In order to awaken Latin Americans to an alternative approach to development, the rhetoric and policies of the Alliance for Progress had to be dramatic enough to garner broad support throughout the hemisphere; a repetition of old slogans and formulas was therefore discarded. The Kennedy administration thus viewed the Latin American appeal for financial assistance as the best means to develop the social and economic infrastructure of the republics, thereby promoting political stability and a more attractive climate for private enterprise. President Kennedy and his advisors were not unaware of the Latin American sensitivity to foreign investment; Kennedy was very cognizant of the dominance of U.S. capital in Cuba before the revolution and the concentrated pattern of American investment in the area. Undoubtedly, the anxiousness of the administration to win the cooperation of Latin American governments with the goals of the Alliance took a precedence over consideration of the role of private enterprise in the Alliance during the early years, but this seemed less an antibusiness bias than a diplomatic maneuver.

It was unlikely, however, that any amount of involvement of the private sector in the planning of the Alliance for Progress would have significantly altered the flight of foreign and domestic capital from the hemisphere in the period following the Cuban

Revolution. And the claim is clearly unfounded that the failure of the Alliance to fulfill its hastily conceived target of $300 million annually of new foreign investment resulted from the hostility of the business community because of its secondary role in the Alliance. While the Alliance sought to attack problems through social and economic reforms, the political instability in Latin America was the major cause of the decline in the flow of foreign capital into the hemisphere. Official statements encouraging foreign investment in the region confronted the skepticism of corporate decision makers, who were justifiably unsure of what the future held for Latin America.

7. Private Enterprise

Again the Crucial Catalyst

THE DISASTROUS FALL in the level of foreign investment in Latin America brought new efforts by the Kennedy administration to encourage private enterprise in the Alliance for Progress. When President Johnson took office, this shift was accelerated. The key role of private enterprise in economic development was reemphasized in order to reassure the U.S. business community of its importance to the Alliance. The Nixon administration bolstered this trend, creating the Overseas Private Investment Corporation as the primary agent to promote private enterprise in the developing countries. In considering the policies of the Johnson and Nixon administrations, one must obviously speculate on whether the "gospel of private enterprise" was again enthroned in Washington; this question will be examined in this chapter.

1964—TURNING POINT FOR INVESTORS

On the third anniversary of the Alliance, President Lyndon B. Johnson declared that the U.S. commitment of public funds was not enough: "We must work together to insure the maximum use of private capital, both domestic and foreign; without it, growth will continue to fall behind."[1] In his foreign aid message of March 19, 1964, he proclaimed that one of the fundamental concepts of a successful foreign assistance program was the full utilization of private initiative in the United States and proposed legislation for a special tax credit to encourage investment in the developing areas.[2] The tax credit idea had been recommended by President Kennedy in 1963, but introduction of the legislation was delayed because of other pending tax legislation.[3]

The Johnson administration's proposal was called the Less-Developed Country Investment Credit Act. It would encourage the flow of private investment to the less-developed countries by permitting a 30 per cent tax credit against the total tax liability of an investor and credit on reinvested earnings over 50 per cent which stay in the host country. To offset an adverse balance-of-payments effect, the tax credit could not exceed the amount of investment made in the form of American manufactured goods. Eligibility was limited to U.S. citizens and domestic corporations which owned at least 25 per cent of the total combined voting power of a qualified enterprise. Only those enterprises which were closely related to economic development and had the greatest risks would be qualified. This restriction specifically excluded the following industries: extraction of minerals, refining, shipping, banking, communications, and insurance.[4] The tax credit would be available for five years but could be extended in individual countries for no more than five additional years upon ratification by the Senate of a tax treaty.

Congressional testimony in 1964 revealed that the Johnson administration had placed a new emphasis on the role of the private sector in economic development and actively sought to expand its involvement in the foreign assistance program. Secretary Rusk told a committee that foreign aid could only do a small part of the task: "American private enterprise must bear a heavier burden of investment in the underdeveloped world. . . ."[5] In

1. U.S., Department of State, *The Department of State Bulletin* 50 (April 6, 1964):536.
2. U.S., President, *Public Papers of the Presidents of the United States*, Lyndon B. Johnson, 1963–64, p. 396.
3. U.S., Congress, House, Committee on Foreign Affairs, *Hearings, Foreign Assistance Act of 1964*, p. 46.
4. Ibid.
5. Ibid., p. 1.

response to the interest of Congress in incorporating the private sector into AID activities, AID had assigned executives with business experience to key missions to assist in "the building of local business institutions, the improvement of local investment climate and the administration of local industrial programs."[6] But an AID official was quick to point out that though it was necessary to show American companies where profits could be made in order to attract needed capital, the main clients of AID remained the recipient underdeveloped countries.[7] Thomas C. Mann, an assistant secretary of inter-American affairs whom businessmen considered responsive to their concerns, listed the problems facing economic and social progress. His list included: "Extremist policies and xenophobic nationalism, [which,] in some countries, have worked to undermine not only needed foreign investment but domestic investment as well, bringing stagnation rather than progress; . . .

"Artificial economic controls and policies exist which promote monopoly at home and the division of markets abroad. We hope for a greater degree of competition within each country, within regional trading blocs, and ultimately, with the outside world."[8] The appointment of Mann was a great assurance to the American business community; they considered him *simpatico* to their position.

Administration spokesmen stressed the role that the Latin American private sector had to perform in the Alliance. However, their comments revealed the cultural differences which Americans felt inhibited the growth of a dynamic Latin American entrepreneurial sector. Walt W. Rostow saw a growing commitment to the social goals of the Alliance, but warned that the attitudes of Latin American businessmen had to change further: "But the private enterprise sector will not truly fulfill its function in a society until it ceases to regard the poorer folk as a social problem and begins to regard them as potential customers, and until the private enterprise sector in Latin America abandons the concept of larger markups and low turnover and moves toward mass production and marketing with low unit profits."[9] Mann stated that it

6. Ibid., p. 358.

7. U.S., Congress, Senate, Committee on Foreign Relations, *Hearings, Foreign Assistance, 1964*, p. 33.

8. House Committee on Foreign Affairs, *Hearings, Foreign Assistance Act of 1964*, p. 269.

9. U.S., Department of State, *The Department of State Bulletin* 50 (March 30, 1964):499.

was the responsibility of the governments of the region to encourage domestic private enterprise by establishing favorable conditions and attractive fiscal and monetary policies. However, he criticized the prevailing outlook of Latin American entrepreneurs who were unwilling to risk their capital in job-producing industries.[10]

Foreign assistance became increasingly employed as a political wedge for the American business community. Particularly, program lending was seen as an "important and flexible weapon" to move resources into the private sector, as Donald Hoagland of AID affirmed: "It can also enable us to negotiate for and obtain, or to enable the government of the country in which the financing is made to institute improvements in their own internal arrangements for the private sector such as the elimination of import controls."[11] Secretary Rusk referred to this approach to promoting U.S. private interests as "incentive programming."[12]

The real possibility that the foreign aid program could be accused of intervening in the domestic affairs of Latin American republics in order to secure benefits for American businessmen did not escape the attention of the congressmen. But when Mann was asked if Latin American governments were sensitive to the terms of U.S. loans, he tended to shrug off the explosive question: "Latin Americans are very conscious of their sovereign rights, and sometimes this becomes a theological, mystical kind of concept."[13] His patronizing attitude, needless to say, ignored the real issue. Program and sector loans were utilized throughout the Johnson years, as indicated from 1968 testimony, as tools "to help bring about changes in government policies—fiscal, monetary, export-import, price and wage—so that they support rather than inhibit private investment and entrepreneurship."[14]

President Johnson received the report of the Advisory Committee on Private Enterprise in Foreign Aid in September 1965. The committee, headed by Arthur K. Watson of International Business Machines Corporation, declared their belief "that non-government resources not only can do more, they must. Other-

10. U.S., Department of State, Bureau of Public Affairs, *The Alliance for Progress*, p. 4.

11. U.S., Congress, House, Committee on Foreign Affairs, *Hearings, Foreign Assistance Act of 1965*, p. 219.

12. Ibid., p. 924.

13. Ibid., p. 159.

14. U.S., Congress, House, Committee on Foreign Affairs, *Hearings, Foreign Assistance Act of 1968*, p. 189.

wise, foreign aid would be doomed to become a costly palliative of indefinite duration."[15] They pointed to the estimated annual resource gap of $5–20 billion required for the economic growth of Latin America and the gap of skills and technology to substantiate their argument for a greater flow of private capital to the less-developed countries. They stated that private initiative was capable of greater speed and flexibility than government agencies and avoided the possible mismanagement of governmental assistance, and that the level of private investment was not tied to the "vagaries of public and Congressional sentiment" as the AID program was. However, they recognized the limitations of the private sector in attracting capital to projects which might involve substantial financial risk; governmental aid for infrastructure investments, if wisely used, could attract private capital. The committee was aware that private enterprise was often on the defensive in the less-developed world and anticipated that mixed public-private enterprises would be more common in the developing areas than was the case in the experience of the United States. The committee recommended a 30 per cent tax credit to stimulate the flow of private investment and declared that the U.S. government should intercede when foreign governments established conditions for foreign investment which caused legitimate concern on the part of potential U.S. investors.

On February 1, 1966, President Johnson again pledged to "expand our efforts to encourage private initiative and enterprise in developing countries."[16] He said that many of the recommendations of the Watson committee were already being implemented and promised to find new ways to utilize the capabilities of the private sector. In a statement to commemorate the fifth anniversary of the Alliance, the president announced: "After a temporary period of setback, there are now most hopeful signs of a renewal of large-scale private foreign investment in Latin American development, often in joint ventures with Latin American associates."[17]

The administration requested a doubling of the investment guaranty issuing authority from $5 billion to a ceiling of $10

15. *Foreign Aid through Private Initiative*, report to the president, July, 1965, p. 1.

16. Presidential Papers of Lyndon B. Johnson, 1966, p. 121.

17. U.S., Department of State, *Department of State Bulletin* 54 (April 4, 1966):538.

billion in order to stimulate private investment in the developing countries. The president's foreign aid message was interpreted as establishing new foreign assistance criteria. The efforts of a country to improve the investment climate for foreign and domestic private investment were to be carefully assessed in evaluating the self-help performance of a country requesting U.S. aid; opposition to private enterprise and unwillingness to sign an investment guaranty agreement were already considered important factors to be taken into account.[18] Congress added new criteria for Alliance for Progress funding in the 1966 Foreign Assistance Act. Title VI of the Act stressed the need to evaluate the degree of progress a recipient country had made toward "recognition of the importance of individual freedom, initiative, and private enterprise" and "the degree to which the recipient country is taking steps to improve its climate for private enterprise."[19] During the 1966 House hearings on the foreign aid bill, Dante Fascell, subsequently the chairman of the Subcommittee on Inter-American Affairs, took cognizance of the new emphasis on the role of U.S. private enterprise in the Alliance in the preceding two years.[20] His assessment of 1964 as the turning point for the involvement of the private sector in the Alliance was shared by other observers.

In 1967 an Office of Private Resources was established in AID "to concentrate on marshalling private investment and the expansion of private sectors in the less-developed world—the best long-term route to rapid growth."[21] However, the Foreign Affairs Committee did not feel that AID had utilized private initiative as much as Congress desired. They were critical because Congress had specified that at least 50 per cent of appropriated AID funds be used for loans to encourage private enterprise and this request was being ignored by AID in preference for financing of roads, power, and public utilities.[22] They felt that there should be more funding of private enterprise through credit institutions and development banks.

18. U.S., Congress, House, Committee on Foreign Affairs, *Hearings, Foreign Assistance Act of 1966*, p. 515.

19. U.S., Congress, House, Committee on Foreign Affairs, *Conference Report, Foreign Assistance Act of 1966*, p. 4.

20. House Committee on Foreign Affairs, *Hearings, Foreign Assistance Act of 1966*, p. 410.

21. Presidential Papers of Lyndon B. Johnson, 1967, p. 168.

22. U.S., Congress, House, Committee on Foreign Affairs, *Report, Foreign Assistance Act of 1967*, p. 10.

At the April 1967 Summit Conference of the Presidents of the Americas at Punta del Este, the United States pledged its support for Latin American integration and industrial development. In the Action Program adopted by the presidents to promote regional integration, foreign private enterprise was allotted an important role. The presidents of the member states of the OAS agreed: "To mobilize public and private resources within and without the hemisphere to encourage industrial development as part of the integration process and of national development plans."[23] Sol M. Linowitz, U.S. representative to the OAS, felt that much of the imagination and vision required for Latin American integration could be provided by the technical knowledge and capital of U.S. investors. He observed that American businesses "[provide] one-tenth of the continent's production, pay one-fifth of all taxes, account for a third of all export earnings, and provide jobs for an estimated 1,500,000 Latin Americans."[24] He did not seem to be aware that Latin Americans, well aware of the overwhelming presence of the United States, might not be as enthusiastic over economic integration if it would lead to a further enhancement of the role of U.S. investors in the economic life of the region.

On January 4, 1968, President Johnson unveiled his action program to deal with the U.S. balance-of-payments deficit. The major cause of the imbalance was the spiraling cost of the war in Vietnam, but increased private loans and investments abroad were also a factor. He announced mandatory controls on direct foreign investment, designed to be most stringent against investments in Western Europe. New investments in the less-developed countries were limited to 110 per cent of the 1965–66 average of the firm; this had the effect of penalizing companies which wanted to expand their investments in 1968 but had had only a nominal investment in the developing areas during the base period.[25] As mentioned earlier, this program was not enthusiastically received by the business community. The U.S. balance-of-payments problem made the administration back away

23. U.S., Department of State, Bureau of Public Affairs, *Commitment for Progress: The Americas Plan for a Decade of Urgency*, p. 16.

24. U.S., Department of State, *The Department of State Bulletin* 56 (May 8, 1967):730.

25. U.S., Department of State, *The Department of State Bulletin* 58 (January 22, 1968):110–14.

from the use of tax credits to stimulate foreign investment in the developing countries.[26]

Johnson's assistant secretary of state for Latin American affairs, Covey T. Oliver, outlined a new role for the foreign investor in Latin America: "The modern investor should be willing to accept a development role. He should be willing to look beyond this year's profit-and-loss sheets to consider the effect of his endeavors on national and regional development efforts.... He must actively search for labor-intensive projects that will ease the strain of underemployment in most areas as well as work to his own profit. He should explore and even suggest joint-ownership arrangements and managerial and technical training programs that will add to the region's pool of administrators and technicians....

"And perhaps most important of all, the foreign businessman working in Latin America must find some way to inculcate into his Latin American counterpart at all levels a similar concern for the well-being of the community, a similar sense of responsibility for neighbors who are less fortunate."[27]

Oliver urged American businessmen to empathize with Latin Americans, to see the United States and its investors as they did—a giant with a large proportion of the wealth, strength, and stability of the world: "They are ashamed, envious, and faintly apprehensive."[28] In one speech, he sought to substantiate the extent to which the early development of the United States had depended on foreign investment. He pointed out that almost $11 million of the money for the Louisiana Purchase had come from European sources, New York had financed the Erie Canal almost entirely with English assistance, and Europeans had purchased $243 million worth of U.S. railway securities.[29] It should be recognized, however, that these were all portfolio investments, common in Latin America prior to World War II and currently preferred by Latin American governments over direct foreign investment.

26. House Committee on Foreign Affairs, *Hearings, Foreign Assistance Act of 1968*, p. 189.

27. U.S., Department of State, *The Department of State Bulletin* 58 (April 15, 1968):503.

28. U.S., Department of State, *The Department of State Bulletin* 59 (September 30, 1968):339.

29. U.S., Department of State, *The Department of State Bulletin* 58 (April 1, 1968):441.

ACTION FOR PROGRESS—A NEW APPROACH?

Shortly after his inauguration, President Nixon was presented a report from the General Advisory Committee on Foreign Assistance Programs, which had been appointed by President Johnson in 1965. Chaired by the president of Cornell, James A. Perkins, the committee reaffirmed "the U.S. commitment to private enterprise in development and is convinced that a decentralized economic system guided by market forces is the right approach to promoting development."[30] They recommended the establishment of an overseas investment corporation and an easing of direct foreign investment controls to expand vitally needed U.S. foreign investment in the developing areas. But private investment was viewed as an "essential complement" to public development assistance, which was required "to support the framework within which private investment can do its part."[31]

The House Subcommittee on Inter-American Affairs, in their hearings on U.S. policy in the 1970s, probed for the perceptions and intentions of the new administration. President Nixon's new assistant secretary for inter-American affairs, Charles A. Meyer, had extensive experience in Latin America as a high official of Sears, Roebuck and Company. He emphasized that the "keynote of future U.S. policies must be realism."[32] His "realism" meant that the United States must recognize "the right of the Latin countries to disagree with us where they feel their interests compel them to do so. Dissent among friends is not disaster, and tolerance of differences is not tragedy."[33] Meyer told the subcommittee that he felt the private sector was "one of the essential pieces of an arch called economic development," but trade and private investment were not in competition with bilateral and multilateral assistance.[34] He cautioned that the United States must recognize "that our private investment can be an overpowering, can overpower, can appear to be overpowering, in relationship to the host country."[35] Therefore, rather than a general en-

30. *Development Assistance in the New Administration*, report to the president, October 25, 1968, p. 26.

31. Ibid.

32. U.S., Congress, House, Committee on Foreign Affairs, *Hearings, New Directions for the 1970's: Toward Strategy of Inter-American Development*, p. 544.

33. Ibid.

34. Ibid., p. 556.

35. Ibid.

couragement of private investment, each case should be examined individually. He recognized that there would be areas of disagreement between the investors and the host governments, but he believed that the versatility of the American private investment sector could cope with such changing circumstances.

President Nixon offered a general outline of his foreign aid policy in his message to Congress on May 28, 1969. At the top of his list of new approaches was: "*We must enlist the energies of private enterprise,* here and abroad, in the cause of economic development."[36] To achieve this objective, he proposed the creation of the Overseas Private Investment Corporation (OPIC), whose statutory purpose would be "to provide businesslike management of investment incentives now in our laws so as to contribute to the economic and social progress of developing nations."[37] Other administration spokesmen elaborated on the role that private investment was to play in the foreign assistance program. Undersecretary Elliot Richardson explained that the administration's emphasis on the private sector was derived from the history of development, which revealed that private enterprise was a "crucial catalyst" for economic growth.[38] Another priority of the Nixon administration was the mobilization of private resources within the developing countries, because without their involvement, "outside assistance is of limited value and development progress suffers."[39]

Secretary Meyer argued before Congress that cuts in the level of Alliance funding would make the United States appear to be an unreliable development partner. He reiterated his faith in the sophistication of the American investor who could discern the difference between actions taken by a soverign government in a field like subsoil assets, and possible actions in other sectors of investment. Meyer observed that in spite of the expropriations in Peru and Bolivia and the nationalization of American copper interests in Chile, investors were still negotiating in the Dominican Republic and Panama for mining agreements. "Perhaps the private sector is more sanguine as to the investment climate in the

36. U.S., Department of State, *The Department of State Bulletin* 60 (June 16, 1969):515.

37. Ibid., p. 516.

38. U.S., Congress, House, Committee on Foreign Affairs, *Hearings, Foreign Assistance Act of 1969*, p. 69.

39. U.S., Congress, Senate, Committee on Foreign Relations, *Hearings, Foreign Assistance Act of 1969*, p. 15.

long term than we give it credit for."[40] He demonstrated considerable empathy with Latin Americans in his reply to a question about whether the United States had failed to meet its Alliance commitments: "I don't think it is a failure on our part that, due to U.S. domestic pressures, we may have diverted a pure development concept to a balance-of-payments objective.

"I don't consider that to be a failure, on our part; but it is as disturbing to our clients in Latin America as it is to us to change the rules on private investment in the middle of the game."[41] This observation is interesting in relation to his statement before the Council of the Americas on May 6, 1969: ". . . perhaps the key long-term consideration today is that capital wants to know the rules of the game, whatever the host country decides they may be."[42]

Nixon's secretary of the treasury, David M. Kennedy, repeated before the board of governors of the Inter-American Development Bank in April 1969 the familiar argument that a climate which permitted domestic and foreign private enterprise to flourish was essential for balanced economic growth. He also had praise for the new foreign investor in Latin America who sought to harmonize business operations with local development goals, "particularly with respect to the fields they seek to enter, to active recruitment of local managerial skills, to association with local capital, and to good corporate citizenship in general.[43]

Almost immediately after his inauguration, President Nixon designated Nelson Rockefeller as his envoy for a fact-finding mission throughout the Western Hemisphere. Some critics charged that the Rockefeller mission was unnecessary since there were an ample number of studies and reports available to the president; others saw the trip as simply affording the administration more time to formulate its Latin American policy. Governor Rockefeller visited twenty of the twenty-three countries on his itinerary in his four trips during May, June, and July; his visit was postponed in Peru, Chile, and Venezuela and he encountered demonstrations in other republics. Governor Rockefeller pre-

40. House Committee on Foreign Affairs, *Hearings, Foreign Assistance Act of 1969*, p. 1157.

41. Ibid., p. 1162.

42. U.S., Department of State, *The Department of State Bulletin* 60 (May 26, 1969):442.

43. U.S., Department of State, *The Department of State Bulletin* 60 (May 19, 1969):428.

sented his report to the president on August 30, but it remained secret, even from Secretary Meyer, until November 9.[44] The president scheduled his "major new pronouncement" on Latin American policy for an address before the Inter-American Press Association on October 31, nine months after he took office. The tardiness in articulating a clear policy toward the hemisphere was not overlooked in Latin America.

In the interim, the Commission on International Development, created by the World Bank and chaired by former Canadian Prime Minister Lester B. Pearson, issued its report. In its assessment of the function of private foreign investment, the views of Douglas Dillon, the U.S. commissioner, were strongly influential. The report acknowledged that political sensitivity had made foreign private investment, on the whole, one of the "least dynamic" elements in the flow of private capital to developing countries; other contributing factors to the limited utilization of private enterprise in the less-developed countries were high risks, ignorance of investment opportunities, administrative inefficiencies, and limited markets. The balance-of-payments argument against foreign investment was soundly rejected: ". . . the correct way to look at the balance-of-payments effects of foreign investment is to ask what the balance-of-payments would have been like in its absence."[45] Likewise, the "popular misunderstanding" that the cost of direct investment was greater than that of fixed interest loans was rebutted by pointing to the additional benefits of technology and managerial and entrepreneurial skills which accompanied private capital. Although it was conceded that there was an absence of detailed empirical studies, the Pearson commission concluded that "direct foreign investment had added substantially to the real national income of developing countries."[46]

Nixon unveiled his "Action for Progress" program on October 31, reportedly after full consideration of the still unreleased Rockefeller Report: "We will not encourage U.S. private investment where it is not wanted, or where local political conditions face it with unwarranted risks. But I must state my own strong belief, and it is this: I think that properly motivated private enterprise has a vital role to play in social as well as economic develop-

44. *New York Times*, October 7, 1969, p. 46.
45. Lester B. Pearson (chairman), *Partners in Development: Report of the Commission on International Development*, p. 101.
46. Ibid., p. 104.

ment in all of the American nations."[47] The president stated that he would modify the U.S. direct investment controls, provide increased aid to local private enterprise, and order a review of the restrictions on foreign assistance loans.

Governor Rockefeller was acutely aware of the rising tide of economic nationalism in the hemisphere. In his report to President Nixon, he asserted that the central problem was that Latin American governments failed to appreciate fully the importance of private investment for economic development. His analysis of the cause of this trend was very perceptive: "Private investment, particularly foreign investment, is regarded with suspicion in many quarters. A great many and probably a majority of the citizens of hemispheric nations regard United States private investment as a form of exploitation or economic colonialism. There is a widespread, mistaken view, that such investment takes more out of the area than it contributes to it. Fear of domination by United States companies is expressed frequently."[48] To cope with this gloomy state of affairs, he recommended the creation of OPIC, encouragement of new modes of foreign investment, and repeal of irritating restrictions of foreign aid. In an interview, Secretary of State William Rogers acknowledged that there had been a rise in nationalism in Latin America. He attributed it in part to the past paternalism of U.S. policies toward the hemisphere, now being rejected by Latin Americans as they took responsibility for their own future.[49] Overall, the secretary believed this new nationalism to be a positive force.

In his 1971 report to Congress, *U.S. Foreign Policy for the 1970's*, President Nixon again emphasized: "*Private investment must play a central role in the development process, to whatever extent desired by the developing nations themselves*."[50] However, he was cognizant of the feelings of economic nationalism in the hemisphere: "Foreign investments are the most exposed targets of frustration, irrational policies, misguided nationalism. . . . The nations of this hemisphere must work out arrangements which can attract the needed technical and financial resources of

47. U.S., President, *Public Papers of the Presidents of the United States*, Richard M. Nixon, 1969, p. 898.

48. U.S., Congress, Senate, Committee on Foreign Relations, *Hearings*, *Rockefeller Report on Latin America*, p. 148.

49. *U.S. News and World Report*, January 26, 1970, p. 34.

50. U.S., President, *U.S. Foreign Policy for the 1970's*: *Building for Peace*, report to the Congress by Richard Nixon, p. 102.

foreign investment. For their part, investors must recognize the national sensitivities and political needs of the 1970's. There is no more delicate task than finding new modes which permit the flow of needed investment capital without a challenge to national pride and prerogative."[51] He appeared to be calling for a more flexible approach on the part of U.S. investors as well as Latin American governments.

Secretary Meyer and the U.S. representative to the OAS explained the administration's Latin American policy to the American Management Association in February 1970. Meyer told the businessmen how the administration had sought to obtain agreement on the important role of private enterprise in economic development and the necessity of clear rules for such investment; however, he reported that at the Caracas meeting on foreign investment no agreement was reached and it was unlikely that consensus would be achieved in the future. Ambassador Joseph Jova explained that a realistic assessment of Latin America indicated that though Latin America needs help from the United States, "their sense of legitimacy depends increasingly on the degree of independence from us."[52] He viewed the Consensus of Viña del Mar as one manifestation of that drive.

On March 4, 1970, the Presidential Task Force on International Development, chaired by Rudolph Peterson of the Bank of America, offered ideas for a new approach to foreign assistance in the 1970s. They were critical of both the heavy emphasis on private enterprise in the post-World War II period and the preference for governmental assistance during the early years of the Alliance for Progress. The task force urged that the United States extend more capital to local development banks, contribute to the evolution of capital and credit markets in the developing countries, encourage regional private investment companies such as the Atlantic Community Development Group for Latin America, and increase the funding of the International Finance Corporation to $400 million so that it could encourage joint ventures. International organizations were considered to be in a strategic position for bridging the gap of misunderstanding and hostility between developing countries and foreign investors concerning the proper roles of the private and public sectors.

51. Ibid., p. 51.

52. Joseph J. Jova, statement at the Seminar on Latin America of the American Management Association.

In his foreign aid message on September 15, 1970, President Nixon pledged to expand and enhance the contribution of trade and private investment in the development process.[53] OPIC, an important component of the new bilateral assistance program, would encourage "constructive investment" in the developing countries. He announced the untying of many of the restrictions on procurement, endorsement of the International Investment Insurance Agency for multilateral investment guaranties, and support for an expansion of the resources and operations of the IFC to promote the role of the private sector in the developing countries. Many of these proposals reflected the thinking of the Peterson task force.

But while some of the statements of Nixon administration officials seem reminiscent of the Eisenhower era, there has been some rethinking of old shibboleths and the myopic emphasis on private enterprise. One of the most judiciously balanced evaluations of the role of foreign capital in Latin American economic development was offered by Nathaniel Samuels, deputy undersecretary for economic affairs.[54] He pointed out that the role of the state in Latin America had deep historical roots and was not a new device to irritate or despoil American investors. The nationalization of utilities and certain key industries was objectively discussed, and the close identification of foreign investors in the past with the land-owning oligarchies was frankly identified as one of the reasons for the nationalists' attacks on foreign capital. While he highlighted the contributions that private enterprise could make in the development process, he called for a pragmatic approach in which government assistance and private capital supplemented and complemented each other. He was even temperate on the touchy issue of repatriation of foreign enterprises, which, based on the U.S. experience, was the normal process as a less-developed country achieved economic growth.

In January 1971 Daniel Szabo, deputy assistant secretary for inter-American affairs, addressed himself to the ambivalence of Latin America toward foreign investment. He told a group of businessmen that U.S. firms "have been strong reeds in the winds of change" and praised American management for its flexibility,

53. U.S., President, *Foreign Assistance for the Seventies*, message to the Congress, p. 3.

54. U.S., Department of State, *The Department of State Bulletin* 62 (February 16, 1970):182–85.

formulation of new modes and forms of investment, and recognition of the pressures on Latin American governments. "New modes of investment must be evolved; we increasingly have to take into account national sensitivities concerning natural resources and certain sectors of the economy."[55] Sidney Weintraub, deputy assistant secretary of international finance and development, told a meeting of Esso executives about the reexamination of U.S. policies toward Latin America occurring within the Nixon administration: ". . . we must pay attention to Latin American economic and social development, since if it is the single most important factor in the lives of the politicians and the people of the countries, we can have no relevant policy without taking these essential aspirations into explicit account. Another is that our style, when it is abrasive, when it is needlessly negative, when it is overbearing, does need alteration. Our investment policy, our reaction to Latin American excesses which damage some of our interests, our trading relations, our attitudes towards institutions in these countries, must all be framed on the basis of what we perceive to be the essential aspirations and facts of life in Latin America."[56] He said that the administration sought to change the abrasive quality of the American diplomatic style, but sometimes the lower profile was interpreted in Latin America as reflecting a lessened interest in the region: "We have tried not to make a low profile and a low voice mean no reaction at all. We wish to be more flexible in how we deal with issues and face problems."

AN ASSESSMENT OF THE ALLIANCE

But what was the pattern of U.S. economic assistance to Latin America during the Alliance for Progress? As discussed earlier, there was a sharp decline in the reliance on Export-Import Bank loans to stimulate economic growth during the initial years of the Alliance, but as the economic burden of the war in Vietnam increased, there was again a greater emphasis on these "hard" loans as shown in Table 6–1. AID commitments to Latin America were 27 per cent of AID's total worldwide commitments from 1962 to 1970 (see Table 7–1). However, these aggregate figures do not

55. Daniel Szabo, remarks to the American Management Association, January 26, 1971.

56. Sidney Weintraub, "An Overview of U.S. Policy towards Latin America," address to meeting of Esso executives, January 29, 1971.

reveal the concentration of aid in a limited number of countries in the hemisphere. Table 7–2 shows that 54 per cent of AID's hemispheric assistance went to three countries during the first nine years of the Alliance—Brazil, Chile, and Colombia—with Brazil receiving over half of these funds. This reflected the agency's policy of making maximum use of limited funds by concentrating

TABLE 7-1

Regional Aid Commitments, Fiscal Years 1962-70 (in Millions of Dollars)[a]

Year	Total Regional Programs ($)	Region: Near East--South Asia ($)	Latin America ($)	Far East ($)	Africa ($)
1962	2,284.1[bc]	1,077.4	478.2	399.3	312.8
1963	2,207.4	947.2	556.0	443.1	261.1
1964	2,087.8	843.3	631.3	351.4	261.8
1965	1,895.8	693.9	588.1	449.9	163.9
1966	2,393.8	859.8	684.1	663.2	176.7
1967	2,118.4	572.5	572.3	770.6	203.0
1968	1,861.8	532.9	532.1	640.0	156.7
1969	1,378.7	372.5	325.9	526.5	153.9
1970	1,539.0	404.7	421.7	557.4	155.2

Source: U.S., President, *The Foreign Assistance Program, Annual Report to the Congress*, fiscal years 1962-70.

a. Includes development loans, technical cooperation, supporting assistance, and contingency fund.

b. Includes $16.4 million in European programs.

c. Columns may not add due to rounding of figures.

assistance in a few countries where development efforts, especially self-help performance, appeared to promise the greatest success. In fiscal 1970, 87 per cent of all AID commitments in the world went to fifteen countries, including Brazil, Chile, Colombia, Costa Rica, Ecuador, and Guatemala.[57]

It should be noted, however, that the flow of foreign assistance did not move automatically toward the countries with large

57. U.S., President, *The Foreign Assistance Program, Annual Report to the Congress*, fiscal year 1970, p. 9.

TABLE 7-2

AID Commitments in Latin America by Country, Fiscal Years 1962–70 (in Millions of Dollars)[a]

Country	1962 ($)	1963 ($)	1964 ($)	1965 ($)	1966 ($)	1967 ($)	1968 ($)	1969 ($)	1970 ($)
Argentina	21.9	99.7	9.8	1.8	1.7	1.6	2.8	1.9	1.0
Bolivia	31.8	35.6	63.8	9.4	28.4	15.5	2.8	10.6	3.0
Brazil	84.5	86.5	230.9	234.8	243.1	213.8	193.0	12.4	88.0
Chile	142.4	41.3	79.5	99.5	93.3	15.5	57.9	35.4	18.0
Colombia	37.9	93.5	79.7	4.0	87.0	104.7	77.5	100.6	75.8
Costa Rica	1.9	13.0	10.0	8.3	2.5	6.9	5.1	13.9	19.5
Dominican Republic	26.0	29.6	0.9	53.7	94.3	53.7	43.5	12.3	5.2
Ecuador	19.9	18.2	20.6	12.1	16.3	3.9	3.6	5.9	23.2
El Salvador	3.1	19.6	11.1	5.8	3.4	2.2	8.2	10.6	10.3
Guatemala	4.2	3.3	5.9	7.3	4.1	11.5	11.2	6.1	29.1
Haiti	6.8	2.1	1.5	1.4	2.4	1.8	2.0	1.9	1.6
Honduras	2.9	7.3	8.7	2.5	12.0	9.1	13.1	2.7	5.5
Mexico	20.6	0.3	22.8	24.9	0.2	0.3	0.2	0.2	1.0
Nicaragua	3.5	3.5	3.9	16.4	16.3	11.4	25.5	1.9	2.3
Panama	12.4	8.8	9.2	11.3	12.8	35.2	19.6	16.0	11.8
Paraguay	1.1	3.0	5.4	2.4	11.7	4.1	2.7	9.7	7.1
Peru	26.6	2.9	36.0	7.4	18.5	22.6	5.4	4.0	11.3

TABLE 7-2 (Continued)

Country	1962 ($)	1963 ($)	1964 ($)	1965 ($)	1966 ($)	1967 ($)	1968 ($)	1969 ($)	1970 ($)
Uruguay	0.3	7.9	6.3	1.1	5.9	2.7	16.3	1.6	16.9
Venezuela	11.1	33.1	1.8	1.8	1.7	1.4	1.4	1.0	1.1
Other Western Hemisphere	5.9	18.4	9.3	22.4	22.2	24.7	9.3	34.0	25.7
Regional	13.4	35.7	77.4	59.7	18.4	29.6	25.2	68.7	64.4
Total	478.2	563.3	694.5	588.0	696.2	572.2	526.3	351.4	421.8

Source: U.S., President, *The Foreign Assistance Program, Annual Report to the Congress*, fiscal years 1962-70.

a. Includes development loans, supporting assistance, technical cooperation, and contingency fund.

U.S. investments; Argentina, Mexico, and Venezuela, which together held 47 per cent of the total U.S. direct investment in the hemisphere in 1969, received only 6 per cent of U.S. foreign assistance from 1962 to 1970. While AID argued that Brazil's prominence in the program was attributed to its large size and population, fluctuations in the flow of assistance in the 1960s certainly reflected U.S. dismay at the inflation and strident nationalism of the Quadros and Goulart regimes in the early 1960s, reassurance and strong support for the military governments which seized power in 1964 to curb inflation and impose order, and coolness again in 1969 as the repressive policies of the Brazilian military brought American public and congressional criticism of AID's high level of support. Brazil's military assistance from the United States was also reduced (see Table 7–3).

The AID program changed over the years to meet the attacks of congressmen and businessmen that it was not adequately considering the role of the U.S. private sector in the development process; this shift also reflected the growing concern over the U.S. balance of payments as Vietnam expenditures increased. Whereas in fiscal 1962 AID's expenditures abroad totaled 55 per cent and expenditures in the United States 45 per cent, by fiscal 1970 AID reported that stringent tying of loans to U.S. procurement had sharply reduced AID's offshore payments to only 10 per cent, while 90 per cent of the agency's total expenditures were in the United States.[58] In fiscal 1960 American companies supplied only 41 per cent of AID-financed commodities—$423 million of a $1,040 million total that year. However, in fiscal 1970, 98 per cent of the $995 million in AID-financed commodities were purchased in the United States.[59] A congressional subcommittee in 1969 candidly pointed out that Export-Import Bank credits under the Alliance should not be considered as a gift to a foreign country: ". . . if anything, they are an 'aid' to American exporters."[60] The Public Law 480 program has helped to export U.S. farm commodities, and between 1964 and 1969, AID financed from 22 to 30 per cent of all cargo shipped on U.S. flag vessels, because of the restriction that not less than 50 per cent of the goods purchased through AID loans had to be shipped in the more costly American vessels.[61]

58. Ibid., p. 21.
59. Ibid., p. 24.
60. U.S., Congress, House, *Report, New Directions for the 1970's: Toward a Strategy of Inter-American Development*, p. 6.
61. *Washington Post*, November 6, 1971, p. A13.

TABLE 7-3

U.S. Military Assistance Program in Latin America by Country, Fiscal Years 1962-70
(in Millions of Dollars)

Area and Country	1962 ($)	1963 ($)	1964 ($)	1965 ($)	1966[a] ($)	1967 ($)	1968 ($)	1969 ($)	1970 ($)
Argentina	2.2	1.3	9.1	12.7	11.8	5.8	1.8	0.8	0.7
Bolivia	1.4	4.1	3.0	2.4	2.8	3.8	2.3	2.0	1.5
Brazil	22.8	9.7	11.4	11.4	17.3	13.0	2.8	1.0	0.9
Chile	8.3	10.1	8.6	9.4	9.3	4.1	1.9	0.8	0.9
Colombia	9.8	9.2	10.0	9.2	12.2	9.1	4.8	8.9	3.0
Costa Rica	0.5	0.5	0.7	0.4	0.2	0.1	..	..	..
Dominican Republic	0.9	4.4	0.6	1.7	2.9	2.8	2.6	2.8	2.0
Ecuador	2.3	4.5	3.8	3.6	2.9	3.2	1.8	2.3	1.9
El Salvador	0.8	1.5	1.2	0.7	0.7	0.4	0.7	0.5	0.5
Guatemala	2.9	2.4	2.0	1.3	1.4	2.2	1.2	2.0	1.2
Haiti	1.2	0.2	..	..	..	..	..	..	..
Honduras	1.0	1.4	0.1	0.9	1.0	0.9	0.8	0.8	0.5
Mexico	0.3	0.4	0.3	0.2	0.4	0.1	..	0.1	0.1
Nicaragua	1.8	1.3	1.4	1.2	1.4	1.1	1.1	0.9	1.0
Panama	0.8	0.5	0.3	0.2	0.6	0.6	0.2	0.3	0.8
Paraguay	0.5	1.3	1.6	1.0	1.5	1.0	1.1	1.1	0.7
Peru	10.0	12.6	9.5	9.4	9.4	4.9	1.4	0.7	0.7

TABLE 7-3 (Continued)

Area and Country	1962 ($)	1963 ($)	1964 ($)	1965 ($)	1966[a] ($)	1967 ($)	1968 ($)	1969 ($)	1970 ($)
Uruguay	1.8	2.4	2.8	3.0	2.3	1.5	1.3	1.5	1.4
Venezuela	0.9	1.3	1.6	1.5	1.1	1.1	1.1	1.0	0.8
Total, Latin America	70.2	69.1	68.0	70.2	79.2	55.7	26.9	27.5	18.6
World Total	1,832.0	1,598.6	1,231.8	1,325.5	1,636.1	952.3	600.8	452.6	390.6

Source: U.S., President, *The Foreign Assistance Program, Annual Report to the Congress*, fiscal years 1962-70.

a. Beginning in 1966, grants for Vietnam, Thailand, and Laos were funded from the regular defense budget.

Latin Americans charge that the possible contributions of the Alliance for Progress to their economic development are undermined by an adverse trade relationship with the United States. As Table 7–4 indicates, while Latin American exports to the United States have increased in absolute terms from 1960 to 1969, the Latin American share of the U.S. market declined from 21 to 12 per cent during this period. State Department officials have testified that, beginning in 1965, the net flow of public and private resources from Latin America to the United States represented a positive impact on the U.S. balance of payments.[62] The growth in world exports from 1960 to 1969 was 75 per cent greater than for Latin America, which led Governor Rockefeller to suggest that access to the U.S. market offered the best opportunity to stimulate hemispheric economic progress.[63] President Nixon announced that his administration would press for a worldwide system of generalized tariff preferences for all developing countries, and pledged support for efforts to promote Latin American trade expansion.

The Latin Americans were unified in their hostile reaction to the Nixon administration's New Economic Policy proclaimed in August 1971, especially the 10 per cent surcharge on imports to the United States and the 10 per cent reduction in the U.S. foreign assistance program. Latin American ministers met in Buenos Aires the week before the seventh annual meeting of the Inter-American Economic and Social Council in September 1971 and adopted a "Manifesto of Latin America."[64] They branded as "unjust" the fact that the Latin American nations should bear the consequences of the measures adopted by the United States to correct its balance-of-payments deficit, since the United States enjoyed a favorable balance of trade with the hemispheric countries; the surcharge was also viewed as a violation of existing commitments by the United States, especially President Nixon's pledge of support for generalized tariff preferences for the developing countries. At the Inter-American Economic and Social Council meeting in Panama, Nathaniel Samuels announced that the United States would not apply the 10 per cent reduction in

62. U.S., Congress, House, Committee on Appropriations, *Hearings, Foreign Assistance and Related Agencies Appropriations for 1970*, pt. 2:1678.

63. Senate Committee on Foreign Relations, *Hearings, Rockefeller Report*, p. 129.

64. Special Commission for Latin American Coordination (CECLA), "Manifesto of Latin America."

TABLE 7-4

Latin American Trade with the United States, Selected Years, 1960-69
(in Millions of Dollars)[a]

	Latin American Exports				Latin American Imports			
			Per cent of Total:				Per cent of Total:	
Year	Total ($)	To U.S. ($)	L.A.[b] Exports (%)	U.S. Imports (%)	Total ($)	From U.S. ($)	L.A. Imports (%)	U.S. Exports (%)
1960	8,000	3,195	40	21	-7,740	-3,353	49	16
1961	8,120	3,200	39	22	-7,980	-3,525	44	17
1965	10,420	3,701	36	17	-8,870	-3,778	43	14
1967	11,070	3,877	35	14	-10,160	-4,123	41	13
1968	11,580	4,288	37	13	-11,190	-4,698	42	14
1969[c]	12,880	4,213	33	12	-12,250[c]	-4,870	40	13

Source: U.S., Department of State, Agency for International Development, *Latin America: Economic Growth Trends*.

a. Total of 19 Latin American republics.

b. Latin America (L.A.).

c. Estimates.

foreign aid to the Latin American AID program, in a futile attempt to win Latin American acceptance for the administration's New Economic Policy.[65] However, the Latin American press response to the Nixon administration's 10 per cent surcharge was harsh, as evident in *Folha* of São Paulo: "The U.S. made its intransigent position prevail in defense of the commercial protectionism rehabilitated by the Nixon Administration. It is undoubtedly a cross-eyed diplomacy . . . Latin America is paying for a sin it did not commit. The U.S. files away, as old stuff, promises of 'more trade, less aid' which now have become 'less trade, less aid.' "[66]

In summary, the Johnson administration moved vigorously to regain the confidence of the American business community. Private enterprise was accorded a central role in the Alliance for Progress and policies were recommended, such as the investment tax credit, to stimulate the flow of U.S. private capital into the developing areas. The criterion of self-help for recipients of U.S. foreign assistance was interpreted as requiring that they should provide inducements to attract foreign investment and conditions in which private enterprise could thrive. Program loans under the Alliance were used for bargaining leverage to enhance the interests of the private sector. Private enterprise was allotted a major task in the regional integration plans agreed upon by the presidents of the Americas in 1967. And, as the threat of Castro receded, the reassured foreign investors again turned to Latin America.

The Nixon administration was criticized in its early months for the delay in formulating a Latin American policy; obviously, the pressures of the war in Vietnam had a priority within the administration. President Nixon, in his Action for Progress, proposed a low profile for the United States in Latin America. While he considered such a posture to be reducing the tensions between the United States and its southern neighbors, others saw it as evidence of a lack of concern for the problems of the hemisphere. The Overseas Private Investment Corporation was created to assume the major responsibility for coordinating and encouraging U.S. foreign investment in the developing countries. Private en-

65. Organization of American States, Inter-American Economic and Social Council, statement by Nathaniel Samuels, special representative of the United States, September 13, 1971.

66. U.S., Department of State "Summary of Latin American Press Reaction to Seventh IA-ECOSOC Meeting in Panama," report to the president, September 1971.

terprise was to play a central role in the development process, as envisioned by the Nixon administration.

However, there were statements by President Nixon and other officials that a greater flexibility would be required on the part of American investors in Latin America. Thus, although the "gospel of private enterprise" had again achieved prominence, there was a recognition of the need for bilateral and multilateral foreign assistance and accommodation by U.S. businessmen to the nationalist sensitivities of Latin Americans.

In 1963 Colombia's Camargo offered a sweeping and penetrating criticism of the rationale behind the U.S. foreign assistance program. He especially scored U.S. presidents for not telling the American people that foreign aid was a long-term investment which did not always produce material benefits for the donor nation and often faced an uncertain future. Then he declared: "What may be an error is to try to convince the people of the United States—quite unnecessarily—that the Alliance for Progress is a policy that really seeks to open markets for them and to get back the $1 billion that were lost in Cuba."[67] While such arguments were usually not heard by the public at large, they seem to have been employed to attract the support of congressional critics and certain elements in the business community to the Alliance for Progress.

67. Alberto Lleras Camargo, "The Alliance for Progress: Aims, Distortions, and Obstacles," p. 470.

8. To Promote and Protect

THE UNITED STATES, imbued with a belief that private enterprise was the key to economic development, enacted in the post–World War II period various measures to encourage and safeguard American foreign investment in the less-developed countries. One of the earliest programs was the investment guaranty program, which sought to ensure U.S. businessmen against the particular political risks attendant with investments in the developing nations. While initially the program had only limited popularity in the business community, the Cuban and Congo expropriations of American properties suddenly gave it a new lease on life.

In the wake of these expropriations, Congress enacted the Hickenlooper Amendment to the Foreign Assistance Act as a deterrent to further nationalization of U.S. property without prompt, fair compensation; if the amendment failed to deter the seizure of American firms, the president was required to curtail all foreign assistance to the offending country. The Nixon administration sought to bolster the contributions of the U.S. private sector to economic development by the creation of OPIC. All these efforts by the U.S. government to promote and protect American foreign investment in the developing nations will be examined in this chapter, in addition to the less publicized endeavors to stimulate U.S. investors to form joint ventures with local partners as a means of reducing the high profile of American investment.

Investment Guaranties—or Else

When President Truman proposed extending the guaranty program of the Economic Cooperation Act of 1948 (which benefited only U.S. investors in Europe) to cover risks arising from inconvertibility and expropriation of American foreign investment, the business community opposed the plan. American businessmen felt that the underdeveloped countries should bear most of the responsibility for improving their investment climate in order to attract foreign capital; governmental guaranties would only weaken the economic incentives which were the foundation of private enterprise. In 1951 the program was expanded to include more countries, but it was not until 1953 that the first Latin American nation—Haiti—signed an investment agreement with the United States.[1] The Calvo Doctrine, which asserted the Latin American belief that foreign governments could not intervene in juridical disputes on behalf of their nationals, inhibited many Latin American republics from entering into such agreements. Hemispheric leaders were also worried that their participation in the program would be attacked by extreme nationalists as collaboration with American Dollar Diplomacy. As of January 1, 1960, Mexico, Brazil, Venezuela, the Dominican Republic, and Uruguay had not signed an investment agreement with the United States; Argentina, Chile, Colombia, and Peru had agreed on convertibility but not expropriation guaranties.[2] A 1958–59 Commerce Department survey of actual or potential U.S. overseas investors led one study to conclude that the investment guaranty program "cannot be regarded as the key stimulant to U.S. private investment, either in the world as a whole or specifically in Latin America."[3]

The Kennedy administration consolidated the guaranty au-

1. U.S., Congress, Senate, Committee on Foreign Relations, *United States–Latin American Relations*, p. 518.

2. U.S., Congress, Senate, Committee on Foreign Relations, *Hearings, International Development and Security*, pp. 287–88.

3. Senate Committee on Foreign Relations, *United States–Latin American Relations*, p. 520.

thorities of the International Cooperation Administration and the Development Loan Fund. AID officials testified in 1961 that there was a backlog of 570 applications for the program, totaling over $2 billion for specific risk guaranties. Fowler Hamilton attributed the sudden popularity of the guaranties to the situations in Cuba and the Congo, which had obviously alarmed foreign investors.[4] The Foreign Affairs Committee was unhappy with AID's explanation of the backlog: "The economic development of the countries eligible for investment guaranties will be retarded if private investment in such countries is delayed."[5] The demands for investment guaranties were still acute in 1963; David Bell again pointed to the Cuban expropriations as the primary cause of the stampede for guaranties.[6] During the 1963 hearings, General Clay testified that his committee did not support a legislative proposal to cut off aid to countries which refused to sign investment guaranty agreements, although the Clay Report doubted "the advisability of continuing aid to countries which refuse to enter into investment guaranty agreements."[7] He felt that discretion should be left to the AID administrator regarding the negotiation of agreements.[8]

However, on the floor of the House an amendment to the Foreign Assistance Act of 1963 was passed to cut off aid to any less-developed country which failed to sign an investment guaranty agreement by December 31, 1964. In conference it was agreed to make the cut-off date December 31, 1965, to provide adequate time to complete negotiations or permit "an orderly closing out of U.S. assistance" to governments unwilling to sign agreements.[9] In 1964 an administration spokesman declared that the restriction had not assisted in the negotiation of agreements; rather "there is a tendency for these countries to get their backs up

4. U.S., Congress, Senate, Committee on Foreign Relations, *Hearings, Foreign Assistance Act of 1962*, p. 417.

5. U.S., Congress, House, Committee on Foreign Affairs, *Report, Foreign Assistance Act of 1962*, p. 9.

6. U.S., Congress, House, Committee on Foreign Affairs, *Hearings, Foreign Assistance Act of 1963*, p. 143.

7. *The Scope and Distribution of United States Military and Economic Assistance Programs*, report to the president, March 1963, p. 19.

8. Committee on Foreign Affairs, *Hearings, Foreign Assistance Act of 1963*, p. 309.

9. U.S., Congress, House, *Conference Report, Foreign Assistance Act of 1963*, p. 18.

and this section does not help us deal with them in terms of getting an agreement signed."[10]

In response to the executive appeal, the deadline for the provision was extended one year, to December 31, 1966. The Johnson administration requested in 1966 that the president be given the discretion to weigh overall U.S. objectives before determining whether or not foreign assistance would be curtailed. The restriction presented a problem to U.S. policies: "For a few aid recipients the internal political situation inhibits the institution of these programs. It is unlikely that agreements could be reached in the future. Important U.S. interests are at stake in certain of these countries."[11] Witnesses also pointed out that once the termination date was reached, the effectiveness of the provision was lost, and a short extension of the termination date only weakened its effectiveness. But, Congress was assured, the lack of an investment guaranty agreement would be a major factor in AID's appraisal of foreign assistance requests.[12]

Lincoln Gordon proposed at a hemispheric meeting in March 1966 the multilateralization of the investment guaranties "through a joint agreement providing uniform procedures whereby individual governments guarantee the investments of their nationals in other participating nations."[13] He optimistically reported that the proposal was endorsed by a large majority of the delegates and CIAP would explore the concept further with interested governments. In fact, the proposal received a quiet hemispheric burial.

But doubts began to be voiced about the extended risk guaranties. Senators questioned whether such guaranties were not a subsidy to business, hence a violation of the spirit of private enterprise by limiting the risk factor; they also wondered if the program might be promoting present or future competition with American industry. AID strongly opposed the Foreign Relations Committee's proposal to reduce the extended risk coverage and its negative attitude toward a request to increase the ceiling for investment guaranties; they argued that such actions would renege on the commitment to the less-developed countries and

10. U.S., Congress, Committee on Foreign Affairs, *Report, Foreign Assistance Act of 1964*.

11. U.S., Congress, House, Committee on Foreign Affairs, *Hearings, Foreign Assistance Act of 1966*, p. 5.

12. Ibid., p. 515.

13. Ibid., p. 396.

American investors.[14] The committee reduced the extended risk coverage from 75 to 50 per cent, citing an additional argument that such protection tended to encourage investments in marginal projects abroad. It also turned down a request to extend the program to cover losses due to civil strife, as too imprecise for an insurance program backed by U.S. taxpayers.[15]

In 1969 Silberstein of the Office of Regional Economic Policy stated his belief that the guaranty program had been a positive factor in promoting the flow of U.S. investment to the less-developed countries. However, he suggested a review of the coercive element of the program. Even though the coercive aspect had been modified by giving discretion to the president, he suggested that the entire restriction should be stricken from the law. The Latin American resentment of such a provision concerned him: "Practically every time an investment guarantee has come up on the legislative table it has been a focus of extreme nationalist attack."[16] He wondered if it might not be wiser to have the U.S. government extend guaranties without an agreement from the host country if such an investment met U.S. foreign policy objectives.

Table 8–1 shows the upward trend in the number of less-developed countries participating in the investment guaranty program and in the amount of overseas coverage issued to American companies. Obviously, the concern of U.S. investors after the Cuban and Congo expropriations enhanced the popularity of the program, increasing pressures on the Department of State from congressmen and the business community to negotiate investment guaranty agreements with additional countries. As of June 30, 1970, most of the Latin American republics had signed investment guaranty agreements, but the hesitancy of some legislatures to ratify the agreements and the absence of Peru and Mexico from the list of participating nations highlights the nationalistic opposition to the program (see Table 8–2). Table 8–3 reveals that American investors in Latin America have shown the greatest interest in the guaranty program, under the impetus of the grow-

14. U.S., Congress, Senate, Committee on Foreign Relations, *Hearings, Foreign Assistance Act of 1967*, p. 148.

15. U.S., Congress, Senate, Committee on Foreign Relations, *Report, Foreign Assistance Act of 1967*, p. 20.

16. U.S., Congress, House, Committee on Foreign Affairs, *Hearings, New Directions for the 1970's: Toward a Strategy of Inter-American Development*, p. 232.

ing economic nationalism of the region; 49 per cent of the $9.5 billion in worldwide political risk investment insurance issued covered U.S. firms operating in the hemisphere. Thus, the potential economic and political liability that the program has accrued for the United States is considerable.

Roderick Groves proposed in 1969 that the U.S. investment insurance program should be expanded "to include *all* United States investments on a compulsory basis in certain, particularly

TABLE 8-1

Aid Investment Guaranty Program, 1963–70

Year	Total Amount in Force (in Billions of Dollars)	Number of Less-Developed Countries Participating
1963	0.9	55
1964	1.4	60
1965	2.0	69
1966	2.9	73
1967	3.7	78
1968	6.0	83
1969	6.8	89
1970	7.8	91

Source: U.S., President, *The Foreign Assistance Program, Annual Report to the Congress*, fiscal year 1970, p. 19.

sensitive regions such as Latin America."[17] Acknowledging that the primary purpose of the current program is to induce new investments in the developing areas, he argued that there is also a need to enlarge its function to protect American foreign investment. He criticized the limitation of restricting insurance coverage to only new investments or new additions to existing investments, since the long-established enterprises are the most vulnerable to expropriation. He also objected to the restriction of the availability of insurance to only those countries which have bilateral agreements with the United States and whose govern-

17. Roderick T. Groves, "Expropriation in Latin America: Some Observations," p. 65.

ments approve the specific investments; this would also include the investments most likely to be nationalized.

Groves was aware that no precise actuarial standard existed to measure the potential liability the U.S. government would incur if it adopted his recommendation; he appeared to rely on the fact that the current program has had a negligible number of claims,

TABLE 8-2

Latin American Countries with Investment Guaranty Agreements (June 30, 1970)

Type of Agreement			
Convertibility	Expropriation	War, Revolution, and Insurrection	Extended Risk Guaranties
Argentina	Argentina[a]	Argentina[a]	Argentina[a]
Bolivia	Bolivia	Bolivia	Bolivia
Brazil	Brazil	Brazil	Brazil
Chile	Chile[a]	Chile[a]	Chile[a]
Colombia[a]	Colombia[a]	Colombia[a]	Colombia[a]
Costa Rica	Costa Rica	Costa Rica	Costa Rica
Dominican Republic	Dominican Republic	Dominican Republic	Dominican Republic
Ecuador	Ecuador	Ecuador	Ecuador
El Salvador	El Salvador[a]	El Salvador[a]	El Salvador
Guatemala	Guatemala	..	..
Haiti	Haiti	..	..
Honduras	Honduras	Honduras	Honduras
Nicaragua	Nicaragua	Nicaragua	Nicaragua
Panama	Panama	Panama (war only)	..
Paraguay	Paraguay	Paraguay	Paraguay
Uruguay[a]	Uruguay[a]	..	..
Venezuela	Venezuela	Venezuela	Venezuela
British Honduras	British Honduras	British Honduras	British Honduras
Trinidad-Tobago	Trinidad-Tobago	Trinidad-Tobago	Trinidad-Tobago

Source: U.S., President, *The Foreign Assistance Program, Annual Report to the Congress*, fiscal year 1970, pp. 68-70.

a. Agreement signed but not ratified; not in full force and effect.

TABLE 8-3

Political Risk Insurance Issued in Latin America since Beginning of Program in 1948 through March 31, 1970 (in Millions of Dollars)

Country	Number of Coverages	Convertibility ($)	Expropriation ($)	War Risk ($)	Combined Expropriation, War Risk ($)	Totals ($)
Argentina	290	420.1	184.4	93.0	24.1	721.6
Bolivia	115	50.5	65.0	24.7	11.3	151.4
Brazil	138	231.6	92.2	52.8	119.4	496.0
Chile	146	749.0	284.6	12.0	390.2	1,435.7
Colombia	247	110.2	89.3	46.9	31.0	277.4
Costa Rica	110	31.0	32.6	16.6	3.4	83.6
Dominican Republic	108	213.8	16.5	36.3	203.3	469.9
Ecuador	184	36.1	24.2	13.1	11.9	85.2
El Salvador	32	8.5	8.2	..	..	16.7
Guatemala	11	1.0	3.4	..	..	4.4
Haiti	33	10.2	11.3	..	..	21.5
Honduras	77	35.0	34.5	1.7	24.0	95.2
Nicaragua	50	9.8	7.5	5.0	4.0	26.4
Panama	24	2.4	12.1	1.2	0.2	16.0
Paraguay	8	4.4	7.2	0.1	..	11.6
Peru	56	98.8	..	..	..	98.8
Venezuela	153	55.2	43.5	33.0	31.8	163.6
Other Western Hemisphere	79	96.3	38.7	34.4	299.2	468.4
Total, Latin America	1,853	2,163.9	955.2	370.8	1,153.8	4,643.4
Worldwide	4,178	4,279.9	2,392.0	1,002.2	1,854.6	9,528.7

Source: Compiled from AID figures, U.S., Congress, House, *Hearings, Foreign Assistance and Related Agencies Appropriations for 1970*.

forgetting that this has been largely because of the restrictions he criticized. But if such insurance had been compulsory, what would have been the basis for establishing the premium for IPC's properties in Peru, especially considering the long history of Peruvian hostility to the original concession? How would this scheme take into account the fact that the real issue was not simply the expropriated properties, which IPC valued at $190 million, but rather the alleged "debt" of $690 million which the Peruvians claim the American firm owes for its exploitation of La Brea y Parinas from 1924 to 1968?[18] What mechanism would be established to determine the true value of long-disputed enterprises and to review legal claims and any existing debts? In the IPC case, Secretary Meyer admitted that the U.S. government had not made such an independent evaluation.[19]

If the suggestion of Groves were adopted, the United States would assume a huge liability and place itself in the middle of every dispute which might arise, since the government would reimburse the expropriated owner and then press the claim against the host government. The opportunity to represent the American investor diplomatically, while examining the legitimacy of the U.S. firm's claim, would be sorely curtailed. The United States would be forced to insure inequitable investments and directly inherit the enmity which the firm may have earned because of its earlier business and political dealings. If premium payments were at all commensurate with the high risks of these investments, the private investors would certainly oppose the program.

Senator J. William Fulbright noted in 1969 that specific risk guaranties totaled $6.8 billion while only $78 million in fees had been collected from insured firms; he cautioned that the potential of a major setback to the taxpayer would be great if only one sizable U.S. investment went sour.[20] Considering that IPC valued its seized assets at $190 million and Gulf Oil Corporation estimated its total investment in Bolivia at $141 million, the U.S. treasury would be assuming a tremendous liability under the suggested expansion of the existing program. The U.S. govern-

18. U.S., Congress, Senate, Committee on Foreign Relations, *Hearings, United States Relations with Peru*, p. 111.
19. Ibid., p. 121.
20. *Congressional Record*, December 12, 1969, p. 16630.

ment also had a liability of $321 million of expropriation guaranties on American investments in Chile which were affected by President Allende's nationalization program.[21]

The United States would acquire this huge burden without any control over the type of investment or its acceptability to the host government. The OPIC program deems ineligible speculative investments, loans with usurious rates of interest, monopolistic ventures, and investors with a bad reputation; it also protects American commercial interests by prohibiting coverage for investments in textiles, certain agricultural crops for export to the United States, and runaway industries. Herbert Salzman, the assistant administrator of the Office of Private Resources, proudly testified that his office was very selective and sensitive about the private projects it insured. He recognized that the U.S. government would be associated with the investments and their actions in the host countries and cited several examples of investors who were refused insurance.[22] While Groves wanted American policies and programs to show more sensitivity to the forces of nationalism, his proposal would remove the discretion of the government in granting investment guaranties and would place the United States in the position of underwriting every investment regardless of the merits of the claim.

The Nixon administration has debated the possibility of the U.S. government getting out of the investment guaranty business, especially in the extractive field. The political liability assumed through the program was of prime concern: "If we give a guaranty, does the U.S. Government thereby obtain a greater right to make its own feelings known about the mode of investment in order to reduce potential future sensitivity? Since the U.S. Government would probably be involved in any case if problems arise later, we do have a certain interest in a country."[23] The sensitive questions raised would appear to be central in any objective evaluation of the political implications of the investment guaranty program. This matter will be explored further when OPIC is examined.

21. U.S., Congress, House, Committee on Appropriations, *Hearings, Foreign Assistance and Related Agencies Appropriations for 1971*, p. 421.

22. U.S., Congress, House, Committee on Foreign Affairs, *Hearings, Overseas Private Investment Corporation*, p. 26.

23. Sidney Weintraub, "An Overview of U.S. Policy towards Latin America," address to meeting of Esso executives, January 29, 1971.

The Hickenlooper Amendment—Protection or Irritant?

The Hickenlooper Amendment to the Foreign Assistance Act of 1962 required the president to suspend all assistance to a country which: "(A) has nationalized or expropriated or seized ownership or control of property owned by any United States citizen or by any corporation, partnership, or association not less than 50 per centum beneficially owned by United States citizens, or (B) has taken steps to repudiate or nullify existing contracts or agreements with any United States citizen or any corporation, partnership, or association not less than 50 per centum beneficially owned by United States citizens, or (C) has imposed or enforced discriminatory taxes or other exactions, or restrictive maintenance or operational conditions, which have the effect of nationalizing, expropriating, or otherwise seizing ownership or control of property so owned," if such a country within six months of the action failed to take appropriate steps for prompt and adequate compensation for the seized property.[24] The president could authorize the U.S. Foreign Claims Settlement Commission to evaluate the full value of the affected property.

The Hickenlooper Amendment was not just a reaction to the Cuban and Congo expropriations, although they did play an influential part in its passage; congressmen were also agitated over the actions of the governor of the Brazilian state of Rio Grande do Sul, who had seized the holdings of American and Foreign Power Company in 1959 and a subsidiary of ITT in February 1962.[25] Harold Geneen, the president of ITT, urged Senator Bourke B. Hickenlooper to attach his amendment to the foreign assistance program, while Ambassador Gordon was attempting to persuade Brazilian President Goulart to settle the case.[26] Simon Hanson, in his bitter critique of the Alliance for Progress, used the case of ITT in Brazil as an example of how the Alliance had come to serve as a means to bail out U.S. firms. He lambasted the public relations campaign of the company on behalf of the Hickenlooper Amendment, especially since rate disputes and poor service were at the heart of the 1962 controversy. An ITT statement issued after

24. U.S., Congress, Senate, Committee on Foreign Relations, *Hearings, United States Relations with Peru*, p. 48.

25. U.S., Congress, Senate, Committee on Foreign Relations, *Report, Foreign Assistance Act of 1962*, p. 25.

26. Jerome Levinson and Juan de Onís, *The Alliance that Lost Its Way*, p. 144.

the matter was settled declared: "The expropriation in Brazil was exaggerated out of all proportion to what was seized—a $7.3 million company that was running in the red! . . ."[27] He also described how the amendment complicated the settlement of the Brazilian seizure of the American and Foreign Power Company.

Secretary Rusk, discussing the Brazilian situation with Congress in 1962, stated that American investments in public utilities presented a special problem, since other U.S. firms were doing quite well.[28] He felt that it was unwise to punish the entire country for the actions of one state, but his greater concern was that the United States could not afford "to settle its interests in other countries on a particular private investment in a particular situation. . . ."[29] If American policy was tied to the private investor overseas, ". . . then I think that we of necessity must reassure ourselves as to the operations, the conduct, the financial structure, and other aspects of those private investors."[30] He believed that a legislative sanction which compelled the severing of diplomatic relations with important countries was a "drastic remedy for a particular problem," which jeopardized the other policy interests of the United States.[31]

An official statement by the Department of State reaffirmed the adherence of the United States to the principle that expropriated parties must receive fair compensation for their foreign investments, but declared that existing diplomatic and legal procedures were adequate to seek redress. Below are the main arguments advanced in the statement against adoption of the Hickenlooper Amendment in 1962: "We believe that the injection of the U.S. foreign assistance program into condemnation proceedings would at best advance the interests of the American citizen whose property is expropriated only marginally, and, on the other hand, it can seriously injure the vital U.S. national interests which the foreign assistance program is designed to further.

"First, the writing of this provision in the Foreign Assistance Act would make it appear that our aid programs are substantially

27. Simon G. Hanson, *Five Years of the Alliance for Progress*, p. 174.

28. House Committee on Foreign Affairs, *Hearings*, *Foreign Assistance Act of 1962*, p. 820.

29. Senate Committee on Foreign Relations, *Hearings*, *Foreign Assistance Act of 1962*, p. 31.

30. Ibid., p. 32.

31. House Committee on Foreign Affairs, *Hearings*, *Foreign Assistance Act of 1962*, p. 811.

motivated by a desire to protect U.S. private investment and that they are, in effect, tools of U.S. capital. . . .

"Second, a vital, and often crucial, element of U.S. foreign policy is placed at the mercy of one unreasonable action by a foreign official, perhaps not even a member of the national government of that country. . . .

"Third, the suggested amendment could also retard some of the economic and social reforms we seek in connection with our aid program, particularly in Latin America. Land reform may well require expropriations of existing estates, some of which may be owned by U.S. nationals. . . .

"Fourth, a requirement that aid be cut off under the suggested circumstances may well commit our whole policy into the hands of one intransigent American citizen, whose action could provoke expropriation and whose obstinancy could prevent a reasonable settlement. . . ."[32] The Department of State concluded its case against the amendment by stressing that "flexibility, rather than a rigid rule, is required."[33]

The arguments against the amendment fell on deaf congressional ears. The Foreign Relations Committee thought that in addition to offering greater security to U.S. foreign investors, "the amendment should serve the collateral purpose of encouraging more American investment in less developed countries."[34] The Committee on Foreign Affairs declared: "Nations should not be regarded as qualifying for U.S. assistance unless they understand the importance of private investment to their economic development and are ready to encourage such investment."[35] Therefore, the committee felt that the seizure of American property without prompt, fair compensation did not reflect an attitude of partnership and mutuality, nor an understanding of how to effectively use U.S. assistance.

After passage of the amendment, the Kennedy administration suspended U.S. assistance to Ceylon when it expropriated U.S. property. The administration's position, stated by Secretary Rusk, was that both private investment and foreign aid were required for

32. Senate Committee on Foreign Relations, *Hearings*, *Foreign Assistance Act of 1962*, pp. 557–58.

33. Ibid.

34. Senate Committee on Foreign Relations, *Report*, *Foreign Assistance Act of 1962*, p. 36.

35. House Committee on Foreign Affairs, *Report*, *Foreign Assistance Act of 1962*, p. 30.

economic development, and the AID effort could succeed only if domestic and foreign private capital were involved in the effort.[36] However, Rusk warned Congress about the limitations of the Hickenlooper Amendment as a deterrent to expropriation: "I think if we get to the point where we have to actually employ the amendment, then in a certain sense it may already be too late, because at that point one does not know whether one can be of any further help to the companies involved on the one side, and there is a possibility of a real deterioration of relations between governments on the other."[37] The most effective feature of the amendment was that it reflected the attitude of the United States regarding the importance of a climate for investment and the role of private enterprise in the aid program. His evaluation of the effect of the amendment in the first year, despite his reservations, was that it had been "a good thing."[38]

Congress tightened and broadened the provisions of the Hickenlooper Amendment in 1963. The Foreign Relations Committee was pleased with the experience of the first year; they concluded that the presence of the amendment had helped to settle one major expropriation case and had avoided several other possible discrimination actions or expropriations.[39] They also emphasized that nationalization had a detrimental effect on a country's economy since it diverted resources from more productive uses and discouraged new private investment. The 1963 Clay Report assessed the Hickenlooper Amendment as a "helpful" addition to the foreign aid program. As late as 1967, administration spokesmen testified that the preventive aspects of the Hickenlooper-Adair Amendment (as it was called by the Foreign Affairs Committee) was "very healthy indeed."[40]

But the failure of the amendment as a deterrent, despite the early declarations, and the manner in which it could complicate delicate negotiations in investment disputes became very evident in subsequent crises. In fact, many of the Department of State

36. U.S., Department of State, *The Department of State Bulletin* 47 (March 11, 1963):365.

37. Senate Committee on Foreign Relations, *Hearings*, *Foreign Assistance Act of 1963*, p. 30.

38. Ibid.

39. U.S., Congress, Senate, Committee on Foreign Relations, *Report*, *Foreign Assistance Act of 1963*, p. 30.

40. U.S., Congress, Senate, Committee on Foreign Relations, *Hearings*, *Foreign Assistance Act of 1967*, p. 331.

warnings in 1962 appeared to be prophetic. Richard Goodwin concluded from his examination of the IPC seizure in 1969 that the Hickenlooper Amendment had kept an agreement from being reached, since the intransigence of IPC was strengthened by the potential sanctions which would have been invoked if the Peruvians had nationalized IPC property.[41] A high official of IPC admitted to Goodwin that their mistake had been in not extending the terms of their 1968 offer to Belaúnde Terry's government four years earlier. An IPC representative told the Foreign Relations Committee that their proposal might have been accepted in 1964, since the political position of Belaúnde had been much stronger then.[42] The Johnson administration's decision to suspend aid to Peru until an agreement was reached with IPC also contributed to the resistance of the American company while ultimately undermining the democratic Belaúnde government. An official of Standard Oil Company of New Jersey explained the intransigence of the company: "Our flexibility is limited by our worldwide commitments."[43]

Describing his government as one of "leftist nationalism," Bolivia's president, General Alfredo Ovando Candía, declared ideological identification with the military government of Peru. In an apparent bid for popular support in October 1969, he decreed nationalization of the properties of Gulf Oil Corporation, the largest foreign firm in Bolivia and its only oil company. Seeking leftist backing, government spokesmen accused Gulf of using imperialist pressures to renegotiate its agreement with the new regime. At a news conference in Washington two weeks after the nationalization, E. D. Brocket, chairman of the corporation, stated that he favored application of the Hickenlooper Amendment to cut off aid to Bolivia. He commented that Bolivia's actions were illegal under Bolivian and international law.[44] Reports now indicate that the Bolivians, realizing they did not have the means either to ship or to market the seized oil, were considering a compromise with Gulf. The shaky state of the Bolivian economy, which would be severely affected by the stoppage of oil production and loss of other foreign investments, encouraged government

41. Senate Committee on Foreign Relations, *Hearings*, *United States Relations with Peru*, p. 92.

42. Ibid., p. 111.

43. Levinson and de Onís, *Alliance that Lost Its Way*, p. 150.

44. *New York Times*, October 31, 1969, p. 63.

action to obtain a prompt settlement. However, the Gulf press conference angered and united Bolivians against the "gringo" threat to the nation.[45] If the Hickenlooper Amendment had not been available, quiet negotiations might even have reached a satisfactory solution for all parties without agitating anti-American feelings and creating a possible diplomatic confrontation.

The *New York Times* disclosed that President Nixon was planning to announce that he would seek the repeal of the Hickenlooper provisions in his Latin American policy speech. But when Bolivia nationalized the Gulf properties two weeks before his address, the president deemed it unadvisable to seek congressional action at that time, for obvious political reasons.[46]

The Latin American reaction to possible application of the amendment was foreseen by the president of Ecuador. He told Governor Rockefeller, during his violent trip through Latin America, that he hoped the United States would not apply the Hickenlooper Amendment in the Peruvian dispute. He feared the reaction in Ecuador would be so bitter and anti-American feeling so strong that Ecuador would not be able to sign the pending contract with Texaco, Inc., which was vital to Ecuador's economic future.[47] Governor Rockefeller concluded that the automatic feature of the Hickenlooper Amendment was extremely dangerous since a private citizen or foreign government could trigger an action by the United States which the government could not control. His report to the president urged the modification or suspension of the Hickenlooper Amendment.

There were indications that the wisdom and usefulness of the Hickenlooper Amendment were being seriously questioned in high government circles. The Peterson task force told President Nixon that the amendment "has outlived its usefulness. It provides no room for flexibility in dealing with this difficult and politically sensitive problem."[48] However, a letter dated November 25, 1969, from Secretary Rogers to Senator Fulbright indicated that the president did not intend to initiate action on the controversial amendment. After presenting both sides of the ques-

45. *Washington Evening Star*, November 8, 1969, p. 3.

46. *New York Times*, November 10, 1969, p. 6.

47. U.S., Congress, House, Committee on Foreign Affairs, *Hearings, Governor Rockefeller's Report on Latin America*, p. 29.

48. *U.S. Foreign Assistance in the 1970's: A New Approach*, report to the president, March 4, 1970, p. 22.

tion, the secretary declined to take a position on the matter or suggest any changes in the current law.[49] But despite the unwillingness to seek repeal of the amendment, the reluctance to employ its heavy-handed sanction in the Peruvian and Bolivian disputes signified the virtual abandonment of the amendment as a viable tool of U.S. policy. Assistant Secretary Meyer told the American Management Association on February 23, 1970: "Gunboat diplomacy. . .is behind us."[50]

OPIC—Spearhead for Investment

Senator Jacob K. Javits of New York has long been an advocate of expanding U.S. private investments abroad. He was the sponsor of the original investment guaranty program in foreign assistance legislation in the late 1940s and played an instrumental role in the creation of the Atlantic Community Development Group for Latin America (ADELA) in 1964, a multinational corporation which channels private investment to Latin America for economic development projects. His proposal for a federally chartered "Peace by Investment Corporation," to tap the resources of American private investors for economic growth in the less-developed countries, was endorsed by the Foreign Affairs Subcommittee on Foreign Economic Policy in 1968.[51]

Impetus for OPIC also came from the International Private Investment Advisory Council (IPIAC) to AID, which had been established in 1966. In December 1968, responding to the Javits Amendment to the Foreign Assistance Act of 1968, which called upon the president to consider the creation of a federally sponsored corporation "designed to mobilize and facilitate the use of U.S. private capital and skills in less developed countries and areas," IPIAC gave strong support for the establishment of a U.S. Overseas Private Enterprise Development Corporation. Private enterprise was deemed a powerful stimulus to modernization; the benefits to the U.S. economy from exports and overseas investment were also acknowledged.[52] President Johnson's Perkins

49. *Congressional Record*, December 12, 1969, p. 16630.

50. *National Journal*, February 28, 1970, p. 428.

51. U.S., Congress, House, Committee on Foreign Affairs, *Report*, *The Involvement of U.S. Private Enterprise in Developing Countries*, p. 3.

52. *The Case for a U.S. Overseas Private Enterprise Development Corporation*, report to the president, December 1968, p. 2.

committee also embraced the idea of an overseas investment corporation.[53]

President Nixon proposed the creation of an Overseas Private Investment Corporation in his 1969 foreign assistance message. Its prime function would be to encourage private investment in the less-developed countries. Fundamentally, OPIC would have the same authority to issue investment guaranties as the existing Office of Private Resources in AID, although in addition it would have the authority to make limited loans. OPIC would also take over the functions of AID's Private Investment Center for Investment Promotion and preinvestment assistance to U.S. investors and would provide financial or technical support for special private enterprise programs of technical, professional, or managerial assistance. The major difference was that OPIC was separated from the administration of AID and organized along corporate lines as a federal agency with six of its eleven directors chosen from private life. According to a witness from the National Association of Manufacturers, this separation from AID and reorganization would ensure a "business-oriented" institution.[54] It might also signal a special clientele relationship.

An examination of the original administration proposal and the bill reported by the Foreign Affairs Committee revealed some of the views of the proponents and the critics of the corporation. Supporters contended that separation from AID, the inclusion of businessmen on its board of directors, and the establishment of a corporate structure would facilitate businesslike decision making, obviating the need for bureaucratic clearances. This step would enhance OPIC's standing and support in the business community. The interests of the government would be protected, since the corporation would be under the policy guidance of the secretary of state. One AID spokesman declared that the central function of OPIC "must be to assist the Administration in seeing that AID's regular programs are applied with an eye to their consequences for private enterprise—both local and foreign."[55] Another acknowledged that OPIC would not change the ambiva-

53. *Development Assistance in the New Administration*, report to the president, October 25, 1968, pp. 26–28.

54. House Committee on Foreign Affairs, *Hearings*, *Overseas Private Investment Corporation*, p. 87.

55. House Committee on Foreign Affairs, *Hearings*, *Foreign Assistance Act of 1969*, p. 191.

lent attitudes of Latin Americans have toward foreign capital.[56]

Some members of the Foreign Affairs Committee, upset over the image of U.S. business in Latin America and the growing friction with nationalistic governments, were critical of the wedding of American foreign policy to business interests. Congressman John Tunney observed that currently the American government can remain somewhat isolated from disputes between a U.S. investor and a foreign government, but it cannot if the government is closely associated through OPIC.[57] Representative F. Bradford Morse criticized the fact that "all too frequently, the objectives of a commercial enterprise do not conform to U.S. national objectives."[58] John Culver wondered whether a code of investment was needed to ensure that the long-range developmental goal of socioeconomic progress was fully embraced by American businessmen abroad. Skeptical of the "enlightened" attitudes of businessmen, he described the recent establishment of a Communist union in Costa Rica after the United Fruit Company for years had opposed and criticized the efforts of American embassy officials to encourage a democratic trade union movement as called for in the Alliance for Progress.[59]

A motion to delete OPIC from the Foreign Assistance Act was defeated, but amendments to the original proposal indicated that the critics were able to modify OPIC's structure and goals. The chairman of the board would be the administrator of AID, to assure close coordination between the corporation and U.S. foreign policy. It was specified that at least one of the six nongovernmental directors should be experienced in small business, one in organized labor, and one in cooperatives. Another key amendment was suggested by an AID official to overcome liberal criticism that the corporation was not adequately oriented toward the developmental needs of the less-developed countries. Listed sixth in the guidelines for the corporation, the original clause read: ". . . to encourage and facilitate efforts by private investors to conduct their operations in less developed friendly countries and areas in a manner that is sensitive and responsive to the special needs of

56. Ibid., p. 1246.

57. House Committee on Foreign Affairs, *Hearings, Overseas Private Investment Corporation*, p. 27.

58. House Committee on Foreign Affairs, *Hearings, Foreign Assistance Act of 1969*, p. 1234.

59. House Committee on Foreign Affairs, *Hearings, Overseas Private Investment Corporation*, p. 112.

those economies and societies." The amended version stated that OPIC would encourage and support *only* those private investments which are sensitive and responsive to the special needs of their economies "and which contribute to the social and economic development of their people." The clause remained sixth on the list of guidelines.[60] According to an official of the Office of Private Resources, his staff preferred the amendment that was closer to their initial draft legislation. It is interesting to note that although the amendment was almost an afterthought and is still low on the list of guidelines, Nixon spokesmen have stressed this clause in discussions on the operation of OPIC.[61] An OAS document also favorably commented upon this provision in the OPIC legislation.[62]

The authorization to create OPIC encountered difficulties in the Senate Foreign Relations Committee. A tie vote of 7–7 in the committee excluded OPIC from the Foreign Assistance Act of 1969. Senator Church explained to his colleagues that the committee had decided not to consider any new substantive legislation and had confined its attention to the existing foreign aid program in order to expedite its passage in the Senate.[63] Senator Javits, a member of the committee, introduced on the floor, with seventeen co-sponsors, an amendment to include OPIC in the foreign assistance bill. Javits lauded OPIC as a resourceful new initiative which would facilitate and encourage the flow of private foreign capital for development and thus relieve the tax burden of foreign aid.[64] The new corporation, Senator Javits explained, would serve the foreign investor in much the same way that the Export-Import Bank had assisted the American exporter. Whereas only 5 per cent of U.S. firms are now active abroad, OPIC would attract new companies into the foreign investment field. This would be to the

60. The administration bill was H.R. 11792. The bill reported from the Committee on Foreign Affairs was H.R. 14580, Public Law 91–175, 91st Cong., 1st sess. The cited clause was in sec. 321 (f) in both bills.

61. Daniel Szabo, remarks to the American Management Association, January 26, 1971.

62. Organization of American States, Special Committee of the Inter-American Economic and Social Council, November 17–19, 1969, documents of the first part of the meeting, p. 25.

63. *Congressional Record*, December 12, 1969, p. 16635.

64. Ibid., p. 16624. The view that private investment reduces the need for U.S. economic aid is in direct conflict with the Latin American sentiment expressed in the Consensus of Viña del Mar: "It should be agreed that private foreign investment should not be considered assistance, nor should it be computed as part of financial cooperation for development."

advantage of the U.S. balance of payments, since the return on American investments abroad could be called a hidden export. The trade balance would also be protected by the fact that these foreign investments would be tied to purchases in the United States. Thus, the senator continued, OPIC would further development in the less-developed countries "so that they may be better customers of ours and so they may be better places to live for their people. . . ."[65]

Senator Fulbright, chairman of the Foreign Relations Committee, took the floor against the proposal, stating that the creation of OPIC was a major policy which required careful and deliberate study. He suggested that the Senate should wait until the Peterson task force on foreign aid submitted its recommendations to President Nixon in March 1970. Fulbright briefly mentioned some of the major issues involved in this policy question: "Is it a device to help American business or the developing countries? What are the political consequences abroad for the United States to assume greater control over the economies of developing countries? . . . Should the United States give 100 per cent, no-risk guarantees to American businessmen to invest abroad when similar programs are not available for stimulating economic growth in the ghettos and poverty areas here at home?"[66] The chairman then declared that he did not oppose legislation benefiting American business, but it should stand separately, not disguised as part of the foreign aid bill. Fulbright referred to Senator Javits's comparison of the role of OPIC to the operation of the Export-Import Bank and noted that the bank had been avowedly designed to help U.S. business and was not created as part of the foreign aid bill. The Senate finally voted 53–34 to accept the Javits Amendment.

OPIC also encountered troubles in the House Appropriations Committee, which refused to appropriate the $75 million that the administration had requested to supplement existing reserves. The Senate Appropriations Committee, however, recommended that the $75 million request be added to the total reserves of OPIC. The Conference Report agreed that $37.5 million should be appropriated for OPIC, half the initial request.

Governor Rockefeller "applauded" the Nixon administration's legislation for OPIC; he pointed out, however, that 80 to 90 per cent of U.S. investment went abroad without

65. Ibid., p. 16628.
66. Ibid., p. 16629.

guaranties. While guaranties were helpful, he felt that the best long-term policy was the wise conduct of private enterprise.[67] But though Rockefeller supported OPIC, he recommended the formation of a private insurance group to take over U.S. foreign investment guaranties under a reinsurance arrangement with OPIC; "This would further remove the U.S. government from direct involvement in protecting U.S. private investment."[68] Such an arrangement would also avoid the bitterness generated by Latin American objections to U.S. intervention in their domestic affairs: "They are very bitter about our not accepting their internal procedures."[69] The Peterson task force strongly endorsed the establishment of OPIC as an effective instrument to encourage U.S. private investment in the less-developed countries.[70]

Although Congress created OPIC in December 1969, it was not formally organized until January 19, 1971, when its executive officers and directors were installed; the delay was due to a controversy between the White House and Senator Javits regarding the appointment of the first president of the corporation. OPIC has interpreted the provisions inserted into its guidelines to meet congressional criticism as offering them a broader mandate. OPIC officials and literature emphasize the selectivity employed in determining whether a proposed new investment can be issued guaranties or loans; these standards include an assessment of developmental impact, risk management, and written approval of the new investment by the host government.

On March 8, 1971, confronting possible bankruptcy because of the question of fair compensation for expropriated American properties in Chile, OPIC approved policy guidelines for "large and sensitive projects." Such projects would include those involving U.S. investment of $25 million or more, public utilities, protected industries, and natural resources. Equity investment insurance would not extend beyond twelve years, and although the amount of insurance could not exceed the original investment, the coverage would be adjusted on a predetermined declining formula. OPIC reserved the right to limit the maximum amount of insurance coverage on investments in excess of $50 million, and

67. House Committee on Foreign Affairs, *Hearings*, *Rockefeller Report*, p. 28.

68. Ibid., p. 152.

69. Ibid., p. 29.

70. *U.S. Foreign Assistance in the 1970's*, report to the president, p. 21.

would insure only the tangible and removable assets of petroleum investments unless the project was of "exceptional developmental significance."[71] Steps would also be taken to ascertain whether agreements between the investor and the host government were fairly and openly negotiated. Table 8–4 shows the number of applications for investment insurance that OPIC rejected from January 1970, to March 1971, and the reasons for the rejections.

In April 1971 the beleaguered new president of OPIC, Bradford Mills, described the potential liability of OPIC in Chile, where it had issued insurance contracts for thirty-two projects. The estimated total liability in Chile under expropriation coverage was $310 million, with insured investors having an additional $85 million of expropriation funds on a standby basis; under inconvertibility, $171 million; and under war risk, $119 million.[72] Contracts for standby coverage with Anaconda for $247.7 million were in contention, as OPIC declared that Anaconda did not pay its premiums and only had an option to insure.[73] Mills would only discuss some of the cases on a classified basis since they involved "privileged business information which the insuring companies would not want us to discuss openly."[74] He informed the congressional committee that while OPIC had not paid out any claims on the Chilean coverage, eight investors had filed preliminary notices or claims because of nationalization steps under way. However, a potential liability of $18 million from Bethlehem Steel Corporation appeared to have been amicably settled with the Chilean government. But OPIC in September 1971 faced a claim of $108.5 million for coverage on ITT's 70 per cent share of the Chilean telephone company, when the Chilean government assumed management control; in October the comptroller general of Chile ruled that American copper companies should receive no compensation for their nationalized holdings because of the "excess profits" they had earned in prior years.

On June 17, 1971, Mills described OPIC's portfolio and problems to the Council of the Americas.[75] He pointed out that of

71. U.S., Department of State, Overseas Private Investment Corporation, "General Policy and Guidelines: Large or Sensitive Projects.

72. U.S., Congress, House, Committee on Appropriations, *Hearings, Foreign Assistance and Related Agencies Appropriations for 1972*, p. 590.

73. *Washington Post*, October 13, 1971, p. A2.

74. House Committee on Appropriations, *Hearings, Foreign Assistance Appropriations for 1972*, p. 589.

75. Bradford Mills, remarks before the Council of the Americas, June 17, 1971.

OPIC's worldwide coverage, Latin America accounted for 50 per cent of OPIC's total inconvertibility coverage, 57 per cent of its insurance against expropriation, and 55 per cent of its global war risk coverage. However, in the previous calendar year the number of new investments registered with OPIC for insurance in the region fell approximately 50 per cent from the 1968 rate; the number of contracts issued declined from twenty-two per month to only three per month during the quarter which ended March 31, 1971; and insurance issued during the last quarter totaled only $8 million compared to an average level of more than $100 million dollars each quarter during the previous four years. Because of economic nationalism, OPIC programs were inoperative in Bolivia, Chile, and Peru, while programs in Argentina, Colombia, Ecuador, and Guyana were being monitored. He told the businessmen that OPIC had to adapt and lead the way in devising new ways to invest in Latin America. He suggested local ownership, especially with large investments or in the natural resource and public utilities industries, multinationalization of investment, and new investments which emphasized technology, management, and services, rather than cash. Thus, OPIC has begun to explore new policies to cope with economic nationalism in the hemisphere.

JOINT VENTURES—HARMFUL OR HELPFUL?

President Truman's International Development Advisory Board recommended that "foreign capital should be encouraged to invest in the underdeveloped countries in partnership with local capital and in a spirit of cooperation rather than of exploitation."[76] The Truman administration, however, did not energetically promote joint ventures. The census of 1950 showed that most of the U.S. investments in Latin America were wholly owned; participation by foreign investors amounted to only 10 per cent, compared to a world average of almost 22 per cent.[77] President Eisenhower's Undersecretary of State Dillon expressed his pleasure that "our business leaders are more and more coming to realize and accept the importance of this principle of local partnership."[78] And in

76. Donald M. Dozer, *Are We Good Neighbors?: Three Decades of Inter-American Relations, 1930–1960*, p. 250.

77. Ibid., p. 254.

78. U.S., Department of State, Bureau of Public Affairs, *Strengthening Friendship and Trust Among the American Republics: President Eisenhower's Visit to Brazil, Argentina, Chile, and Uruguay, February–March, 1960.*

TABLE 8-4

Written Applications for OPIC Investment Insurance Rejected during January 1970–March 1971

Summary		
Total applications received		666
Total applications rejected		97
Reasons for Rejection		
Statutory ineligibility of investor or country under Foreign Assistance Act		17
Paragraph 221--No bilateral agreement with foreign government	(3)	
Paragraph 223(c)--Investor not U.S. citizen or corporation	(2)	
Paragraph 620(f)--Communist country	(1)	
Paragraph 620(n)--Shipping to North Vietnam	(8)	
Paragraph 620(m)--Developed country	(2)	
Paragraph 620(t)--Severed diplomatic relations	(1)	
Foreign government approval refused		12
Premature application (no definite project)		4
Country program suspended		12
OPIC policies		52
Projects not sufficiently developmental	(18)	
Government control of project	(7)	

TABLE 8-4 (Continued)

Reasons for Rejection		
Irrevocable commitment before registration	(5)	
Balance of payments (ineligible foreign procurement)	(3)	
Military field	(1)	
Overrun after contract issued	(1)	
Agricultural product in surplus	(8)	
Export to U.S. intended	(5)	
Natural resource policy	(2)	
Investor's reputation	(1)	
Incomplete application	(1)	
Total		97

Source: U.S., Congress, House, *Hearings, Foreign Assistance and Related Agencies Appropriations for 1972*, p. 593.

1960, President Eisenhower commented favorably on the growing number of partnerships with local entrepreneurs.[79] But despite these public indications of support for the concept of joint ventures, the Eisenhower administration did not vigorously promote them.

Joint ventures were strongly endorsed by the Kennedy administration. Theodore Moscoso testified that the best guaranty for foreign investors, even better than the investment guaranty program, was for American companies to take local partners; because "a firm which becomes identified with a country rather than identified with a foreign country will have a much better opportunity for successful development."[80] Another official stated that AID acted "as a catalytic agent in the formation of new joint ventures" in the less-developed countries;[81] he believed that AID's task was serving as "missionaries for the joint venture in the less developed countries."[82] It was not only good politics, it was good business to have a local partner. As Kennedy's ambassador to Brazil, Lincoln Gordon encouraged joint ventures as a means to transfer modern techniques.[83]

In 1969 Governor Rockefeller told the Foreign Relations Committee: "There is no question . . . that the local participation in ownership of international investments is psychologically and economically very important."[84] His action recommendations to President Nixon included proposals for open-end investment trusts for local participation in shares of foreign-owned companies, improved mechanisms to bring together private U.S. investors and Latin American companies seeking American partners, establishment of a contract arrangement for high-risk but necessary projects which would later sell the equity to the American participants and local investors, and alteration of U.S. tax laws which discourage joint ventures. The Peterson task force also encouraged local participation in the ownership of U.S. subsidiaries abroad, although they questioned the usefulness of rigid

79. Ibid.

80. Senate Committee on Foreign Relations, *Hearings*, *Foreign Assistance Act of 1962*, p. 416.

81. House Committee on Foreign Affairs, *Hearings*, *Foreign Assistance Act of 1963*, p. 453.

82. House Committee on Foreign Affairs, *Hearings*, *Foreign Assistance Act of 1964*, p. 396.

83. Lincoln Gordon, *A New Deal for Latin America*, p. 50.

84. House Committee on Foreign Affairs, *Hearings*, *Rockefeller Report*, p. 25.

equity formulas.[85] They suggested that increased funding of the World Bank's IFC, which was charged with the responsibility of bolstering the private sector in the developing countries, would facilitate the formation of joint ventures, and recommended that OPIC make greater use of its guaranty program to promote joint ventures.[86] But the Department of State has avoided taking a public position on this issue, arguing that companies that desire to invest abroad should make their own decision on ownership matters. However, officials in the Department of Commerce have mentioned the possibility of forming joint ventures to American businessmen considering investments in the hemisphere.

Some Nixon administration officials were favorable toward joint ventures, although not unaware of their limitations. Secretary Meyer told the Council for Latin America in May 1969: "Increasingly, the Latin American countries are urging, even insisting on, cooperative ventures with local partners. . . . I believe the joint ventures are a natural outcome of local capital formation, and I think that we should constantly search for ways in which they can feasibly be developed. Sometimes, however, they cannot be carried through in practice without greatly restricting the areas available to foreign capital or doing injustice to local interests. Partnership implies, semantically, common objectives and common expectations between partners. These conditions do not always exist. It would be unfair to expect a small country, let alone a small local investor, to share the costs of an expensive and highly risky operation."[87] However, Secretary Meyer told the Foreign Relations Committee in 1969 that it was his personal view that joint ventures were "the way of the future."[88] An AID official, while raising the question of whether it was arrogant on the part of the U.S. government to encourage private investors to form joint ventures as the best means to operate in a foreign country, was very concerned about the effects of U.S. investment disputes upon U.S. policies. As he characterized the issue: ". . . the U.S. government is in on the crash landing but not on the takeoff."[89] It is interesting that Assistant Secretary of the Treasury John Petty,

85. *U.S. Foreign Assistance in the 1970s*, report to the president, p. 21.

86. Ibid., p. 22.

87. U.S., Department of State, *The Department of State Bulletin* 60 (May 26, 1969):442.

88. Senate Committee on Foreign Relations, *Hearings*, *United States Relations with Peru*, p. 121.

89. Weintraub, address of January 29, 1971.

in an August 1970 speech in Mexico City, offered the increasing moves of American investors toward balanced joint ventures as one defense of U.S. private investment in Latin America.[90]

In conclusion, the policies that the United States has adopted to stimulate and protect American foreign investments in the less-developed countries have often disregarded the resistance and hostility toward foreign capital in Latin America. The vigorous promotion of investment guaranty agreements has often politically embarrassed friendly governments when they tried to ratify the agreements in their national legislature. Even though congressional statements have stressed that guaranties would further economic development, the tenor of the discussions has revealed that the major concern has usually been the protection of American investors and an ideological desire to bolster private enterprise.

The Hickenlooper Amendment, hastily adopted as a deterrent to expropriation of American property, has proved to be cumbersome and ineffective in practice. Fearful that its implementation in an investment dispute might endanger other investors and interests of the United States, the president has managed to ignore, with the tacit consent of Congress, the mandatory provisions for employment of the heavy-handed sanction. The State Department's early call for flexibility in such disputes appears to be the operating principle behind the response of the United States to the expropriations in Peru, Bolivia, and Chile.

The Overseas Private Investment Corporation, while not a dramatic policy departure, was created to coordinate and streamline existing programs to encourage U.S. foreign investment in the less-developed countries. However, the obvious sensitivity of Latin America to foreign capital and the recent attacks on American firms caused a congressional debate on whether U.S. foreign investment ought to be uncritically encouraged in the hemisphere. Joint ventures, while not eagerly embraced by American investors, have been promoted by U.S. officials as a means to reduce the high profile of American investment in Latin America. However, the success of joint ventures seems to rest primarily upon the selection of suitable local partners in the host country.

Congress has been the most forceful defender of the interests of American foreign investors, adding restrictions to the foreign

90. John R. Petty, "The U.S.–Latin American Trade and Payments Relationship," p. 92.

assistance bills to promote and safeguard the concerns of the private sector, even over the protests of the executive branch. The president, responsible for the broader political and economic interests of the United States, has resisted provisions which limit the flexibility of the government to respond to conflicts between American firms and sovereign nations. While both Congress and the president have voiced the belief that private enterprise is the best stimulus to economic growth, the president, confronting the reality of Latin American economic nationalism, has been more sensitive to the skepticism of the hemisphere and the role of foreign investment in the development process.

But investment guaranties present a disturbingly large liability to the U.S. treasury because of the nationalization of sizable American holdings insured by OPIC, and the mandatory provisions of the Hickenlooper Amendment could spark a plethora of retaliatory attacks on American firms throughout the hemisphere. More and more the argument has been raised that if the United States assumes the responsibility of encouraging and insuring U.S. foreign investment, the government ought to have the authority to scrutinize and control the type of investments and the operations of American companies in the less-developed areas. While this is obviously an infringement on the laissez-faire concept, many argue that investment guaranties and intervention in the domestic affairs of another nation on behalf of private interests are also violations of the sanctity of that principle. The issue is whether the policies of the United States should be so closely wedded to the business sector that an individual company, through its past actions or an intransigent attitude, could embroil the U.S. in a bilateral dispute which might have hemispheric ramifications. Somehow, the U.S. government must find ways to balance its responsibilities to American investors, neighboring countries, and the overall interest of the United States. The next two chapters will consider the business community's approach to these matters.

9. The Troubled American Businessman

IN THE PRECEDING CHAPTERS, the dichotomy of views between Latin Americans and U.S. investors regarding foreign investment has been discussed. We have examined the growth of economic nationalism, conflicting perceptions of the role of private enterprise in economic development, and past U.S. policies to promote American investment.

But what is the present thinking of the American business community as it is assailed by the latest wave of economic nationalism in Latin America? How do businessmen feel it will affect prospects for foreign investment in future years? What official and corporate policies are contemplated to cope with the unrest and resentments aimed at the high profile of the American investor in the hemisphere? These are some of the questions which have been posed to officials of American companies with investments in Latin America.

Survey Methodology

While a Congressional Fellow of the American Political Science Association, I undertook a survey on behalf of Senator Fred Harris to ascertain the views of American businessmen on U.S. economic policy in Latin America. One facet of the study concerned the role of private enterprise in economic development. The Council of the Americas was chosen as the universe for the survey since its corporate membership represented about 85 per cent of American investment in the hemisphere. The selection of members for the council undoubtedly excluded many of the smaller investors operating in Latin America. Because their firms had smaller investors in the hemisphere, it was felt that they had probably not felt nationalist pressures to the extent of the larger U.S. investors included in this study. In June 1970 the council was contacted and their staff offered full cooperation with the study. They were especially pleased to have the opportunity to develop more interest in Latin America on Capitol Hill at a time when hemispheric affairs were not receiving much attention from U.S. policy makers, and American properties were in jeopardy in Peru, Bolivia, and Chile.

The Council of the Americas supplied a mailing list of its corporate members and their individual representatives. The mailing list was checked for its active current membership and noncorporate members were deleted; the universe for the study consisted of 213 American corporations (see list in Appendix). A questionnaire was mailed to each firm with an accompanying letter from Senator Harris, a member of the Finance Committee, which considers legislation dealing with international trade and foreign investment; respondents were assured of anonymity. The letters were addressed to the highest official representing each company's interests in the Council of the Americas; the assistance of the staff of the council was extremely helpful in this matter. It was assumed that if the questionnaire were sent to the highest official involved in a firm's Latin American operations, he or a subordinate would be interested enough in the topic of the survey to reply. It was felt that the nature of the survey—dealing with current problems of American investors in Latin America—and the official capacity of Senator Harris would ensure that the survey was well received. These assumptions were justified.

The survey was mailed on August 5, 1970, to the 213 council members; 100 completed questionnaires were returned, a response rate of 48 per cent. Council staff members indicated that this response was above average. From the remarks of council officers at their annual meetings urging greater member participation, it would appear that while the membership of the Council of the Americas is large, few companies take an active role in council affairs. It must be noted, however, that an additional eight firms replied that they felt their companies' business interests in Latin America would not be applicable to the survey; also, two other completed questionnaires were received after the survey was processed in December 1970.

The response rate of this survey can be compared with several other studies of business elites and national leaders interested in the foreign aid program. For *American Business and Public Policy*, Bauer, Pool, and Dexter sent their questionnaires on foreign trade policy to businessmen who had been interviewed on the subject the previous year by the National Opinion Research Center; over two-thirds of their sample replied.[1] The mail questionnaire for this survey did not have the advantage of such a preliminary interview to evoke an interest in the study. For another study, James Rosenau mailed questionnaires to national leaders from all segments of American society who attended a 1958 White House conference on the foreign aid program; a total of 61 per cent responded. However, he stated: "It must be emphasized at the outset that no claim to representativeness is made on behalf of the data presented herein. While the proportion of returned questionnaires is remarkably high, and despite considerable evidence that the conferees who responded were in no way a biased sample of those who attended the Conference, the inherent value of the data lies in the uniqueness of the respondents and not in their representativeness."[2] His universe consisted of 1,067 conferees who were interested in foreign aid and attended the conference out of an initial group of 1,772 invitees. Guy Meeker's survey on the fade-out venture was sent to 340 U.S. companies and had a response rate of 26 per cent;[3] it was felt that the number of replies to this questionnaire to business elites constituted a satisfactory rate.

In the universe of this study, membership in the Council of the Americas can only be assumed to mean that an individual firm has investments in Latin America. Membership in the council provides the firm with additional information on the investment climate in Latin America, bolsters the efforts of American busi-

1. Raymond A. Bauer, Ithiel de Sola Pool, and Lewis Anthony Dexter, *American Business and Public Policy*, p. 116.

2. James N. Rosenau, *National Leadership and Foreign Policy*, p. 49.

3. Guy B. Meeker, "Fade-out Joint Venture: Can It Work for Latin America?" p. 28.

ness to promote private enterprise in the hemisphere, and provides the firm with access to U.S. and Latin American policy makers through the activities of the council and its officials. While there is general agreement that the council's prime objective is "to identify U.S. business as a positive force in the development of the countries in which it operates," the level of member participation in the operation of the council varies considerably.[4] The fact that the entire corporate membership was chosen for the universe—and corporate members comprise about 85 per cent of American investment in the hemisphere—speaks for the representativeness of the survey on one level. It was impossible, however, to examine the representativeness of the respondents compared to the total universe because of the lack of information regarding the nature and extent of the Latin American investments of the other fims.

Conducting the survey under the auspices of a U.S. senator provided a unique opportunity to study the American business community. The Bauer study noted that professors were automatically associated with the liberal side of the trade issue by both protectionists and free traders; the interviewers had a difficult time assuring businessmen that they were neutral on the substance of the trade issue.[5] While they were "painfully aware" of these biases, no effort was made to evaluate how they may have affected the attitudes of the respondents. Since this study was conducted for a U.S. senator, who as a member of the Finance Committee was concerned with international trade and foreign investment (which was pointed out in the cover letter), the questionnaire afforded business executives the opportunity to have an input into the policy-making process. Indeed, many of the returned questionnaires were accompanied by letters which expressed appreciation for the chance to voice their ideas and satisfaction at the senator's interest in Latin American affairs; some sent lengthy letters with in-depth analyses of the problems of foreign investors. It was obvious that many felt U.S. economic policy in the hemisphere was receiving insufficient attention in Washington. This opportunity to influence a policy maker provided the survey with many thoughtful replies from executives of some of the largest firms in the nation. It is doubtful that many modified their comments contrary to their

4. Council for Latin America, "How Can My Company Get the Most Out of Membership in the Council for Latin America?"

5. Bauer, Pool, and Dexter, *American Business and Public Policy*, p. 148.

own self-interests to sway an official, since the replies could be anonymous and their recommendations might influence future policy decisions. Hence, it is likely that the respondents provided the senator with the type of input they would like to see implemented in U.S. policies toward Latin America. On February 11, 1971, I held a meeting in the Capitol with members of the Council of the Americas (selected to represent various types of investors), council staff, and Senator Harris. The preliminary findings of the survey were presented and discussed. This gave the businessmen the opportunity to elaborate upon their comments and the general findings of the survey, and to personally state their concerns to the senator.

Profile of the Respondents

Table 9–1 reveals the positions of the respondents in the companies which replied to the survey. As mentioned above, the questionnaire was addressed to the highest official representing each firm in the Council of the Americas. The official capacity of

TABLE 9-1

Position of Respondents in Company

Position	Total Sample N=100 (%)
Chairman of the board	9
President[a]	20
Senior or executive vice-president	11
Vice-president	29
General manager or director	10
Others in executive positions	7
Economist, financial or trade expert	11
Public relations or governmental relations	3

a. Three respondents were presidents of their firms' Latin American or international divisions.

each respondent was determined from the notation on the questionnaire to that effect or from any accompanying letter. It was assumed that if the staff had prepared many of the answers, particularly those requiring quantitative data, and the questionnaire was sent back by a high company official, he had read and approved the reply as accurately reflecting his corporation's position. Since many of the members of the Council of the Americas represent the largest industrial and financial corporations in the United States, Latin America may not be a central concern of the presidents of these corporate giants. Instead, a senior vice-president or vice-president for international operations or Latin America may have been designated as the company's representative to the Council of the Americas. Therefore, using the mailing list of the council restricted the potential respondents to those who were actively and operationally concerned with their firm's Latin American investments. Although using the list meant, perhaps, that executives on a lower level were contacted , it had the advantage of assuring that the respondents would be knowledgeable about their company's Latin American interests and aware of the political situation in the hemisphere.

The type of Latin American investments of each respondent firm was ascertained from a question requesting them to indicate the approximate percentage of investment in each of nine categories. In compiling Table 9–2, firms were classified in a particular category if they had over 50 per cent of their investment in that sector of economic activity. This meant that twelve firms could not be classified as having their investments primarily in one economic sector because they had diversified their investments, had not indicated the percentage of their investment in several areas, or did not answer the question. It can readily be seen that manufacturers predominate the sample, which is representative of the membership of the entire Council of the Americas. It also reflects the burgeoning activity in the manufacturing sector during the last few decades, as shown earlier. The respondents in the extractive category include ten mining and five petroleum companies; it is recognized that a smaller percentage of the petroleum corporate members of the council replied to the questionnaire than companies engaged in mining activities. Their replies were aggregated both to assure anonymity and to reflect the general sentiments of companies engaged in the sensitive areas of extractive enterprises.

The nature of a firm's Latin American investment was assumed to be a key variable in evaluating the attitudes of the respondents. The extractive industries have been the targets of nationalists for many years and much of the current economic nationalism in Latin America is aimed at U.S. interests in the sensitive sectors of petroleum and mining activities. Some observers feel that the extractive industries, because of their economic and political power, have been less willing than others to modify their corporate policies in the face of this nationalism and

TABLE 9-2

Type of Latin American Investment

Industry Sector	Number (100)
Manufacturing	48
Extractive	15
Finance and insurance	10
Service	9
Agriculture	4
Trade	2
No response (not ascertained)	12

appear more determined to have the U.S. government resort to severe sanctions to protect their interests. Manufacturers, on the other hand, are considered to have a lower profile which permits them to blend more easily into the local environment. They are more likely to be engaged in import-substitution activities and may contribute more directly to local employment and the training of nationals in skills readily transferable to other economic enterprises. Since they may be newer to the region than extractive enterprises, they probably do not have a history of close relations with discredited earlier regimes which granted concessions under questionable circumstances. These and other hypotheses will be examined by making the nature of the investment—manufacturing or extractive—an independent variable in the analysis of the survey.

It was hypothesized that the "old-timers" who had weathered nationalist attacks in the past would have different attitudes toward the current problems of investors than corporate newcomers to hemispheric affairs. However, when the number of years of experience was made an independent variable, there were few significant differences of opinion in the total sample. Since the size of a firm was a key variable in the Bauer study of American business, the extent of a company's investment in Latin America was considered an important variable in this analysis. Different indicators of size were sought for this survey because there was no accurate list of the number of employees in Latin America for each firm and there was an additional problem of how to assess the differences in the number of U.S. nationals and indigenous employees in the Latin American subsidiaries. Three variables to determine size were investigated: the firm's Latin American investment in dollars, the Latin American investment as a percentage of all its overseas investment, and the Latin American investment as a percentage of total assets. The best indicator of a firm's interest in Latin America was considered to be the dollar amount of its investment. The larger the size of the investment, the higher the firm's profile and vulnerability to economic nationalism; the larger the investment, the greater the concern about Latin American politics by high executives in the parent company. Tables 9–3 and 9–4 indicate the years of experience a firm has had with investments in Latin America and the dollar amount of its investment.

Although almost half of the total sample had been active in the region for over thirty years, the extractive companies had the most experience with the vagaries of Latin American political and economic life and presented the highest profile in the hemisphere. This corresponds to earlier discussions of the lucrative concessions granted to extractive firms by regimes anxious to increase their revenues and the greater capital demands of extractive enterprises. Only 17 per cent of the respondents stated that their Latin American investment comprised over 50 per cent of all their overseas investment; however, 40 per cent of the extractive firms indicated that they had a great deal of interest in Latin American policy since they had over 75 per cent of their overseas investment in Latin America. Of the extractive industries, 35 per cent had over 25 per cent of their total assets in Latin America (see Appendix). Therefore, it was hypothesized that because of their longer exposure and more visible presence in the hemisphere, the extractive firms may have felt greater pressures to adopt corporate policies to meet nationalist demands. Subsequent findings will disclose whether these assumptions were valid.

It should be noted that the respondents represented many of the largest corporations in the United States, many with vast overseas holdings. Some of the corporate members of the Council of the Americas who were sent questionnaires were: Anaconda

TABLE 9-3

Years of Experience in Latin America

Years	Total Sample N=100 (%)	Manu-facturing N=48 (%)	Extractive N=15 (%)	Other N=37 (%)
Under 10 years	11	8	..	22
10 to 20 years	29	38	27	19
20 to 30 years	12	10	7	14
Over 30 years	45	42	67	41
No response (not ascertained)	3	2	..	4

Company, Bank of America, Chrysler Corporation, Ford Motor Company, General Electric Company, W. R. Grace & Company, ITT, IBM, Koppers Company, Inc., Standard Oil Company of New Jersey, Sears, Roebuck and Company, and Texaco, Inc. I examined the rankings by *Fortune* in May 1970 of the 500 largest industrial corporations and the largest banks of the nation, utilities, transportation, and life insurance companies, to classify the companies which replied to the survey. While it was difficult to compare the diverse nature of the companies, I concluded that 42 of the respondents could be classified as giants of U.S. business, ranking among the top 100 corporations in the United States, and 29 others could be ranked within the 500 largest American corporations.

TABLE 9-4

Size of Latin American Investment
(in Millions of Dollars)

Size of Investor	Total Sample N=100 (%)	Manu-facturing N=48 (%)	Extractive N=15 (%)	Other N=37 (%)
Small investors (under $5 million)	19	8	7	38
Medium investors ($5-25 million)	33	48	13	22
Large investors (over $25 million)	38	40	67	24
No response (not ascertained)	10	4	13	16

The Business Community Assesses Economic Nationalism

The expropriation of American properties in Latin America was on the front page of U.S. newspapers in the years immediately preceding this survey. This study examined whether the respondents felt that such a threat endangered their investment in Latin America and, if so, what type of corporate and official U.S. policies would best protect their investment. The survey began with a question asking the respondents to rank, on a scale from one to six, a list of issues frequently mentioned as the most critical impediments to foreign investment in Latin America. Thus, the salience of their fear of expropriation could be assessed in relation to other problems that affect the investment climate in Latin America. Although conditions varied from country to country, it was postulated that a general assessment of the fears of investors in the region would provide a background for evaluating policies such as the Hickenlooper Amendment, which have hemispheric ramifications. The same broad overview of the problems confronting businessmen was evident in most of the reports submitted to the president on U.S. economic policy in the hemisphere.[6]

The issue that had the highest salience to the respondents was their concern over Latin American restrictive economic policies, closely followed by worry over the political instability of the region (see Table 9–5). Next came their concern over hostility toward private enterprise, both indigenous and foreign, and then that endemic problem in Latin America—inflation. Significantly, the respondents ranked the danger of expropriation very low on the list of adverse considerations affecting the investment climate of the region. It appeared that they were most agitated over the gradual "nibbling away" at their profits and managerial prerogatives by nationalist governments; restrictions on profit remittances, inconvertibility, and local participation demands were a more immediate problem than imminent nationalization. It should be pointed out, however, that the Hickenlooper

6. In coding the data, the ranking of an issue as either the number one or two concern of an investor was interpreted to mean that it had a high salience for that firm. The ranking of a problem as three or four placed the issue in the medium salience category, and the rank of five or six indicated it was of low salience to the corporate respondent.

TABLE 9-5

Salience of Problems Confronting U.S. Investors in Latin America[a]

Attitudes	Total Sample (N=100)				Manufacturing (N=48)				Extractive (N=15)				Other (N=37)			
	High (%)	Medium (%)	Low (%)	NR[b] (%)	High (%)	Medium (%)	Low (%)	NR (%)	High (%)	Medium (%)	Low (%)	NR (%)	High (%)	Medium (%)	Low (%)	NR (%)
Restrictive economic policies	54	34	5	7	50	38	6	6	60	20	7	13	57	35	..	5
Political instability	53	33	9	5	52	35	6	6	47	27	20	7	57	32	8	3
Hostility to private enterprise	31	34	27	8	33	35	25	6	27	47	20	7	30	27	32	11
Inflation	26	35	33	6	31	31	31	6	7	33	53	7	27	41	27	5
Danger of expropriation	18	36	37	9	15	38	42	6	33	33	20	13	16	35	38	11
Discriminatory tax rates	8	14	70	8	8	10	75	6	7	33	53	7	8	11	70	11

a. Totals may not add due to rounding of figures.

b. NR--no response.

Amendment is totally useless as a means to cope with and deter restrictions on American capital; its sanction can only be employed when American properties are seized by a foreign recipient of U.S. foreign assistance. Thus, an investment climate of a relatively laissez-faire marketplace, though desired by investors, was seen as succumbing to the restrictive policies of economic nationalism.

Table 9–5 compares the salience of these problems to manufacturers and extractive companies in the area. Both groups of respondents were primarily concerned over the restrictions placed on foreign enterprises operating in Latin America. Not surprisingly, the danger of expropriation was the third major concern of extractive firms, with their high profile and activities in the most sensitive sector of a host country's economy. Manufacturers ranked the danger of expropriation, on the other hand, as one of their least concerns. This may be attributed to their lower profile, import-substitution activities, and the feeling of nationalists that manufacturers tend to "exploit" the host country less than extractive industries. It is interesting that manufacturers appeared considerably more worried over inflation than extractive companies, which from long experience with inflation in the hemisphere have been better able to adapt their operations to cope with this ever-present factor in Latin American economic life; manufacturers are less able to adjust their prices to keep pace with the inflationary spiral.

It was hypothesized that the larger the dollar amount of a company's investment in Latin America, the more concerned it would be about the threat of expropriation and increased hostility to private enterprise. This survey found that no matter what the size of a firm, the danger of nationalization was not a highly salient fear of the company. However, a corporation's worry about hostility to private enterprise showed a direct correlation to the amount of its investment in Latin America. Whereas only 16 per cent of the small investors indicated that such hostility was a major concern to them, 27 per cent of the medium-sized investors and 45 per cent of the large investors ranked this as a very serious problem. Therefore, the firms with the highest profile in the hemisphere felt the threat of economic nationalism as the level of anti-American rhetoric rose (see Appendix). Since most of the extractive industries were classified as large investors, it was decided to examine the separate responses of the twenty-three medium-sized manufacturing investors and the nineteen large manufacturing investors to determine how attitudes differed within the same economic sector. Consistent with the above findings, 47 per cent of the large manufacturing investors ranked hostility to private enterprise as a highly salient problem, while only 30 per cent of the medium-sized manufacturing investors ranked it so high (see Appendix).

In order to solicit the thoughts of businessmen on economic nationalism in the hemisphere, an open-ended question asked what they felt was the cause for the growing economic nationalism and hostility to foreign investment in Latin America as reflected in the Consensus of Viña del Mar, and what they saw as the most fruitful approach to make foreign private investment mutually attractive. I was interested in determining how their recommendations corresponded to those of the recent Rockefeller and Peterson reports; the Peterson Report had used the expression "most fruitful approach" in discussing its policy recommendations. Since this was an open-ended question, multiple responses were appropriately coded.

The businessmen felt that the major reason for the growing tide of economic nationalism in Latin America stemmed from frustration and dissatisfaction with the slow pace of economic development. These resentments were often encouraged by demagogues and ambitious politicians and then directed against the highly visible U.S. investor, rather than at their own leaders who had failed to initiate meaningful reforms. Forty-two of the respondents cited this as the cause of the latest wave of anti-American sentiment. Below are some of the replies of the businessmen:

> Nationalism has always been, and will continue to be, a strong force in Latin America. So-called economic nationalism is but one facet of that force. Xenophobia is another. . . . The rise of a literate middle class, and the increase in literacy among the peasants permit demagogues, self-seekers, and sincere reformers to manipulate public opinion, unfortunately, in a negative way from our point of view.
>
> Coupled with this development, there has been a real effort to use the U.S. as a "whipping boy" on whom to place the blame for the ills of most of Latin America. This we must

> expect to continue until the countries mature and conditions change. [Manufacturer.]
>
> The growing visibility of foreign investment particularly during these times of great social unrest makes foreign investment a convenient target. [Manufacturer.]
>
> The developed countries are developing, in general, at a faster rate than the developing countries, thus attainment falls short and this causes deep-seated and continuing frustration. . . . For various reasons internal problems such as social unrest, political instability, graft and corruption, domination of the economy by the wealthy elite, the disproportionate role of the military, etc., are too close to home, too sensitive and too inflammatory to serve as an outlet. For this reason, foreign investment, which has no local constituency, can be used as a convenient target. In this view, foreign investment will be a favorable whipping boy for some time to come and must stiffen its spine and learn to live within the shadow of continued deprecation. [Trade.]

Thus, the American businessman saw himself as the scapegoat for the failure of Latin American governments to fulfill the socioeconomic expectations of their people.

Another frequently mentioned reason was that Latin Americans feared foreign, especially American, economic domination and exploitation. This was based on their previous experiences with foreign investors and their governments, who intervened and exploited the natural wealth of the weaker host country. From this perspective, economic nationalism was viewed as the assertion of Latin American independence from outside forces and the fervent desire of Latin Americans to protect their national patrimony. Thirty firms felt that these considerations contributed to the current manifestations of economic nationalism.

> There is the feeling . . . that U.S. companies make huge profits and exploit the economies of the host countries. This feeling is apparently based on unhappy past experiences with some local and U.S. business enterprises which did not act as responsible citizens. [Manufacturer.]
>
> The natural desire to keep possession and control over their own natural resources which constitute their most valuable assets. Ostensible cause is the fear of Latins that economically strong outside interests may gain political leverage and thus influence national policy. [Service.]
>
> Size of foreign investment vastly disproportionate to total

> GNP. Type of investment (high profile) normally touches very basic resources or needs (copper, oil, telephones). [Manufacturer.]

As can be observed, the past conflicts and the high profile of extractive industries and public utilities in sensitive sectors of the host country's economy were identified by some respondents as the source of the antagonism. The question of whether a corporate giant with a vast investment in a developing country can truly blend into the environment is a serious one. These enterprises often bring back painful memories of the colossus image of the United States.

The respondents also saw the lack of Latin American understanding of the role of private enterprise and its contribution to economic development as another reason for the hostility toward foreign investment. Twenty-three businessmen cited this factor, often with bitterness toward local politicians who would not publicly acknowledge the benefits of private enterprise to the host country's economy. In part, this sentiment failed to recognize the traditional dominant role of the state in Latin American economic affairs and the cultural factors which undermine many of the norms and appeals usually associated with a vigorous private sector.

> The cause for the growing economic nationalism and hostility to foreign investment in Latin America is based mainly on the lack of knowledge of the public of the important role that foreign investment has been playing in developing their economic infrastructure. Very little has been said about the contribution in taxes that foreign enterprises have been making in the Latin American countries. Also nothing or very little has been mentioned concerning the existence of primary industries in this area which today represents a steady source for labor. In several instances, local people in these countries are totally unaware of how important it has been for the improvement of their standards of living. [Finance and Insurance.]
>
> The main cause as I see it of growing economic nationalism is that none of the government officials in most Latin American countries have the guts to stand up and defend contracts that they or their predecessors have made with foreign capital. Most of them think it is not politically convenient for them to defend private capital and they are all trying to tell the

> public what they think the public wants to hear which I believe is basically wrong. [Extractive.]
>
> Perhaps the fundamental problem facing U.S. private enterprise in Latin America is that there is a general lack of understanding of its motives and operations by the general public, government officials, politicians and the press. [Manufacturing.]

The problem, then, as discussed earlier, is the conflicting images of the costs and benefits of private enterprise to an underdeveloped country. The different perceptions are derived from political, historical, and cultural reasons, which all too often becloud the fundamental issue of the economic contributions of private foreign investment.

It was interesting that nine respondents specifically referred to the hostility of Latin American businessmen toward foreign investment; fearing competition from the larger and more sophisticated U.S. firms, these businessmen would encourage attacks on foreign businesses. It was also mentioned that local businessmen and elites would often promote nationalist attacks on foreign enterprises as a means to garner greater personal rewards from the ventures and the economic growth of their country.

> The fact that as a country does achieve a measure of economic development there is a natural tendency for the local businessmen to feel that they could profitably assume a larger role in the lucrative industries which have attracted foreign investments to their countries. [Manufacturing.]
>
> Where the foreign investor (particularly the American investor) doesn't score high is with the local private businessmen who rightly see us as competitors who are more expert, better equipped, better financed. Why should they like us? [Manufacturing.]

Therefore, rather than being an ideological and political ally of the foreign investor, the local businessman may see his personal interests as being best advanced by the nationalist assault on foreign capital. Only nine respondents specifically referred to leftist pressures or socialist opposition to all private enterprise as the motivating force behind the present hostile investment climate. This indicates that the respondents were cognizant of the antipathy toward foreign capital among all segments of the Latin American public.

TABLE 9-6

Latin Americans Prefer Non-U.S. Investment

Attitudes	Total Sample N=100 (%)	Manu-facturing N=48 (%)	Extractive N=15 (%)	Other N=37 (%)
Yes	55	60	67	43
No	31	31	13	38
Not necessarily	10	4	13	16
No response (not ascertained)	4	5	7	3

Another indicator of the American businessman's realization of his lack of popularity in the hemisphere was probed by asking if he felt Latin Americans were more receptive to foreign private enterprise from countries other than the United States. Of the respondents, 55 per cent declared that non–U.S. investors were preferred (see Table 9–6).

Those who saw a preference for non–U.S. capital referred to the dominant presence of the United States in the hemisphere, the historic colossus image, and a desire of the Latins to seek a balance by diversifying their source of capital. Some businessmen frankly admitted that European and Japanese investors were more flexible and offered better concessions and terms.

Yes, because they are basically afraid of increasing the dominance by U.S. interests and, thus, cultivate others, whose policies may be no different or even worse, to secure more of a balance. [Trade.]

Yes—and we should *encourage* this to minimize the political / emotional threat inherent where U.S. investment dominates as completely as it does in Latin America. [Extractive.]

Yes. For many years in many Latin countries, the U.S. engaged in less than admirable dollar diplomacy. The "Colossus of the North" still looms large in many countries. Latins wish to diversify; take their eggs out of one basket. More importantly, Latins have stronger cultural ties to many European countries and frequently obtain a more appropriate technology at a lower price. [Manufacturing.]

Latin Americans view diversification of foreign investment as one means to reduce the overwhelming presence of American investment and thus enable the host country to assert its sovereignty and bargain as an equal with foreign firms. While it is obvious that many firms fear such a development, others think the long-term effect would be to reduce the tension between nationalist governments and American investors, thereby permitting a more normal relationship to evolve.

The Corporate Response

The American business community's perception of the antipathy toward foreign capital in Latin America had not resulted in a frantic rush to disinvest in the region at the time of this survey. When respondents were asked whether their firm was planning to significantly expand or decrease its investment in Latin America in the near future, the prevailing attitude seemed to be a cautious increase in the level of investment in the hemisphere. Of the companies, 51 per cent were planning to expand their investments, albeit in many cases very selectively; of the corporations, 39 per cent had a wait-and-see approach and intended to maintain their current level of investment; only 5 per cent of the respondents said that their firms would decrease the amount of their Latin American holdings (see Appendix). While the American investor was worried about the new restrictions on foreign enterprise, he seemed to feel that either the tide would change or he could accommodate himself to the new investment climate, no matter how distasteful some of the regulations might seem. A survey conducted by the Department of Commerce in December 1970, of 4,500 large U.S. corporations with approximately 4,500 foreign affiliates, indicated that American investors were prudently expanding their investments in the hemisphere (see Table 9–7).

In response to the question about what would be the most fruitful approach to make foreign investment mutually attractive, thirty-five respondents stressed the need to educate Latin Americans on the role and requirements of private enterprise. They also urged individual companies to bolster their public relations programs and to advertise their firm's contributions to the local economy. This seemed to parallel the response of Detroit auto manufacturers and large U.S. oil companies to the growing concern among the American public regarding environmental and consumer protection. The establishment of joint ventures was viewed by twenty-five respondents as one of the most effective approaches to counter economic nationalism; cooperation with local economic development programs was suggested by twenty-three other firms.

It would appear that the Council of the Americas has wisely defined its primary mission as helping private enterprise in the hemisphere become "recognized as a positive force for the future

TABLE 9-7

Estimates of Plant and Equipment Expenditures by Foreign Affiliates of U.S. Corporations in Latin America: Summary of Surveys (in Millions of Dollars)[a]

Major Industry Division	1966 ($)	1967[b] ($)	1968[b] ($)	1969[b] ($)	1970[c] ($)	1971[d] ($)
Mining and smelting	229	288	456	497	448	388
Petroleum	268	306	405	501	583	620
Manufacturing	452	505	575	611	739	823
Other industries	143	183	220	247	301	325
Total	1,092	1,282	1,656	1,856	2,071	2,156

Source: U.S., Department of Commerce, *Survey of Current Business*, March 1971, p. 28.

a. Includes other Western Hemisphere.

b. Actually reported in June of following year.

c. Estimated in December of 1970.

development of Latin America." The council's commissioning of the study by Herbert May on the effects of U.S. foreign investment and dissemination of the findings of the report in Latin America has obviously met the expectations of many of its corporate members. The realization of the need for U.S. corporations to take the publicity offensive signals a reversal from earlier corporate policies of quietly blending into the environment, thereby reflecting cognizance of a need to meet aggressively the growing antipathy toward foreign enterprise. Prime Minister Pierre Trudeau of Canada once remarked that living so close to the United

States was like sleeping with an elephant; the council's policy seems to be that the American elephant can be hidden behind a rosebush of public relations. But aggressive salesmanship of foreign investment could draw attention to the high profile of American firms in the hemisphere, aggravating an already tense situation. Such a policy also ignores the "psychological value" of economic nationalism, which may dismiss or play down the contributions of foreign capital to economic growth.

The corporate executives were asked if their firm had adopted any new management policies to make their Latin American investments more integrated into the local environment and more acceptable to the host government and people. Forty-five respondents replied that they were making an effort to train and place local nationals in top management posts. This appeared to be consistent with the finding of the May Report that only 7.5 per cent of the managerial staff and only 2.6 per cent of the technical and professional staff of U.S. manufacturing affiliates in Latin America were from the United States. Twenty-one businessmen said that their firm had established or was considering joint ventures as a means to become more integrated into the local environment. Below are some of the replies which indicate that U.S. companies are moving in the direction of becoming good "corporate citizens."

> It has been our company's policy to develop a worldwide manufacturing organization with plants in the major countries. We believe that for companies which are able to do so, local manufacturing for exports offers an excellent way to be recognized as a "good citizen." In addition, it has always been our policy to have local company management. In the first three levels of management of our 24 companies in Latin America, more than 95% are local nationals. [Service.]
>
> For quite a few years now we have tried to have a social conscience as far as educating, training and improving the lot of the local people where we operate. We have constantly decreased the number of foreigners and operate with a very minimum foreign staff now which we hope in time will be all local people. Where we do not have local ownership, we have tried very diligently in the last few years to obtain local capital and will continue trying to do so. [Extractive.]
>
> We have had over a 20 year period an extensive program to integrate into the local economy. For instance, our U.S. personnel have been reduced from 200 to 5. [Extractive.]

> Yes, through development of new local sources of supply, the training of local nationals, and an extensive program of aid to education, including school construction and equipment donations. [Manufacturing.]

It is evident that many of these policies have been in effect for a number of years, while in other cases they were initiated as a response to the present political situation in the hemisphere. A major facet of the corporate good-citizen role appears to be an emphasis on having a direct linkage to the local development effort through close cooperation with governmental plans and priorities.

10. The Investor's View of Hemispheric Policy

IN THIS CHAPTER, the attitudes of the business community toward specific corporate and official U.S. policies in the hemisphere will be examined. The members of the Council of the Americas were asked to respond to the following questions: Is the Hickenlooper Amendment, which was designed to deter the expropriation of U.S. property, considered an effective policy tool or has it outlived its usefulness? Are joint ventures a practical way to reduce the Latin American sensitivity to American investment? Was the creation of the Overseas Private Investment Corporation important to your firm? Should the level of foreign assistance funding in the hemisphere continue to decline?

Safeguarding the Investor

A list of policies often suggested as the most effective means to protect U.S. investment in Latin America was presented to the respondents, who were asked to rank them on a scale from one to eight, from the policies they considered the most effective to the least effective. The proposals were selected to represent all shades of political opinion.[1] Perhaps the most startling result was that rigid enforcement of the provisions of the Hickenlooper Amendment, to cut off all foreign aid to a country which expropriates U.S. property without prompt and adequate compensation, was overwhelmingly considered by the businessmen as the least effective means to protect U.S. investment in Latin America. Of the firms, 81 per cent ranked it as the least effective approach to protect private enterprise in Latin America; sixty-three respondents ranked it eighth—last—on the list of possible means to protect American investments in the hemisphere. As can be seen in Table 10–1, the efficacy of the Hickenlooper Amendment was doubted by both manufacturers and extractive industries.

Close cooperation with host governments to make foreign private investment more integrated into national plans for development was evaluated overall by the respondents as the most effective means to protect U.S. business interests in the hemisphere. Manufacturers were slightly more enthusiastic over this approach than extractive industries, but both ranked this approach high. While 55 per cent of the total sample felt that the establishment of firm rules of the game for foreign investment in individual Latin American countries was the next best approach, respondents in extractive companies favored firm rules more than manufacturers. This undoubtedly represents the insecurity of the extractive industries, which are the most susceptible to the whims and restrictive policies of nationalist regimes. Surprisingly, 67 per cent of the extractive firms ranked joint ventures as a highly effective means to protect U.S. investment in Latin America, while only 48 per cent of the manufacturers scored it so positively; I had assumed that a reverse relationship would exist. This meant that the extractive respondents saw firm rules of the game and joint ventures to reduce their high profile as their best form of protection, even surpassing close cooperation with the host governments. The long-sought-after hemispheric investment code, while still desirable, appeared to be considered an unlikely possibility in the face of the historic opposition of the region to any policy which would infringe upon their sovereignty—the Calvo

1. The replies were coded so that a ranking of one, two, or three indicated that the firm's respondent thought a suggested approach could be highly effective, a rank of four or five represented a moderately effective approach, and a rank order of six, seven, or eight signified that the proposal was considered among the least effective means to protect U.S. investment in Latin America.

TABLE 10-1

Most Effective Means to Protect U.S. Investment[a]

	Total Sample (N=100)				Manufacturing (N=48)				Extractive (N=15)				Other (N=37)			
Attitudes	High (%)	Moderate (%)	Least (%)	NR[b] (%)	High (%)	Moderate (%)	Least (%)	NR (%)	High (%)	Moderate (%)	Least (%)	NR (%)	High (%)	Moderate (%)	Least (%)	NR (%)
Close cooperation with host governments	66	17	10	7	71	15	8	6	60	13	20	7	62	22	8	8
Firm rules of the game in individual countries	55	21	19	5	52	23	21	4	67	7	13	13	54	24	19	3
Local participation	53	24	16	7	48	23	23	6	67	13	7	13	54	30	11	5
Hemispheric investment code	37	39	17	7	40	48	8	4	40	27	20	13	32	32	27	8
International Investment Insurance Agency	27	42	23	8	27	35	31	6	13	53	20	13	32	46	14	8
Reduce investment in sensitive areas	26	20	45	9	31	17	46	6	13	33	40	13	24	19	46	11
Increase foreign assistance	16	17	59	8	8	23	63	6	13	20	60	7	22	11	59	8
Rigid enforcement of Hickenlooper Amendment	5	6	81	8	6	6	81	6	..	13	73	13	5	..	84	8

a. Totals may not add due to rounding of figures.

b. NR--no response.

Doctrine. The known resistance of Latins to the proposed International Investment Insurance Agency of the World Bank, also deemed valuable from the U.S. investor's point of view, probably made its adoption seem unlikely.

Although some respondents had referred to the historic antipathy of Latin Americans toward the high-profile extractive companies and public utilities in reply to earlier questions on economic nationalism, only 26 per cent of the firms felt that a reduction of U.S. investment in the sectors of Latin American economies most sensitive to nationalist sentiment would be an effective policy. This contradiction between the overall assessment of the causes of economic nationalism and the policy recommendations appears to correspond with a conclusion in the Bauer study: "It is a part of the unwritten code of business to avoid actions which will gratuitously injure others. . . . Under that code, businessmen without a vested interest in foreign trade are reluctant to advocate a policy in which they believe if others will thereby suffer injury."[2]

The extractive firms, quite naturally, were more skeptical of this approach than manufacturers. However, one could assume from the extractive companies' high rating of joint ventures that they were certainly not oblivious to the need to reduce their high profile. While 31 per cent of the manufacturers supported the idea of a reduction of U.S. investment in sensitive sectors, paradoxically they were cooler toward joint ventures, which could affect their enterprises, than the extractive firms. Although this approach was not scored as a highly effective means to protect U.S. investment, Department of Commerce statistics on the decrease in U.S. direct investment in extractive and public utilities vis-à-vis the sharp increase in the manufacturing sector in the last twenty years, indicate that in practice this policy has been adopted by many U.S. corporations. It was shown above that the lack of social and economic development was considered by the respondents to be a major factor contributing to economic nationalism and attacks on U.S. investors in the hemisphere. But when the businessmen were asked to evaluate the option of increasing U.S. foreign assistance as a means to promote a stable social, economic, and political environment for investment, they

2. Raymond A. Bauer, Ithiel de Sola Pool, and Lewis Anthony Dexter, *American Business and Public Policy*, p. 218.

ranked this approach as one of the least effective means to protect U.S. investment. This inconsistency will be examined later.

The Hickenlooper Amendment—Illusory Protection

As noted above, American investors ranked the rigid enforcement of the Hickenlooper Amendment very low as an effective means to protect U.S. investments in Latin America. To probe their views more fully on this matter, they were asked if they agreed with Peterson's Task Force on International Development that the Hickenlooper Amendment had "outlived its usefulness." The low estimation of the value of the Hickenlooper Amendment was verified by the fact that 76 per cent of the businessmen stated that they agreed with the Peterson Report. However, extractive firms were far less willing to surrender its alleged protection than manufacturers, even though none of the extractive respondents ranked it as a highly effective means of protection. They apparently feared that the repeal of the amendment might signal an open season on U.S. extractive investments. There were no significant differences of opinion when size and years of experience in the area were made independent variables (see Table 10–2).

Thirty-three respondents saw the Hickenlooper Amendment as an ineffective deterrent and an irritant to U.S.–Latin American relations. The amendment's existence was viewed as a symbol of gunboat diplomacy which resurrected the big-stick image of the United States; its application would adversely affect other U.S. policies and interests in the hemisphere.

> The IPC case points out that its effectiveness must be seriously questioned. The Hickenlooper Amendment didn't serve to clarify the IPC situation or speed it to a final decision. [Service.]
>
> Better remove the Act from the books. This is the last attempt at a "big stick" politics. That period is past. Better secure "justice" on a longer range basis through the economic laws of nature. Capital goes where it is wanted and well treated. [Extractive.]
>
> It was never useful and always counterproductive. It is morally wrong, completely unworkable and will only serve to solidify the opposition of the political leaders who seek to move unilaterally against private foreign investors. All U.S.

> investors in Latin America have and will continue to be victimized by the Hickenlooper Amendment until we remove this modern version of 19th century "Gunboat" diplomacy. [Extractive.]

As can be readily discerned, the utility of the Hickenlooper Amendment either as a deterrent or as a sanction to bring about settlement of an investment dispute was seriously questioned by many businessmen.

Another major criticism of the amendment was that the present law is too inflexible because of its mandatory provisions, which hamper the president's discretion in dealing with sensitive issues. Twenty respondents cited this objection to the Hickenlooper Amendment. While many of the businessmen judged the amendment to be too inflexible with its mandatory, heavy-handed sanction, some of them objected less to the existence of such a policy tool than to the fact that the present law was unworkable in actual investment disputes. Therefore, the objection to the amendment in its present form cannot be interpreted as a mandate for its repeal. They recognized that the automatic feature might jeopardize negotiations for a fair settlement in instances of expropriation and could have the additional harmful effect of provoking attacks on other American investments in the host country. One respondent stated this viewpoint quite well: "Our position in dealing with the Latin American countries should be based on a policy of negotiations, not on the adoption of measures which effectively will mean retaliation." Fourteen other respondents

TABLE 10-2

Has Hickenlooper Amendment Outlived Its Usefulness?

Attitudes	Total Sample N=100 (%)	Manu-facturing N=48 (%)	Extractive N=15 (%)	Other N=37 (%)
Has outlived usefulness	76	75	53	86
Has not outlived usefulness	21	21	47	11
No response (not ascertained)	3	4	14	3

felt that the Hickenlooper Amendment has never been tested since it has never been invoked. Their opinion was that since it was the law, it should be enforced; if it was not enforced, it should be repealed.

The attitudes of the respondents toward the Hickenlooper Amendment, when the salience of the danger of expropriation was held constant, were also examined. Significantly, 61 per cent of the firms which ranked fear of expropriation as a major concern of their company agreed that the Hickenlooper Amendment had outlived its usefulness (see Appendix). Clearly the deterrent value of the amendment was seriously doubted by those firms which felt the greatest threat of expropriation.

JOINT VENTURES—RELUCTANT POPULARITY

The American business community has begun to consider the possibility of joint ventures as one means to reduce the high profile of U.S. investment in the hemisphere. Of the companies surveyed, 60 per cent indicated that they had had experience with joint ventures; however, this experience was not necessarily in Latin America. A higher percentage of the extractive firms said that they had been involved in joint ventures, as noted in Table 10–3. Size appeared to be an important variable; although only 47 per cent of the small investors had had such experience, 58 per cent of the medium investors and 68 per cent of the large companies had tried joint ventures. Corporations which had been in Latin America over twenty years had had slightly more experi-

TABLE 10-3

Experience with Joint Ventures

Attitudes	Total Sample N=100 (%)	Manu-facturing N=48 (%)	Extractive N=15 (%)	Other N=37 (%)
Experience	60	60	73	54
No experience	17	17	13	19
No response (not ascertained)	23	23	..	27

ence with joint ventures (see Appendix). The high percentage of respondents not replying to this question perhaps indicates the unwillingness of some firms to even consider abandoning the wholly-owned subsidiary as a principal means of conducting overseas business.

The respondents were then asked if joint ventures were a practical way to reduce nationalist sensitivities to U.S. investment in Latin America. Of the companies, 68 per cent saw joint ventures as a practical means to reduce nationalist sensitivities to American foreign investment in the hemisphere, although many were quick to point out the problems involved with joint ventures. The support for joint ventures appeared to corroborate the findings of the Meeker study, which found that 86.7 per cent of the firms surveyed accepted joint ventures as a general policy.[3] Consistent with the earlier finding that the extractive industries ranked local participation higher on the list of effective means to protect U.S. investment than did manufacturers, a greater percentage of the extractive companies viewed joint ventures as a practical way to reduce nationalist resentments. Again, this was contrary to my hypothesis that the extractive companies would more vehemently oppose joint ventures than manufacturers. It undoubtedly reflects the fact that they are being compelled to form joint ventures in more and more countries by the host governments (see Table 10–4). Although the largest investors had more experience with joint ventures, support of the practicality of joint ventures was inversely proportionate to the size of the firm. While 79 per cent of the smaller companies saw them as a practical way to reduce nationalist sensitivities, only 53 per cent of the larger firms were so optimistic. Within the manufacturing sector, the same relationship existed between medium and large investors, with 60 per cent of the medium investors and only 42 per cent of the larger companies endorsing the practicality of joint ventures (see Appendix).

Of the respondents who indicated that the threat of expropriation was of great salience, 77 per cent replied that joint ventures were a practical way to protect U.S. investments from nationalist pressures. However, a confusing picture emerged when the salience of hostility to private enterprise was made the independent variable. Only 48 per cent of the firms which were greatly con-

3. Guy B. Meeker, "Fade-Out Joint Venture: Can It Work for Latin America?" p. 29.

TABLE 10-4

Practicality of Joint Ventures

Attitudes	Total Sample N=100 (%)	Manu-facturing N=48 (%)	Extractive N=15 (%)	Other N=37 (%)
Practical	68	58	73	78
Impractical	14	19	7	11
Mixed assessment	4	15	20	3
No response (not ascertained)	14	8	..	8

cerned over the rising hostility toward private enterprise considered joint ventures a practical way to cope with the problem, while 81 per cent of the respondents who were not overly worried about that development favored joint ventures as a means to reduce nationalist antipathy toward foreign capital. Therefore, joint ventures were not seen as a panacea to handle the problem of economic nationalism in Latin America, but they did offer one means to reduce the tension between hemispheric governments and U.S. investors. The problems most often mentioned were the unavailability of local capital, the difficulty of finding satisfactory local partners, management differences over rapid payouts and reinvestments for growth, and the need to protect technology. Some respondents feared that they would be forced to become partners with the oligarchy or have partners who were less responsive to development needs than their U.S. counterparts. Two respondents pointed out how joint ventures could either be a great advantage to the foreign investor or a disaster:

> If one is starting a new grass roots development, joint ventures are often impractical because Latin American investors insist on constant and regular dividend payments which are normally impossible during the first three to five years of any new venture. Latin American investors also want a high dividend payout when profits are being earned, which limits growth of the local enterprise and subjects the U.S. investor to dividend taxes on monies that are needed to expand the local business. Whether joint ventures are practical ways or not depends on the specifics of the investment. It obviously re-

duces exposure to economic nationalism but often entails additional encumbrances on investment possibilities that may be of only marginal attractiveness in the first place. [Manufacturer.]

When each partner has something unique to contribute to the operation, and the partners can agree on common goals, joint ventures of foreign and local investors can be highly successful and may serve to reduce local hostilities which might be generated by a wholly-owned subsidiary of a foreign company. On the other hand, the following possible negative aspects of joint ventures should also be recognized: Joint ventures may absorb scarce local capital which might have been invested in other productive activities; the local partners may actually be less responsive to the country's development needs than are foreign investors; and the operation may not be successful simply because the partners have different immediate objectives. In my Company's experience, some joint ventures have been successful operations, while others have been plagued with difficulties such as those mentioned above. It seems clear that it would be unwise for host countries to adopt rigid rules requiring local participation in new foreign investment. [Extractive.]

These respondents summarized most of the pro and con arguments on the issue. It becomes clear that the success or failure of a joint venture depends primarily on the individual partners involved and their ability to work out their differences in management approaches. However, businessmen hesitate to abandon their traditional form of investment—the wholly-owned subsidiary.

OPIC—A Benefit to Whom?

One of the major tools of the Nixon administration to promote private enterprise in the developing countries was the establishment of the Overseas Private Investment Corporation in the Foreign Assistance Act of 1969. The corporation would be responsible for informing the American business community of investment opportunities in the less-developed countries and would assume the task of issuing investment guaranties. One of the major arguments of its supporters during the congressional debate was that OPIC would encourage overseas investment by the smaller U.S. firms which would not otherwise be aware of the investment opportunities and would be leery of investing in a strange environment.

The survey asked the respondents how important they felt the investment guaranty and insurance programs of OPIC would be in determining whether or not their firm expanded its investments in Latin America. In other words, were the guaranties an adequate safeguard to encourage foreign investment in the face of Latin American economic nationalism? It was assumed that the larger companies, with diversification of their investments on a worldwide basis, would not consider OPIC important in their investment decisions. Table 10–5 shows that a majority of the firms

TABLE 10-5

Importance of OPIC to Firm[a]

Attitudes	Total Sample N=100 (%)	Manu-facturing N=48 (%)	Extractive N=15 (%)	Other N=37 (%)
Important	52	63	60	35
Unimportant	37	25	40	51
Unfamiliar with program	8	10	..	8
No response (not ascertained)	3	2	..	5

a. Totals may not add due to rounding of figures.

saw OPIC as an important factor in their plans to expand their Latin American investment; rather remarkably, only 8 per cent indicated that they were unfamiliar with the relatively new program. Contrary to the arguments of OPIC's friends, the smaller investors did not consider the program vitally important to their investment plans. Rather, OPIC was considered more important by the medium and large investors in the hemisphere. Within the manufacturing sector, 63 per cent of the firms with investments totaling over $25 million saw OPIC as important in their expansion decisions, compared to 52 per cent of the medium-sized manufacturing investors (see Appendix). However, the companies which had been in the region for less than twenty years were more enthusiastic about the program than the old-timers. Since OPIC was to promote new U.S. investment in the developing countries, this would seem to meet the expectations of the proponents of the program. While 63 per cent of the newer firms felt that OPIC was important in their investment plans, only 44 per cent of the more experienced investors considered it a major factor. It would appear that the investment guaranty program, which took on new life in the early 1960s, did reassure many businessmen regarding investment in the hemisphere. These newcomers to the region took advantage of the investment insurance and viewed OPIC as an extension of the guaranty program.

THE PRIVATE SECTOR AND FOREIGN AID

The recent decline in foreign assistance funding and Nixon administration statements stressing the role of private enterprise in economic development evoke memories of the gospel of private enterprise popular in the 1950s. A statement by an Eisenhower administration official, that private capital should be the primary source of foreign assistance in the economic development process, was paraphrased in a question to the American business community in 1970: "Should the U.S. government rely on private capital as the primary source of foreign assistance in the economic development process?" Not surprisingly, 62 per cent of the respondents said that private enterprise should be the major source of foreign aid, although some did acknowledge that governmental assistance for infrastructure projects would be needed. The thinking of both manufacturers and extractive firms paralleled the general findings (see Table 10–6). The ideological belief in the role of private enterprise as the most dynamic agent in economic growth was manifest in their replies. In other cases, there was a recognition of the limited availability of public capital to meet the tremendous needs of the less-developed countries, although governmental aid was assigned an important task in the infrastructure area. The firms which felt that private enterprise should not be depended upon as the major force for economic development almost unanimously pointed to the tremendous capital requirements for the developing countries in sectors unattractive to the private investor.

The attitudes of the respondents toward the AID program were also probed. They were asked if the downward trend in the level of U.S. foreign assistance to Latin America in recent years should be reversed. Opinions were closely divided (see Table

TABLE 10-6

Should Private Capital Be Primary Source of Foreign Aid?[a]

Attitudes	Total Sample N=100 (%)	Manu-facturing N=48 (%)	Extractive N=15 (%)	Other N=37 (%)
Yes	62	65	67	57
No	21	21	13	24
Need both	15	15	13	16
No response (not ascertained)	2	..	7	3

a. Totals may not add due to rounding of figures.

10–7). The respondents who felt that the downward trend of U.S. foreign assistance should be reversed argued that foreign aid was the only source of the capital necessary for economic growth. Since Latin America is in the back yard of the United States, foreign assistance was deemed crucial to foster political stability in the region and to bolster U.S. national security. The businessmen who were satisfied with the decline in foreign assistance appropriations were especially critical that foreign aid had not fulfilled the goals of the program and often brought more enemies than friends. They stressed the fact that countries should learn to

TABLE 10-7

Should Decline in Foreign Aid Be Reversed?[a]

Response	Total Sample N=100 (%)	Manu-facturing N=48 (%)	Extractive N=15 (%)	Other N=37 (%)
Yes	37	33	27	46
No	38	40	40	35
Maintain reasonable level	14	15	13	14
No response (not ascertained)	11	13	20	5

a. Totals may not add due to rounding of figures.

help themselves, rather than always leaning on Uncle Sam. The larger companies were slightly less inclined to think that private capital should or could be the primary source of foreign assistance. The difference was greatest within the manufacturing sector, where 74 per cent of the medium-sized manufacturing investors were advocates of private enterprise having the major role, compared to 37 per cent of the large manufacturers. A similar distinction was evident in their respective attitudes on the question of reversing the decline in the foreign assistance program; while 53 per cent of the large manufacturing investors felt that the downward trend of aid should be reversed, only 17 per cent of the medium manufacturing investors favored reversal of the falling level of Alliance for Progress funding (see Appendix).

One may speculate, as Bauer did in his study, that larger companies take a broader approach to the foreign policy question. Because of their larger staffs and global interests, they can become more deeply involved in the general policies of the U.S. government. Smaller companies may be too preoccupied with their subsidiaries in just a few countries to assess the overall impact of programs like foreign aid. Possibly the smaller firms also cling more tenaciously to a rigid conception of private enterprise which emphasizes a minimum of governmental involvement.

The division of sentiment on the issue of foreign aid to Latin America is probably the reason that the Council of the Americas has never testified formally before a congressional committee on behalf of the foreign assistance program. Again, it is ironic that although many of the respondents identified frustration at the slow pace of Latin American economic development as a major cause of the current wave of economic nationalism, they did not strongly support the U.S. foreign assistance program which was designed to help promote economic growth. Instead, the business community's early alienation from the Alliance for Progress and emphasis on self-help have reinforced their traditional belief that the private sector should play the central role in the development process.

SELF-INTEREST AND COMMUNICATION

Bauer found in his study of American business attitudes on trade policy that "almost any criterion of self-interest is correlated with a tendency to communicate with Congress."[4] There was a strong

4. Bauer, Pool, and Dexter, *American Business and Public Policy*, p. 202.

relationship between communication with Congress on foreign trade and the importance of tariffs and foreign competition to the firm. Protectionists, who perceived their economic interests as being directly affected by trade legislation, were more likely to write to their congressman than liberal free traders were. An ideological belief which reinforced a firm's self-interest tended to increase the likelihood of correspondence; an isolationist's belief in protection enhanced the chances that a company would write if it felt the need for protection. They also found that executives from large firms were more likely to write, partly because of their greater staff assistance.

The foreign assistance program generated the greatest amount of communication from the businessmen in this survey. Whereas only about one-fourth of the respondents stated that they had communicated with Congress concerning the protection of U.S. investment in Latin American and OPIC, 41 per cent had written to Congress about foreign aid to Latin America in the previous several years. Of the firms which felt that the downward trend in Alliance appropriations should be reversed, 51 per cent communicated with a congressman or senator on the issue, compared to 29 per cent of the respondents who supported the present decline in foreign aid funding for the hemisphere. It would appear that the friends of the Alliance for Progress felt more strongly about the need to bolster the program than the critics of AID (see Appendix).

The survey also examined the question of whether an investor who was very worried about the growing hostility toward private enterprise and danger of expropriation communicated with Congress on the need to protect U.S. investment. No significant relationship could be found between the salience of either of those fears to a respondent's communication in the previous few years regarding the protection of U.S. hemispheric investments. The businessmen were asked if they or their firm had written to a congressman or senator concerning the creation of OPIC. Of the firms which had indicated that OPIC was important to their company's investment plans, 35 per cent stated that they had communicated with Congress about the program; only 19 per cent of the businesses which felt that OPIC would not be important in their expansion decisions had contacted a national legislator. The larger investors were more inclined to communicate with Congress on the foreign aid program and OPIC than were the small investors (see Appendix). Bauer's hypotheses were thus supported in the case of OPIC, where firms which considered the program important to their expansion plans communicated with Congress. However, the self-interest of companies which worried about the growing hostility and threat of expropriation did not lead to communication appealing for greater protection of U.S. investments in Latin America.

It is harder to assess the larger amount of communication on the foreign assistance program in Latin America. Undoubtedly, the dispute over the optimistic goals of the Alliance and the desire for a greater role for private enterprise in the program generated more communication. However, it would seem that the firms which supported the Alliance for Progress and felt that foreign assistance was vital for development of the infrastructure of Latin American republics would encourage greater political stability and a friendlier attitude toward the United States and the private sector.

In conclusion, the hypothesis that extractive firms were more "hard-line" than manufacturing investors was not substantiated in this survey. The extractive companies shared with manufacturers a skeptical view of the utility of the Hickenlooper Amendment, were more positive toward joint ventures, had adopted programs to train local nationals for top management positions, and emphasized the need for close cooperation with the host government's economic development plans. Because of their high profile, extractive industries had been subjected to nationalist attacks for many years, compelling them to consider new forms of investment which might reduce nationalist sensitivities. It was in their enlightened self-interest to present a new image of the corporate good citizen; unfortunately, these changes often followed years of a less progressive outlook, not quickly forgotten in the host country.

The idea that a firm's high profile would provoke economic nationalism was verified in the replies of the businessmen; the companies with the largest investment in the region saw themselves as the most exposed to hostility. But the respondents realistically assessed their greatest threat not as outright expropriation, but as restrictive economic policies which limited their traditional prerogatives and perhaps doomed the wholly-owned subsidiary in the hemisphere. Nationalization was recognized as a remote threat in most instances because of the reaction it would evoke from the U.S. government and the international financial community; however, restrictions on foreign capital were being adopted in many countries which were still anxious for foreign investment—but on their terms.

The Hickenlooper Amendment was deemed an inflexible tool for the settlement of investment disputes; however, this judgment did not imply that the businessmen desired its repeal. Despite the obvious weakness of the amendment as a deterrent, many clung to the illusion of protection it afforded, fearing that repeal might give rise to another round of expropriations. They undoubtedly felt that the legislative commitment of the United States to protect their interests offered some solace; although the amendment was not effective as a deterrent, pressure from the U.S. government might assist in negotiations to receive some compensation for nationalized properties.

It was notable that although the business community identified Latin American frustration at the slow pace of social and economic progress as the cause of economic nationalism, with the U.S. investor being made the scapegoat for the failure to meet popular expectations, they appeared unable to translate this awareness into support for the foreign assistance program. One cannot be sure if this was due to ideological myopia—their strong faith in private capital as a development agent—or disillusionment with the administration and the limited impact of the program. I suspect that the former reason was most prevalent. It is ironical that as foreign assistance is reduced, the deterrent threat of the Hickenlooper Amendment to cut off all foreign aid is minimized and a bargaining tool for favorable governmental policies is lost. The respondents from the larger companies seemed more cognizant of these factors than the smaller investors, but while the larger companies had expressed to Congress their support of foreign assistance, they were unable or unwilling to convince the Council of the Americas to take a forthright position on the issue. It is unclear whether the desire for organizational unity prevented such a policy declaration or whether the smaller firms were so vehemently opposed to the AID program (as undermining the foundations of private enterprise) that such a stand would not receive favorable passage in the council.

It was also interesting that although many investors recognized the Latin American fear of economic domination and exploitation by large U.S. companies, they were unwilling to endorse any policies which would discourage American investment in the most sensitive sectors of the Latin American economies. Again, basic mores of American business militated against such a policy course, even though there was acknowledgment that the highly visible presence of some firms, unwilling to accommodate nationalist demands, might lead to retaliatory actions which could affect all investors in the region. They religiously adhered to the idea of a minimum of governmental intervention—except in promoting and protecting private enterprise—even though in the long run such a policy might adversely affect their own corporate interests. The ideology of the American business community also encountered the Latin American skepticism toward private enterprise; the investor's frustrated lament that Latin Americans did not understand the advantages of private enterprise completely ignored the different cultural perceptions of the role of private capital in economic development. The advocacy of a massive public relations effort overlooked the fact that the crux of the issue was in differing historical experiences and cultural values, and in the political and psychological attributes of economic nationalism which nullified the economic arguments advanced by American investors. In other words, there was a basic clash of perceptions over the costs and benefits of foreign investment to the developing countries.

11. Some Policy Proposals

A Look at the Past and Future

THIS CONCLUDING CHAPTER will draw parallels between economic nationalism in the United States during the early stages of its economic development, and the current nationalist fervor in Latin America. British investment in the United States and Britain's dominant political and economic role in the Western Hemisphere generated many of the same resentments among Americans that the high profile of the United States now arouses in Latin Americans. Some policy prescriptions will then be suggested, based upon the analysis of economic nationalism in this study, the conflicting views of private enterprise, and the survey of the Council of the Americas.

LESSONS FROM U.S. ECONOMIC NATIONALISM

Too often Americans tend to forget the early stages of development of the United States. Particularly, we overlook the manifestations of strident economic nationalism that Americans directed against the economic and political power of Great Britain, which bore a striking resemblance to the current wave of economic nationalism in Latin America aimed at the overwhelming presence of the United States. Edward Crapol has traced the anglophobia of the United States during the late nineteenth century, and his observations on American economic nationalism offer many provocative parallels to developments in Latin America.

Resentment toward England's role in the Civil War embittered both the North and the South, while the United States confronted England for economic and political hegemony in the hemisphere. Farmers in the West and South saw the prices of their wheat and cotton being determined in Liverpool, and bitterly resented their colonial status: "They complained incessantly of their inferior status at the colonial end of an imperial relationship, with the Northeast and Great Britain serving as metropolitan centers."[1] This argument brings to mind the charge of the Economic Commission for Latin America that the industrialized center countries have kept the less-developed peripheral countries in a subordinate role by an unfavorable trade situation. Americans displayed an ambivalent attitude toward Britain; there was hostility toward Britain's commercial and economic supremacy in the hemisphere and admiration of the success of the British. Latin Americans today show an ambivalence toward the United States: antipathy toward the economic and political dominance of the United States and admiration of American power and prosperity.

There were conspiratorial interpretations of British efforts to block American progress. Certain groups saw efforts for tariff reform as a scheme to weaken U.S. industrial growth and delay economic and financial independence. The bitterness was especially acute in enterprises with large amounts of British capital: cattle ranches, farms, cotton plantations, irrigation projects, railroads, grain elevators, stockyards, mines, and land companies. Almost 1,500 British firms had investments in the trans-Mississippi West, and British investment in the United States by 1899 totalled almost $2,625 million.[2] Nationalist demands for curbs on alien ownership resulted in federal and state restrictions on foreign ownership. A joint resolution passed by the New Hampshire legislature in 1885 voices this sentiment: "American soil is for Americans, and should be exclusively owned and controlled by American citizens."[3] A similar resentment of U.S. in-

1. Edward P. Crapol, "America for Americans: Economic Nationalism and Anglophobia, 1880–1900," unpublished, p. 2.
2. Ibid., pp. 5–6.
3. Ibid., p. 7.

vestment in Latin America, combined with a conspiratorial view of the role of Wall Street in thwarting the economic growth of the region, is certainly present in Latin American economic nationalism. The New Hampshire resolution could very easily be reworded to represent President Salvador Allende's call for the nationalization of American copper interests in Chile. It is the same feeling which leads Latin Americans to press for joint ventures, divestiture, and expropriation as means to regain control over their economy. The American perception of Great Britain as an obstacle to the expansion of trade to Central and South America also has a parallel in the Latin American fear that U.S. companies will garner the bulk of the benefits of regional integration efforts; the Andean Code is a contemporary response to this fear. President Grover Cleveland became a popular hero when he challenged Britain during the Venezuelan crisis of 1895–96 by asserting the Monroe Doctrine. Fidel Castro enjoyed great popularity in the hemisphere when he withstood the pressures of the United States, and military regimes in Peru and Bolivia tapped the same sentiment to garner popular support when they nationalized U.S. oil interests.

Anglophobia had virtually disappeared by the end of World War I when the United States emerged as a world creditor; British investments in the United States were virtually liquidated by the 1920s. England's policies of sympathizing with the United States in the Spanish-American War, concessions on the Panama Canal, acknowledgement of American hegemony in the Caribbean, and support of the Open Door policy all served to diminish anti-British feeling. One lesson this might suggest for U.S. policy makers today is the need to reduce the awesome economic and political presence of the United States in Latin America and embark on a course which would recognize the Latin American desire to assert independence. As with the British, such a policy shift would require major concessions and, in a like manner, will probably result only from the growing power and resentment of the junior partner.

Flexibility and Long-Term Perspective

This study has focused on the conflicting images of the role of private enterprise in economic development. It should be clear from preceding chapters and from the survey of the Council of the Americas that one of the major sources of conflict in U.S.–

Latin American relations is the difference in views on foreign private investment. Latin Americans recall the past interventions of the United States on behalf of its private interests, fear domination and exploitation by large U.S. firms, and look to the state for protection and leadership in the development process. U.S. officials and businessmen stress the positive contributions of private capital to economic growth, the need for a minimum of restrictions over domestic and foreign investment, and the dangers of the state's assuming a major role in the economic life of the country. The respective positions have hardened around beliefs derived from historical and political experiences, with each side ignoring or shunting aside the criticisms and arguments of the other. Latin American governments have adopted stringent policies to govern foreign capital and have nationalized American properties, while the United States has embraced economic sanctions to deter such actions.

But such policies ignore the interdependence of the nations of the inter-American system. Latin America is a market for U.S. goods, provides the United States with many raw materials and foodstuffs, and offers investment opportunities for American companies. Despite the rhetoric about U.S. investors abandoning the region for opportunities elsewhere, the notion of defensive investment recognizes that investment may be necessary to protect a company's Latin American market. The market potential of Latin America, especially as regional integration plans are realized, is an attraction for U.S. companies. Latin Americans are grimly aware of the prominent role of the United States in their economic affairs. The more realistic leaders, despite nationalist actions against foreign investment, recognize the need for private capital to augment limited domestic and international capital sources. However, they seek this capital under more restrictive terms than in the past.

Undoubtedly, this mutual need will result in more accommodating policies by both Latin American governments and American investors. In order to attract capital-intensive industries and receive new technology, Latin Americans will have to offer favorable terms to the foreign investor. The greater the need for a particular investment or technology, the better the bargaining position of the foreign firm. Companies which offer to enlarge the host country's exports, stimulate local sources of supply, and transfer technology and managerial skills will be the most welcome. Their operational autonomy within the host country, however, will be largely dependent upon their level of technological input; companies like IBM will continue to receive favorable concessions. This means that American corporations must reassess their traditional reliance on the wholly-owned subsidiary and begin to consider local participation, management contracts, and licensing and royalty agreements. The rhetoric of the past is unlikely to sway Latin American governments, whose emphasis on the psychological value of economic nationalism will override the strictly economic and ideological arguments of U.S. investors.

The Nixon administration stressed a "realistic" approach in dealings with regimes of all ideological hues; a realistic approach to Latin America's perception of private enterprise is also needed. The Hickenlooper Amendment has been shown to be an irritant in U.S.-Latin American relations, an ineffective deterrent, and an inflexible tool in actual investment disputes. Implementation of such a political blunderbuss, or other economic sanctions, can endanger additional American interests in the host country and throughout the hemisphere. An essential feature of U.S. diplomatic and corporate statesmanship must be a flexible approach to such disputes and an emphasis on a negotiated settlement. The U.S. government, while justifiably representing its investors, must not become so aligned with an investor's claims (as in the IPC case) that its role as a mediator is undermined. The history of the investor's relations with the host government, the accuracy of its claim, and its corporate operations in the host country should all be assessed objectively. The American government should not assume the odious chore of bill collector for firms whose past actions have led to the crisis.

The Hickenlooper Amendment must eventually be repealed, but considering the recent wave of economic nationalism, such an action would create dismay in the business community. Businessmen already consider the Nixon administration's policy of a low profile in the hemisphere as offering no profile at all; they feel that the U.S. government has abandoned them after they were encouraged to invest in the region through investment guaranties and the illusory protection promised by the Hickenlooper Amendment. They believe that they are being made the scapegoat for the failures of official U.S. policies and the unwillingness of Latin American governments to cope with their internal problems. But the existence of the Hickenlooper Amendment in the Foreign Assistance Act becomes increasingly less useful as a deterrent, as the level of foreign assistance appropriations declines and the president and Congress tacitly agree to ignore the amendment's statutory provisions. The wisest course of action would be to quietly delete the measure from the Foreign Assistance Act; a modification to make it more flexible is unnecessary, since the president already has the authority to reduce foreign assistance to AID recipients, as evidenced in the cases of Peru, Chile, and Brazil. And as several corporate executives have pointed out, if a country is intent upon nationalizing all foreign investment, there is little the United States can do short of military intervention. Each investment dispute must be judged on its own merits, with consideration of the full range of American interests involved. The Hickenlooper Amendment precludes such an evaluation. The tough stance of Secretary of the Treasury John Connally, that "the U.S. can afford to be tough with Latin Americans because we have no friends left there any more," is dangerous to the inter-American system.[4] It is a self-fulfilling prophecy, since such a hard-line approach can only provoke more attacks on U.S. investors and arouse nationalist sentiment against the colossus of the North. It also reflects the narrow thinking embodied in the gospel of private enterprise, which refuses to recognize different perceptions of the role of private capital in the development process.

One approach in the effort to reduce Latin American sensitivity to foreign investment is to encourage joint ventures. Although not a panacea, joint ventures help to reduce the high profile of American investment, assist in the development of a local private sector, reduce capital flight, and assure the host government that the enterprise will contribute to local development goals. However, the U.S. government should discourage rigid equity formulas which might forestall new investment in sectors vital to economic growth.

Joint ventures could be encouraged in several ways. Existing tax and antitrust laws which discourage the formation of joint ventures should be modified; it does little good for administration officials to laud joint ventures when there are fiscal restraints on joint-venture operations. Another method of promoting joint ventures would be to offer a graduated tax credit up to 30 per cent when an American firm owns only 50 per cent equity in a venture with

4. *Business Week*, July 10, 1971, p. 65.

local private, not public, participation. There should be a five- to seven-year time limit for the tax credit, contingent upon whether the joint venture contributes to the host country's development goals, as certified in writing by the host government. OPIC could be charged with the responsibility of seeking and screening prospective partners to protect American foreign policy interests and American investors; it already has the authority to insure the U.S. share of joint ventures and is responsible for investment promotion.

This recommendation is narrower in focus than the tax credit proposal of President Johnson in 1964 to increase the flow of private investment in the less-developed countries; it is similar in that it would likewise exclude the extractive industries and public utilities. The objective would be to promote American foreign investment in less sensitive forms of ownership and in sectors closely attuned to the development plans of the host country. It would exclude joint ventures with the host government because of the particular problems involved, as in the Chilean government's partnership with American copper companies. The balance-of-payments effect of such a proposal would be difficult to predict, since if Latin Americans offered adequate inducements, a substantial amount of U.S. capital would be reinvested in the area. However, in the initial years, considerable American capital would be repatriated to expand the domestic output of American industry. While one may criticize this proposal as too costly, it is necessary to weigh the costs against those of expropriated U.S. investments and lost markets for American exports.

It is to the advantage of U.S. interests in Latin America that additional financial and technological assistance be provided to Latin American businessmen. A bolstered Latin American private sector would feel less threatened by foreign investors and would help to demonstrate the contributions that private enterprise can make to economic development. Greater financial assistance should be extended for the creation of local capital markets and local development banks; the World Bank's IFC should be utilized to channel more loans to competent Latin American businessmen for productive enterprises and joint ventures.

The fact that the investment guaranty program under OPIC is facing bankruptcy, due to the claims of American investors in Chile, has raised questions regarding the desirability of the encouragement by the United States of foreign private investment overseas. During the May 1971 hearings on U.S. policies and programs in Brazil, Senator Church asked: "Should it be our policy as a Government to encourage investment elsewhere if the purpose is simply to maximize the profit of the corporation? How does it serve our national interest as a matter of policy to encourage the investments of private capital in foreign countries? We not only encourage it, we guarantee it; we use public credit of various kinds to protect it."[5] An AID official replied that foreign investment has an important effect on the U.S. balance of payments and strengthens the markets for American exports.[6] Existing programs to promote foreign investment in the developing countries were rationalized during earlier hearings in terms of the impact of economic growth, the need to encourage free economies, and the imperative of expanding U.S. investment abroad for its effect on American jobs and productivity. OPIC is now grappling with this problem. Officials have begun to speak out forcefully on the need for American investors to adopt new forms of investment and are exploring new ways in which OPIC can use its guaranty and loan authority to assist American overseas investors in such efforts. But the basic question of whether we should indiscriminately promote foreign investment is often finessed; no one wants to tackle such a thorny issue.

The new policies of OPIC tend to minimize its role in insuring large, sensitive investments, and its guidelines emphasize acceptability to the host government. But would a diversification of the sources of foreign capital in Latin America serve the long-range interests of the United States? The comments of some of the council respondents seemed to imply that if Latin America were not as dependent upon U.S. capital, with the real or imagined fear of domination and exploitation, they would be more receptive to American investment. Latin American governments are zealously seeking to assert their independence vis-à-vis the United States, and no matter how unattainable that goal might be, considering the economic and political power of the United States, the extremely visible presence of large American investments serves to irritate nationalist feelings. Only when the high profile of the American investor in the area is reduced will Latin Americans

5. U.S., Congress, Senate, Committee on Foreign Relations, *Hearings, United States Policies and Programs in Brazil*, p. 244.

6. Ibid.

believe they can speak as juridical equals in hemispheric councils. It should be noted that Jean-Jacques Servan-Schreiber also raised the threat of U.S. economic hegemony through foreign investment in Europe, and the Canadian government has taken steps to restrict American investment. Such nationalist sensitivities to the prominent role of foreign investors in the local economy are not characteristic only of Latin Americans; they are global and were once manifest in our own country.

The United States should exert more leadership in urging the creation of the International Investment Insurance Agency of the World Bank. Together with the International Center for the Settlement of Investment Disputes of the bank, it offers a means to safeguard foreign investors without involving the U.S. government. President Nixon has expressed his support for such a multilateral program, but American efforts for its establishment appear half-hearted. The United States has emphasized the need for risk diversification and the participation of most, if not all, of the major capital-exporting members of the World Bank. The administration argues that if over half of the insured investments were from the United States, the program would appear to be devoted primarily to the protection of American investors. While the Nixon administration has deferred to World Bank President Robert McNamara's lead in this matter, the bank views its role as mainly rendering staff support for the proposal. The draft program was designed so that it could be initiated with five capital-exporting members and ten capital-importing members. In the beginning the program could offer coverage on risks which bilateral programs do not encompass, insure multinational investments, and perhaps offer insurance for investments in countries which find bilateral programs unacceptable. A long-range goal might be direct insurance of foreign investment, with the International Center for Investment Disputes mediating any conflicts.

In 1964 Latin American representatives in Tokyo objected that the Center would confer a special privilege on foreign investors who enjoy the same rights and protection as their own nationals—the Calvo Doctrine. However, Latin American governments have accepted arbitration as a condition for World Bank loans, and outstanding claims and expropriation are considered under the economic performance criteria for loans of the bank. The Pearson Commission suggested linking the International Investment Insurance Agency to the Center and using incentives of higher coverage and / or lower premiums to insure investments in countries which accede to it.[7] Considering how some of the initial objections to the current American investment guaranty program were overcome, the administration might employ the same inducements for acceptance of an international program which would reduce the danger of bilateral conflicts over investment disputes. If the United States firmly stated its position, including whether contributions from the less-developed countries were a condition for entry, there would be a basis for negotiations. Once established, the program could be expanded to include additional governments.

The American business community, whose skills and pragmatism have often been tested, faces one of its greatest challenges. Against the rising tide of economic nationalism it must demonstrate corporate statesmanship in experimenting with new forms of investment, close identification with the aspirations of the host countries, and flexibility when investment disputes arise. The response of many of the companies surveyed indicated that U.S. investors are changing their management policies and adopting new ways of doing business in Latin America. Shrill American objections aimed at restrictive nationalist economic policies can only serve to strengthen the resolve of Latin American leaders, because to back down would show their weakness or sympathy with foreign investors. Quiet negotiations, progressive management, and a realistic assessment of the pressures on Latin American leaders is required. If American business could accommodate itself to the Mexican Revolution and the present Mexican restrictions on foreign capital, surely it can live with the new Andean Code, no matter how disagreeable some features may be. After all, it does establish firm rules of the game and an opportunity to invest in an expanding market.

The U.S. government must recognize that our neglect of Latin America has partly brought about the attacks on our investors. We must, therefore, rededicate ourselves to the goals of social and economic development embodied in the Alliance for Progress. Private enterprise has an important role to play in the economic development of the region, but it must be complementary with the efforts of bilateral and multilateral U.S. assistance programs. A

7. Lester B. Pearson (chairman), *Partners in Development: Report of the Commission on International Development*, p. 109.

true partnership of the American business sector, Latin American governments, and the U.S. government is needed. Only together can they achieve the mutual respect and understanding that is vital among hemispheric partners dedicated to the development of the Americas.

Selected Bibliography

Books

Adams, Richard N.; Lewis, Oscar; Gillin, John P.; Patch, Richard W.; Holmberg, Allan R.; and Wagley, Charles. *Social Change in Latin America Today*. New York: Vintage Books, 1960.

Adler, John H., ed. *Capital Movements and Economic Development*. New York: Macmillan Co., 1967.

Alba, Victor. *Alliance Without Allies*. New York: Frederick A. Praeger, 1965.

Anderson, Charles W. *Politics and Economic Change in Latin America*. Princeton, N.J.: D. Van Nostrand Company, 1967.

Apter, David E. *Ideology and Discontent*. New York: Free Press, 1964.

Arevalo, Juan José. *The Shark and the Sardines*. New York: L. Stewart, 1961.

Asher, Robert E. *Development Assistance in the Seventies*. Washington, D.C.: Brookings Institution, 1970.

Bailey, Norman A. *Latin America in World Politics*. New York: Walker & Co., 1967.

Bauer, Raymond A.; Pool, Ithiel de Sola; and Dexter, Lewis Anthony. *American Business and Public Policy*. New York: Atherton Press, 1968.

Beaulac, William L. *A Diplomat Looks at Aid to Latin America*. Carbondale: Southern Illinois Press, 1970.

Behrman, Jack N. "Foreign Associates and Their Financing." In *U.S. Private and Foreign Investment*, edited by Raymond F. Mikesell. Eugene: University of Oregon Books, 1962.

Bernstein, Marvin D., ed. *Foreign Investment in Latin America*. New York: Alfred A. Knopf, 1966.

Bivens, Karen K., and Lovell, Enid B. *Joint Ventures with Foreign Partners:*

International Survey of Business Opinion and Experience. New York: National Industrial Conference Board, 1966.

Brandenburg, Frank. *The Making of Modern Mexico.* Englewood Cliffs, N.J.: Prentice-Hall, 1964.

Burr, Robert N. *Our Troubled Hemisphere: Perspectives on United States–Latin American Relations.* Washington, D.C.: Brookings Institution, 1967.

Camargo, Alberto Lleras. "The Alliance for Progress: Aims, Distortions, and Obstacles." In *Government and Politics in Latin America*, edited by Peter G. Snow. New York: Holt, Rinehart, & Winston, 1967.

Campos, Roberto de Oliveira. *Reflections on Latin American Development.* Austin: University of Texas Press, 1967.

Cardoso, Fernando H. "The Industrial Elites." In *Elites in Latin America,* edited by Seymour M. Lipset and Aldo Solari. New York: Oxford University Press, 1967.

Carr, Edward Hallett. *Nationalism and After.* London: Macmillan Co., Ltd., 1967.

Caves, Richard E., and Johnson, Harry G., eds. *Readings in International Economics.* Homewood, Ill.: Richard D. Irwin, 1968.

Clissold, Stephan. *Latin America: A Cultural Outline.* New York: Harper & Row, 1966.

Del Rio, Angel. *The Clash and Attraction of Two Cultures.* Translated and edited by James F. Shearer. Baton Rouge: Louisiana State University Press, 1965.

Dell, Sidney. *A Latin American Common Market?* New York: Oxford University Press, 1966.

Deutsch, Karl W. *Nationalism and Its Alternatives.* New York: Alfred A. Knopf, 1969.

Deutsch, Karl W. *Nationalism and Social Communication.* 2d ed. Cambridge: Massachusetts Institute of Technology Press, 1966.

Doob, Leonard W. *Patriotism and Nationalism: Their Psychological Foundations.* New Haven, Conn.: Yale University Press, 1964.

Dozer, Donald M. *Are We Good Neighbors?: Three Decades of Inter-American Relations, 1930–1960.* Gainesville: University of Florida Press, 1959.

Eisenhower, Dwight D. *Waging Peace.* New York: Doubleday & Co., 1965.

Eisenhower, Milton. *The Wine Is Bitter.* New York: Doubleday & Co., 1963.

Emerson, Rupert. *From Empire to Nation: The Rise to Self-Assertion of Asian and African Peoples.* Cambridge, Mass.: Harvard University Press, 1962.

Form, William H., and Blum, Albert A. *Industrial Relations and Social Change in Latin America.* Gainesville: University of Florida Press, 1965.

Franko, Lawrence G.; Dixon, Michael; and Marulanda R., Carlos Arturo. *Entrepreneurship and Industrialization in Latin America.* Austin: Bureau of Business Research, University of Texas Press, 1966.

Furtado, Celso. *Economic Development of Latin America: A Survey from Colonial Times to the Cuban Revolution.* London: Cambridge University Press, 1970.

Gabriel, Peter P. *The International Transfer of Corporation Skills.* Boston: Division of Research, Graduate School of Business Administration, Harvard University, 1967.

Gannon, Thomas A., ed. *Doing Business in Latin America.* New York: American Management Association, 1968.

García Calderon, Francisco. "Commercial and Cultural Intervention." In *Intervention in Latin America,* edited by C. Neale Ronning. New York: Alfred A. Knopf, 1970.

Geiger, Theodore. *The Conflicted Relationship.* New York: McGraw-Hill Book Co., 1967.

Geyer, Georgie A. *New Latins.* New York: Doubleday & Co., 1970.

Gil, Federico G. *Latin American–United States Relations.* New York: Harcourt Brace Jovanovich, 1971.

Glade, William P. *The Latin American Economies.* New York: American Book Co., 1969.

Gordon, Lincoln. *A New Deal for Latin America.* Cambridge, Mass.: Harvard University Press, 1963.

Hagen, Everett E. *On the Theory of Social Change.* Homewood, Ill.: Dorsey Press, 1962.

Hanson, Simon G. *Five Years of the Alliance for Progress.* Washington, D.C.: Inter-American Press, 1967.

Hayes, Carlton J. H. *Essays on Nationalism.* New York: Russell & Russell, Publishers, 1966.

Hayes, Carlton J. H. *Nationalism: A Religion.* New York: Macmillan Co., 1960.

Hays, Samuel P. *The Response to Industrialism, 1885–1914.* Chicago: University of Chicago Press, 1957.

Heilperin, Michael A. *Studies in Economic Nationalism.* Publications de L' Institut Universitaire de Hautes Etudes Internationales, no. 35. Paris: Librairie Minard, 1962.

Hirschman, Albert O. *How to Divest in Latin America, and Why.* Essays in International Finance, no. 76. Princeton, N.J.: Princeton University, 1969.

Hirschman, Albert O. *Journeys Toward Progress.* New York: Twentieth Century Fund, 1963.

International Chamber of Commerce. *International Joint Business Ventures in Developing Countries.* Report of the Commission on International Investments and Economic Development, Brochure 256. Paris, December 1968.

Johnson, Harry G., ed. *Economic Nationalism in Old and New States.* Chicago: University of Chicago Press, 1967.

Johnson, John J., ed. *Continuity and Change in Latin America.* Stanford, Ca.: Stanford University Press, 1964.

Johnson, John J. *Political Change in Latin America: The Emergence of the Middle Sectors.* Stanford, Ca.: Stanford University Press, 1958.

Johnstone, Allan W. *United States Direct Investment in France.* Cambridge: Massachusetts Institute of Technology Press, 1965.

Kautsky, John H., ed. *Political Change in Underdeveloped Countries: Nationalism and Communism.* New York: John Wiley & Sons, 1962.

Kedourie, Elie. *Nationalism.* New York: Frederick A. Praeger, 1960.

Kennedy, John F. *The Strategy of Peace.* Edited by Alan Nevins. New York: Harper & Brothers, 1960.

Kindleberger, Charles P. *American Business Abroad: Six Lectures On Direct Investment.* New Haven, Conn.: Yale University Press, 1969.

Kohn, Hans. *Nationalism: Its Meaning and History.* Princeton, New Jersey: D. Van Nostrand Company, 1955.

Kohn, Hans. *The Idea of Nationalism: A Study of Its Origins and Background.* New York: Macmillan Co., 1944.

La Feber, Walter. *The New Empire: An Interpretation of American Expansion 1860–1898.* New York: Cornell University Press, 1963.

Lambert, Jacques. *Latin American Social Structure and Political Institutions.* Berkeley: University of California Press, 1967.

Levin, Jonathan V. *The Export Economies.* Cambridge, Mass.: Harvard University Press, 1960.

Levinson, Jerome, and de Onís, Juan. *The Alliance that Lost Its Way.* Chicago: Quadrangle Books, 1970.

Lieuwen, Edwin. *U.S. Policy in Latin America.* New York: Frederick A. Praeger, 1965.

Lipset, Seymour M., and Solari, Aldo, eds. *Elites in Latin America.* New York: Oxford University Press, 1967.
Madariaga, Salvador de. *Latin America between the Eagle and the Bear.* New York: Frederick A. Praeger, 1962.
Martz, John D., ed. *The Dynamics of Change in Latin American Politics.* Englewood Cliffs, N.J.: Prentice-Hall, 1965.
Mason, Edward S., ed. *The Corporation in Modern Society.* Cambridge, Mass.: Harvard University Press, 1959.
Masur, Gerhard. *Nationalism in Latin America: Diversity and Unity.* New York: Macmillan Co., 1966.
May, Ernest R. *American Imperialism: A Speculative Essay.* New York: Atheneum Publishers, 1968.
May, Herbert K. *Problems and Prospects of the Alliance for Progress.* New York: Frederick A. Praeger, 1968.
McCormick, Thomas J. *China Market: America's Quest for Informal Empire, 1893–1901.* Chicago: Quadrangle Books, 1967.
McMillan, Claude. "Industrial Leaders in Latin America." In *Industrial Relations and Social Change in Latin America,* edited by William H. Form and Albert A. Blum. Gainesville: University of Florida Press, 1965.
Mecham, J. Lloyd. *A Survey of United States–Latin American Relations.* Boston: Houghton Mifflin Co., 1965.
Mecham, J. Lloyd. "Latin American Constitutions: Nominal and Real." In *The Dynamics of Change in Latin American Politics,* edited by John D. Martz. Englewood Cliffs, N.J.: Prentice-Hall, 1965.
Mikesell, Raymond F. *The Economics of Foreign Aid.* Chicago: Aldine Publishing Co., 1968.
Mikesell, Raymond F., ed. *U.S. Private and Foreign Investment.* Eugene: University of Oregon Books, 1962.
Minogue, Kenneth R. *Nationalism.* New York: Basic Books, Publishers, 1967.
Montgomery, John D., and Smithies, Arthur, eds. *Public Policy.* Cambridge, Mass.: Harvard University Press, 1966.
Morrison, DeLesseps. *Latin American Mission.* New York: Simon & Schuster, 1965.
Nash, Manning. "Economic Nationalism in Mexico." In *Economic Nationalism in Old and New States,* edited by Harry G. Johnson. Chicago: University of Chicago Press, 1967.
Nystrom, J. Warren, and Haverstock, Nathan A. *The Alliance for Progress.* Princeton, N.J.: D. Van Nostrand Company, 1966.
Pazos, Felipe. "The Role of International Movements of Private Capital in Promoting Development." In *Capital Movements and Economic Development,* edited by John H. Adler. New York: Macmillan Co., 1967.
Pearson, Lester B. (chairman). *Partners in Development: Report of the Commission on International Development.* New York: Praeger Publishers, 1969.
Perloff, Harvey S. *Alliance for Progress.* Baltimore: Johns Hopkins University Press, 1969.
Plank, John, ed. *Cuba and the United States: Long Range Perspectives.* Washington, D.C.: Brookings Institution, 1967.
Pratt, Julius W. *America's Colonial Experiment.* New York: Prentice-Hall, 1950.
Ratinoff, Luis. "The New Urban Groups: The Middle Classes." In *Elites in Latin America,* edited by Seymour Lipset and Aldo Solari. New York: Oxford University Press, 1967.
Ronning, C. Neale, ed. *Intervention in Latin America.* New York: Alfred A. Knopf, 1970.
Rosenau, James N. *National Leadership and Foreign Policy.* Princeton, N.J.: Princeton University Press, 1963.

Royal Institute of International Affairs. *Nationalism.* New York: Augustus M. Kelley, Bookseller, 1966.

Schlesinger, Arthur M., Jr. *A Thousand Days.* Greenwich, Conn.: Fawcett Publications, 1965.

Servan-Schreiber, Jean-Jacques. *The American Challenge.* New York: Avon Books, 1967.

Shapiro, Samuel, ed. *Cultural Factors in Inter-American Relations.* Notre Dame, Ind.: University of Notre Dame Press, 1968.

Silvert, K. H., ed. *Expectant Peoples: Nationalism and Development.* New York: Vintage Books, 1967.

Slater, Jerome. *The OAS and United States Foreign Policy.* Columbus: Ohio State University Press, 1967.

Snow, Peter G., ed. *Government and Politics in Latin America.* New York: Holt, Rinehart & Winston, 1967.

Snyder, Louis L. *The New Nationalism.* New York: Cornell University Press, 1968.

Sorensen, Theodore C. *Kennedy.* New York: Bantam Books, 1965.

Steel, Ronald. *Pax Americana.* New York: Viking Press, 1967.

Stein, Stanley J., and Stein, Barbara H. *The Colonial Heritage of Latin America: Essays on Economic Dependence in Perspective.* New York: Oxford University Press, 1970.

Sundelson, J. Wilner. "A Business Perspective." In *Cuba and the United States,* edited by John Plank. Washington, D.C.: Brookings Institution, 1967.

Symmons-Symonolewicz, Konstantin. *Modern Nationalism.* New York: Polish Institute of Arts and Sciences in America, 1968.

United Nations. Economic Commission for Latin America. *Development Problems in Latin America.* Austin: University of Texas Press, 1970.

Uno, F.D. "The Latin American Investment Climate." In *Doing Business in Latin America,* edited by Thomas A. Gannon. New York: American Management Association, 1968.

Urquidi, Victor. "The Implications of Foreign Investment in Latin America." In *Obstacles to Change in Latin America,* edited by Claudio Veliz. New York: Oxford University Press, 1965.

Van Alstyne, R. W. *The Rising American Empire.* Chicago: Quadrangle Books, 1960.

Veliz, Claudio, ed. *Obstacles to Change in Latin America.* New York: Oxford University Press, 1965.

Vernon, Raymond, ed. *How Latin America Views the U.S. Investor.* New York: Frederick A. Praeger, 1966.

Wagner, R. Harrison. *United States Policy Toward Latin America.* Stanford, Ca.: Stanford University Press, 1970.

Whitaker, Arthur P. *Nationalism in Latin America, Past and Present.* Gainesville: University of Florida Press, 1962.

Whitaker, Arthur P., and Jordan, David C. *Nationalism in Contemporary Latin America.* New York: Free Press, 1966.

Wionczek, Miguel S. "A Latin American View." In *How Latin America Views the U.S. Investor,* edited by Raymond Vernon. New York: Frederick A. Praeger, 1966.

Williams, Edward J. *Latin American Christian Democratic Parties.* Knoxville: University of Tennessee Press, 1967.

Williams, William Appleman. *The Tragedy of American Diplomacy.* Rev. ed. New York: Dell Publishing Company, 1962.

Wood, Bryce. *The Making of the Good Neighbor Policy.* New York: Columbia University Press, 1961.

Wythe, George. *Industry in Latin America.* 2d ed. New York: Greenwood Press, 1969.

Articles in Periodicals

Adler, F. Michael. "The High Cost of Foreign Investment Restraints." *Columbia Journal of World Business* 3 (May–June 1968): 73–81.

Alexander, Robert J. "Nationalism: Latin America's Predominant Ideology." *Journal of International Affairs* 15, no. 2 (1961): 108–14.

Anderson, Charles W. "The Changing International Environment of Development and Latin America in the 1970's." *Inter-American Economic Affairs* 24 (Autumn 1970): 65–87.

Angell, Alan. "Chile: From Christian Democracy to Marxism?" *Current History* 60 (February 1971): 84–89ff.

Baklanoff, Eric N. "U.S. Mineral Investments in a Nationalist Setting: Chile's Copper Mining Industry, 1944–1967." *Proceedings of the Council of Economics*, American Institute of Mining, Metallurgical, and Petroleum Engineers, Inc. (1968), pp. 240–55.

Behrman, Jack N. "The Case of the Cautious Matchmaker." *Columbia Journal of World Business* 1 (Spring 1966): 31–40.

Bronheim, David. "Relations between the United States and Latin America." *International Affairs* 46 (July 1970): 501–61.

Cameron, Juan. "Threatening Weather in Latin America." *Fortune*, October 1969, pp. 99–101ff.

Campos, Roberto de Oliveira. "The Dilemma of Private Investment." *Inter-American Economic Affairs* 24 (Winter 1970): 81–84.

Cardoso, Fernando Henrique. "¿'Teoría de la dependencia' o análisis concreto de situaciones de dependencia?" *Commercio Exterior* 22 (April 1972): 360–65.

Chandler, Geoffrey. "The Myth of Oil Power: International Groups and National Sovereignty." *International Affairs* 46 (October 1970): 710–18.

Collado, Emilio G. "Economic Development through Private Enterprise." *Foreign Affairs* 41 (July 1963): 708–20.

Davis, Stanley M. "U.S. versus Latin America: Business and Culture." *Harvard Business Review* 47 (November–December 1969): 88–89.

Delaney, Robert F. "Latin American Opinion: Myth and Reality." *Columbia Journal of World Business* 5 (January–February 1970): 71–78.

Dos Santos, Theotonio. "The Structure of Dependence." *American Economic Review* 60 (May 1970): 231–36.

Ferrer, Esteban. "Peru: The General as Revolutionary." *Columbia Journal of World Business* 5 (November–December 1970): 37–45.

Gabriel, Peter P. "The Investment in the LDC: Asset with a Fixed Maturity." *Columbia Journal of World Business* 1 (Summer 1966): 109–20.

Gallagher, John, and Robinson, Ronald. "The Imperialism of Free Trade." *The Economic History Review* 6 (August 1953): 1–15.

Galtung, John. "A Structural Theory of Imperialism." *Journal of Peace Research* 2 (1971): 81–117.

Goodwin, Richard. "Letter from Peru." *The New Yorker*, May 17, 1969, pp. 41–109.

Gordon, Lincoln. "Private Enterprise and International Development." *Harvard Business Review* 38 (July–August 1960): 134–38.

Grayson, George W., Jr. "Peru's Military Populism." *Current History* 60 (February 1971): 74–78ff.

Groves, Roderick T. "Expropriation in Latin America: Some Observations." *Inter-American Economic Affairs* 23 (Winter 1969): 46–66.

Hornbostel, Peter A. "Investment Guaranties: Bureaucracy Clogs the Flow." *Columbia Journal of World Business* 4 (March–April 1969): 37–48.

Hufbauer, G. C., and Adler, F. Michael. "Foreign Investment Restraints:

Objective—Removal." *Columbia Journal of World Business* 4 (May–June 1969): 29–37.

Huntington, Samuel P. "Foreign Aid for What and for Whom." *Foreign Policy* 1 (Winter 1970–71): 161–89.

Hyson, Charles D., and Weigel, Dale R. "Investment in the LDCs: The Unresolved Debate." *Columbia Journal of World Business* 5 (January–February 1970): 33–41.

Jackson, B. Ward. "Foreign Aid: Strategy or Stopgap?" *Foreign Affairs* 41 (October 1962): 90–104.

Javits, Jacob K. "The Fortunes of ADELA." *Columbia Journal of World Business* 1 (Spring 1966): 123–28.

Johnson, John J. "The New Latin American Nationalism." *Yale Review* 55 (Winter 1965): 187–204.

Johnson, Leland L. "U.S. Business Interests in Cuba and the Rise of Castro." *World Politics* 17 (April 1965): 440–59.

Kendall, Donald. "Corporate Ownership: The International Dimension." *Columbia Journal of World Business* 4 (July–August 1969): 59–65.

Lauterbach, Albert. "Executive Training and Productivity: Managerial Views in Latin America." *Industrial and Labor Relations Review* 17 (April 1964): 357–79.

Linowitz, Sol M. "Why Invest in Latin America?" *Harvard Business Review* 49 (January–February 1971): 120–29.

Meeker, Guy B. "Fade-Out Joint Venture: Can It Work for Latin America?" *Inter-American Economic Affairs* 24 (Spring 1971): 25–42.

Mesa-Largo, Carmelo. "The Revolutionary Offensive." *Transaction* 6 (April 1969): 22–29ff.

Meynen, Johannes; Friedmann, Wolfgang; and Weg, Kenneth. "Joint Ventures Revisited." *Columbia Journal of World Business* 1 (Spring 1966): 19–30.

Petty, John R. "The U.S.–Latin American Trade and Payments Relationship." *Inter-American Economic Affairs* 24 (Autumn 1970): 88–96.

Robock, Stephan. "It's Good for Growth, but Who's Swallowing?" *Columbia Journal of World Business* 2 (November–December 1967): 13–24.

Rockefeller, David. "Closing the Second Gap." *Columbia Journal of World Business* 1 (Spring 1966): 73–78.

Rockefeller, Rodman C. "Turn Public Problems to Private Account." *Harvard Business Review* 49 (January –February 1971): 131–38.

Salera, Virgil. "Liquidate U.S. Direct Investments?" *Inter-American Economic Affairs* 24 (Summer 1970): 31–40.

Salera, Virgil. "On Host Countries' Direct Investment 'Guidelines'." *Inter-American Economic Affairs* 23 (Winter 1969): 67–81.

Sanders, Thomas G. "The Church in Latin America." *Foreign Affairs* 48 (January 1970): 285–99.

Streeten, Paul. "Obstacles to Private Foreign Investment in the LDCs." *Columbia Journal of World Business* 5 (May–June 1970): 31–39.

Sunkel, Oswaldo. "National Development Policy and External Dependence in Latin America." *Journal of Development Studies* 6 (October 1969): 23–48.

Vernon, Raymond. "The Political Economy of Private International Investment." *Economic Development and Cultural Change* 5 (1957): 266–75.

Weffort, Francisco C. "Notas sobre la 'teoría de la dependencia': ¿Teoría de clase o ideología nacional?" *Commercio Exterior* 22 (April 1972): 355–60.

Weisskopf, Thomas E. "Capitalism, Underdevelopment and the Future of the Poor Countries." *Review of Radical Political Economies* 4 (Spring 1972): 1–35.

Whitehead, Laurence. "Aid to Latin America: Problems and Prospects." *Journal of International Affairs* 24, no. 2 (1970): 181–202.

Whyte, William F. "Culture, Industrial Relations and Economic Development: The Case of Peru." *Industrial and Labor Relations Review* 16 (July 1963): 583–94.

Periodicals

Business Week. November 22, 1969, and July 10, 1971.
Christian Science Monitor. 1969–70.
The Economist. January 9, 1971.
El Universal. September 25, 1969.
National Journal. February 28, 1970.
New York Times. 1969–70.
U.S. News and World Report. January 26, 1970.
Washington Evening Star. November 8, 1969.
Washington Post. 1969–71.

United States Congressional Documents

U.S. Congress. Senate Committee on Foreign Relations. *United States–Latin American Relations*. Compilation of studies prepared for Subcommittee on American Republics Affairs, 86th Cong., 2d sess., August 31, 1960.
U.S. Congress. House Committee on Foreign Affairs. *Hearings, International Development and Security Act*. 87th Cong., 1st sess., 1961.
U.S. Congress. Senate Committee on Foreign Relations. *Hearings, International Development and Security Act*. 87th Cong., 1st sess., 1961.
U.S. Congress. House Committee on Foreign Affairs. *Hearings, Foreign Assistance Act of 1962*. 87th Cong., 2d sess., 1962.
U.S. Congress. Senate Committee on Foreign Relations. *Hearings, Foreign Assistance Act of 1962*. 87th Cong., 2d sess., 1962.
U.S. Congress. Joint Economic Committee. *Report, Economic Policies and Programs in South America*, of the Subcommittee on Inter-American Economic Relationships. 87th Cong., 2d sess., January 1962.
U.S. Congress. Senate Committee on Foreign Relations. *Report, Foreign Assistance Act of 1962*. 87th Cong., 2d sess., May 28, 1962.
U.S. Congress. House Committee on Foreign Affairs. *Report, Foreign Assistance Act of 1962*. 87th Cong., 2d sess., June 7, 1962.
U.S. Congress. House. *Conference Report, Foreign Assistance Act of 1962*. 87th Cong., 2d sess., July 20, 1962.
U.S. Congress. Joint Economic Committee. *Hearings, Economic Developments in South America*, before the Subcommittee on Inter-American Economic Relationships. 87th Cong., 2d sess., 1962.
U.S. Congress. House Committee on Foreign Affairs. *Hearings, Foreign Assistance Act of 1963*. 88th Cong., 1st sess., 1963.
U.S. Congress. House Committee on Foreign Affairs. *Report, Foreign Assistance Act of 1963*. 88th Cong., 1st sess., August 8, 1963.
U.S. Congress. Senate Committee on Foreign Relations. *Hearings, Foreign Assistance Act of 1963*. 88th Cong., 1st sess., 1963.
U.S. Congress. Senate Committee on Foreign Relations. *Report, Foreign Assistance Act of 1963*. 88th Cong., 1st sess., October 22, 1963.
U.S. Congress. House. *Conference Report, Foreign Assistance Act of 1963*. 88th Cong., 1st sess., December 6, 1963.

U.S. Congress. House Committee on Foreign Affairs. *Hearings, Foreign Assistance Act of 1964.* 88th Cong., 2d sess., 1964.
U.S. Congress. House Committee on Foreign Affairs. *Report, Foreign Assistance Act of 1964.* 88th Cong., 2d sess., June 1, 1964.
U.S. Congress. Senate Committee on Foreign Relations. *Hearings, Foreign Assistance, 1964.* 88th Cong., 2d sess., 1964.
U.S. Congress. House. *Conference Report, Foreign Assistance Act of 1964.* 88th Cong., 2d sess., October 1, 1964.
U.S. Congress. Joint Economic Committee. *Hearings, Private Investment in Latin America*, before the Subcommittee on Inter-American Relationships. 88th Cong., 2d sess., 1964.
U.S. Congress. Joint Economic Committee. *Report, Private Investment in America*, of the Subcommittee on Inter-American Relationships. 88th Cong., 2d sess., 1964.
U.S. Congress. House Committee on Foreign Affairs. *Hearings, Foreign Assistance Act of 1965.* 89th Cong., 1st sess., 1965.
U.S. Congress. House Committee on Foreign Affairs. *Report, Foreign Assistance Act of 1965.* 89th Cong., 1st sess., May 7, 1965.
U.S. Congress. Senate Committee on Foreign Relations. *Hearings, Foreign Assistance Act of 1965.* 89th Cong., 1st sess., 1965.
U.S. Congress. House Committee on Foreign Affairs. *Hearings, Foreign Assistance Act of 1966.* 89th Cong., 2d sess., 1966.
U.S. Congress. Senate Committee on Foreign Relations. *Hearings, Foreign Assistance, 1966.* 89th Cong., 2d sess., 1966.
U.S. Congress. House. *Conference Report, Foreign Assistance Act of 1966.* 89th Cong., 2d sess., August 31, 1966.
U.S. Congress. House Committee on Foreign Affairs. *Hearings, Foreign Assistance Act of 1967.* 90th Cong., 1st sess., 1967.
U.S. Congress. Senate Committee on Foreign Relations. *Hearings, Foreign Assistance Act of 1967.* 90th Cong., 1st sess., 1967.
U.S. Congress. Senate Committee on Foreign Relations. *Report, Foreign Assistance Act of 1967.* 90th Cong., 1st sess., August 9, 1967.
U.S. Congress. House Committee on Foreign Affairs. *Hearings, Foreign Assistance Act of 1968.* 90th Cong., 2d sess., 1968.
U.S. Congress. House Committee on Foreign Affairs. *Report, The Involvement of U.S. Private Enterprise in Developing Countries.* 90th Cong., 2d sess., April 2, 1968.
U.S. Congress. Senate Committee on Foreign Relations. *Hearings, Foreign Assistance Act of 1968.* 90th Cong., 2d sess., 1968.
U.S. Congress. House Committee on Foreign Affairs. *Hearings, Foreign Assistance Act of 1969.* 91st Cong., 1st sess., 1969.
U.S. Congress. House Committee on Foreign Affairs. *Hearings, New Directions for the 1970's: Toward a Strategy of Inter-American Development*, before the Subcommittee on Inter-American Affairs. 91st Cong., 1st sess., 1969.
U.S. Congress. House Committee on Foreign Affairs. *Report, New Directions for the 1970's: Toward a Strategy of Inter-American Development*, by the Subcommittee on Inter-American Affairs, 91st Cong., 1st sess., 1969.
U.S. Congress. House Committee on Foreign Affairs. *Hearings, Governor Rockefeller's Report on Latin America*, before the Subcommittee on Inter-American Affairs. 91st Cong., 1st sess., 1969.
U.S. Congress. House Committee on Foreign Affairs. *Hearings, Foreign Direct Investment Controls*, before the Subcommittee on Foreign Economic Policy. 91st Cong., 1st sess., 1969.
U.S. Congress. House Committee on Foreign Affairs. *Hearings, Overseas Private*

Investment Corporation, before the Subcommittee on Foreign Economic Policy. 91st Cong., 1st sess., 1969.

U.S. Congress. Senate Committee on Foreign Relations. *Hearings, Foreign Assistance Act of 1969.* 91st Cong., 1st sess., 1969.

U.S. Congress. Senate Committee on Foreign Relations. *Hearings, Rockefeller Report on Latin America.* before the Subcommittee on Western Hemisphere Affairs. 91st Cong., 1st sess., 1969.

U.S. Congress. Senate Committee on Foreign Relations. *Hearings, United States Relations with Peru,* before the Subcommittee on Western Hemisphere Affairs. 91st Cong., 1st sess., 1969.

U.S. Congress. House Committee on Appropriations. *Hearings, Foreign Assistance and Related Agencies Appropriations for 1970,* before a subcommittee of the Committee on Appropriations. 91st Cong., 1st sess., 1969, pt. 2.

U.S. Congress. Joint Economic Committee. *Hearings, A Foreign Economic Policy for the 1970's,* before the Subcommittee on Foreign Economic Policy of the Joint Economic Committee. 91st Cong., 1st sess., 1969, pt. 1.

U.S. Congress. Joint Economic Committee. *Hearings, A Foreign Economic Policy for the 1970's,* before the Subcommittee on Foreign Economic Policy. 91st Cong., 2d sess., 1970, pt. 4.

U.S. Congress. House Committee on Appropriations. *Hearings, Foreign Assistance and Related Agencies Appropriations for 1971,* before a subcommittee of the Committee on Appropriations. 91st Cong., 2d sess., 1970.

U.S. Congress. Senate Committee on Foreign Relations. *Hearings, Foreign Assistance Legislation, Fiscal Year 1972.* 92d Cong., 1st sess., 1971.

U.S. Congress. Senate Committee on Foreign Relations. *Hearings, United States Policies and Programs in Brazil,* before the Subcommittee on Western Hemisphere Affairs. 92d Cong., 1st sess., 1971.

U.S. Congress. House Committee on Appropriations. *Hearings, Foreign Assistance and Related Agencies Appropriations for 1972,* before a subcommittee of the Committee on Appropriations. 92d Cong., 1st sess., 1971.

United States Executive Department Documents

U.S. Department of Commerce. Office of Business Economics. *U.S. Investments in the Latin American Economy,* by Samuel Pizer and Frederick Cutler. Washington, D.C.: Government Printing Office, 1957.

U.S. Department of Commerce. Office of Business Economics. *Survey of Current Business* 40–51 (1960–71).

U.S. Department of Commerce. Office of Business Economics. *U.S. Business Investments in Foreign Countries,* by Samuel Pizer and Frederick Cutler. Washington, D.C.: Government Printing Office, 1960.

U.S. Department of State. *The Department of State Bulletin* 21–62 (1949–70).

U.S. Department of State. *Our Foreign Policy in Latin America,* December 1953. Washington, D.C.: Government Printing Office, 1953.

U.S. Department of State. *Objectives of U.S. Foreign Policy in Latin America.* Department of State Publication 6131, November 1955. Washington, D.C.: Government Printing Office, 1955.

U.S. Department of State. Bureau of Public Affairs. *Strengthening Friendship and Trust Among the American Republics: President Eisenhower's Visit to Brazil, Argentina, Chile, and Uruguay, February–March, 1960.* Department of State Publication 6974, April 1960. Washington, D.C.: Government Printing Office, 1960.

U.S. Department of State. Bureau of Public Affairs, Office of Media Services. *The*

Alliance for Progress. Foreign Affairs Outline 7, June 1964. Washington, D.C.: Government Printing Office, 1964.

U.S. Department of State. Bureau of Public Affairs. *Commitment for Progress: The Americas Plan for a Decade of Urgency*. Department of State Publication 8237, May 1967. Washington, D.C.: Government Printing Office, 1967.

U.S. Department of State. Agency for International Development, Office of Statistics and Reports. *Latin America: Economic Growth Trends*, January 1971. Washington, D.C.: Government Printing Office, 1971.

U.S. Department of State. Agency for International Development, Office of Statistics and Reports. *U.S. Overseas Loans and Grants and Assistance from International Organizations, Obligations and Loan Authorizations July 1, 1945–June 30, 1970*. Special report prepared for the House Foreign Affairs Committee, May 14, 1971. Washington, D.C.: Government Printing Office, 1971.

U.S. President. *Public Papers of the Presidents of the United States*. Dwight D. Eisenhower, 1953–54. Washington, D.C.: Office of the *Federal Register*, National Archives and Records Service.

U.S. President. *Public Papers of the Presidents of the United States*. John F. Kennedy, 1960–63. Washington, D.C.: Office of the *Federal Register*, National Archives and Records Service.

U.S. President. *Public Papers of the Presidents of the United States*. Lyndon B. Johnson, 1963–69. Washington, D.C.: Office of the *Federal Register*, National Archives and Records Service.

U.S. President. *Public Papers of the Presidents of the United States*. Richard Nixon, 1969. Washington, D.C.: Office of the *Federal Register*, National Archives and Records Service.

U.S. President. *The Foreign Assistance Program, Annual Report to the Congress*, fiscal years 1962–70.

U.S. President. *U.S. Foreign Policy for the 1970's: A New Strategy for Peace*. Report to the Congress by Richard Nixon, February 18, 1970. Washington, D.C.: Government Printing Office, 1970.

U.S. President. *U.S. Foreign Policy for the 1970's: Building for Peace*. Report to the Congress by Richard Nixon, February 25, 1971. Washington, D.C.: Government Printing Office, 1971.

U.S. President. *Foreign Assistance for the Seventies*. Message to the Congress. House of Representatives, Document 91–385, 91st Cong., 2d sess., September 15, 1970.

Reports to the President of the United States

Report to the President on Foreign Economic Policies, November 10, 1950. Washington, D.C.: Government Printing Office, 1950.

Partners in Progress. Report to the President by the International Development Advisory Board, March 1951. Washington, D.C.: Government Printing Office, 1951.

Minority Report. Report to the president by the Commission on Foreign Economic Policy, January 1954. Washington, D.C.: Government Printing Office, 1954.

Report to the President and to the Congress. Commission on Foreign Economic Policy, January 23, 1954. Washington, D.C.: Government Printing Office, 1954.

Expanding Private Investment for Free World Economic Growth. A special report prepared at the request of the Department of State under the direction of Ralph I. Straus, special consultant to the undersecretary of state for economic affairs, April, 1959. Washington, D.C.: Government Printing Office, 1959.

Proposals to Improve the Flow of U.S. Private Investment to Latin America. Report of the Commerce Committee for the Alliance for Progress, March 1963. Washington, D.C.: Government Printing Office, 1963.

The Scope and Distribution of United States Military and Economic Assistance Programs. Report to the president of the United States from the Committee to Strengthen the Security of the Free World, March 20, 1963. Department of State. Washington, D.C.: Government Printing Office, 1963.

Foreign Aid through Private Initiative. Report of the Advisory Committee on Private Enterprise in Foreign Aid. Agency for International Development, July, 1965. Washington, D.C.: Government Printing Office, 1965.

The Case for a U.S. Overseas Private Enterprise Development Corporation. The International Private Investment Advisory Council, December 1968. Washington, D.C.: Government Printing Office, 1968.

Development Assistance in the New Administration. Report of the president's General Advisory Committee on Foreign Assistance Program, October 25, 1968. Reprinted by the Agency for International Development. Washington, D.C.: Government Printing Office, 1968.

U.S. Foreign Assistance in the 1970's: A New Approach. Report to the president from the Task Force on International Development, March 4, 1970. Washington, D.C.: Government Printing Office, 1970.

"Summary of Latin American Press Reaction to Seventh IA-ECOSOC Meeting in Panama." Report to the president of the seventh annual meetings of the Inter-American Economic and Social Council, Annex 4. Panama City, Panama, September 10–20, 1971.

COUNCIL OF THE AMERICAS SOURCES (FORMERLY COUNCIL FOR LATIN AMERICA)

Council for Latin America. *Annual Report to the Members*, 1968–69, 1969, and 1970.

Council for Latin America. "Are We Taking More Out of Latin America than We Are Putting In?" Report 5, August 1969.

Council for Latin America. Memo from Enno Hobbing to Council for Latin America members on the views on foreign investment expressed by Chilean foreign minister and CECLA spokesman Gabriel Valdés Subercaseaux to the American Chamber of Commerce in Santiago, July 1969. August 12, 1969.

Council for Latin America. Letter from José de Cubas (president-designate of Council for Latin America) to the Chilean foreign minister, Gabriel Valdés Subercaseaux. Report 5, August 1969.

Council for Latin America. "The Investment Climate in Latin America." Report 5, September 1969.

Council for Latin America. "The Role of Private U.S. Investment in Latin American Economic Development." Report 5, October 1969.

Council for Latin America. "The Matter of Joint Ventures." Report 5, November 1969.

Netto, Antonio Delfim. Address at the fifth annual membership meeting, December 1969. Council for Latin America, Report 6, January 1970.

Council for Latin America. "Building Markets and Dignity." Report 6, January 1970.

Council for Latin America. "Fifth Annual Membership Meeting, December, 1969." Report 6, January 1970.

Council for Latin America. "Expanding Latin America's Exports." Report 6, April 1970.

Council for Latin America. "The Effects of United States and Other Foreign Investment in Latin America." Report by Herbert K. May, January 1970. Reproduction.

Council for Latin America. "How Can My Company Get the Most out of Membership in the Council for Latin America?" Membership pamphlet. New York, n.d.

Council of the Americas. "The Business Sectors Constitute the Most Dynamic Forces; The Medellín Meeting: An Intellectual Breakthrough for Hemispheric Development." Report, June 1970. Reproduction.

INTER-AMERICAN SOURCES

Bermudez, Francisco Morales. Address at the third plenary session, eleventh meeting of the board of governors, Inter-American Development Bank. Punta del Este, Uruguay, April 22, 1970.

Campos, Roberto, and Ferrer, Aldo. "Foreign Investment and Latin American Economic Development." Organization of American States. Inter-American Economic and Social Council. Paper prepared for the sixth annual meeting of the IA-ECOSOC at the Expert and Ministerial Levels, June 14–23, 1969. Port of Spain, Trinidad and Tobago (CIES / 1371), May 20, 1969.

Colombian-American Chamber of Commerce newsletter. July 16, 1969.

De Santamaria, Carlos Sanz. Address to the National Press Club. Washington, D.C., April 15, 1970.

Lleras Restrepo, Carlos. Address to the National Press Club. Washington, D.C., June 13, 1969. Mimeographed.

Organization of American States. Inter-American Economic and Social Council. Documents of the first part of the meeting of the Special Committee of the IA-ECOSOC, November 17–29, 1969. Washington, D.C. (CIES / Com. Esp. / 56), December 29, 1969.

Organization of American States. Inter-American Economic and Social Council. "The Role of Foreign Private Investment in the Development of Latin America." Paper prepared for the sixth annual meetings of the IA-ECOSOC at the Expert and Ministerial Levels, June 14–23, 1969. Port of Spain, Trinidad and Tobago (CIES / 1371), April 28, 1969, and May 20, 1969.

Organization of American States. Inter-American Economic and Social Council. "Report of the Rapporteur of Subcommittee II on External Financing and Foreign Private Investment." Part 2 of the meeting of the Special Committee of the IA-ECOSOC, January 26–February 2, 1970. Caracas, Venezuela (CIES / Com. Esp. / 81), February 4, 1970.

Organization of American States. Inter-American Economic and Social Council. Statement by Nathaniel Samuels, special representative of the United States, at the seventh annual meetings of the IA-ECOSOC. Panama City, Panama (CIES / 1680), September 13, 1971.

Pan American Union and the Agency for International Development, U.S. Department of State. *Alianza para el Progreso: The Record of Punta del Este*. Documents from the special meeting of the IA-ECOSOC at the Ministerial Level. Punta del Este, Uruguay, August 5–17, 1961.

Prebisch, Raul. *Change and Development: Latin America's Great Task*. Report to the Inter-American Development Bank. Santiago, Chile, July 1970.

Prebisch, Raul. Exposición del Sr. Raul Prebisch, Director General del Instituto Latino-Americano de Planificación Económica y Social, Comisión Económica para America Latina. Decimotercer Periodo de sesiones. Lima, Peru, April 23, 1969.

Unpublished Sources

Alliance for Progress weekly newsletter, June 22, 1970.
Brandenburg, Frank. "The Development of Latin American Private Enterprise." Planning Pamphlet 121. Washington, D.C.: National Planning Association, May 1964.
Crapol, Edward P. "America for Americans: Economic Nationalism and Anglophobia, 1880–1900." Paper presented to the Southern Historical Association. Washington, D.C., November 1969.
International Bank for Reconstruction and Development, press release no. 57. Excerpt from the statement by Felix Ruiz. Tokyo, September 9, 1964.
Jova, Joseph J. Statement at the Seminar on Latin America of the American Management Association. New York, February 1970.
Keilany, Ziad. "Structuralism in Latin America: A Radical Approach to Modernization." Unpublished manuscript.
Meyer, Charles A. Address to the sixth meeting of the Inter-American Economic and Social Council, Organization of American States. Port of Spain, Trinidad, June 20, 1969. U.S. Department of State press release 171, June 20, 1969.
Meyer, Charles A. Address to the meeting of the Special Committee of the Inter-American Economic and Social Council, Organization of American States. Washington, D.C., November 18, 1969. Mimeographed.
Mikesell, Raymond F. "Promoting United States Private Investment Abroad." Planning Pamphlet 101. Washington, D.C.: National Planning Association, October 1957.
Mills, Bradford. Remarks before the Council of the Americas, Washington, D.C., June 17, 1971. Reproduction.
Nixon, Richard M. Message from President Nixon to the chairman of the eighth special meeting of the Inter-American Economic and Social Council, Organization of American States. Caracas, Venezuela, February 4, 1970.
Szabo, Daniel. Remarks to the American Management Association, New York, January 26, 1971. Reproduction.
Special Commission for Latin American Coordination (CECLA). "Manifesto of Latin America." Transmitted by letter from Juan Alberto Quilici to Walter J. Sedwitz, September 6, 1971. Reproduction.
U.S. Department of Commerce. Office of Business Economics. "United States Direct Investments in the Latin American Republics by Country and Major Industries, at Year End 1955–67." Mimeographed.
U.S. Department of State. Translation of the "Consensus reached at the CECLA Ministerial Meeting at Viña Del Mar." May 29, 1969. Mimeographed.
U.S. Department of State. American Embassy, Bogotá, Colombia. "Economic Trends Report." September 17, 1969. Mimeographed.
U.S. Department of State. American Embassy, Caracas, Venezuela. "Petroleum: Service Contracts." October 10, 1969. Mimeographed.
U.S. Department of State. Overseas Private Investment Corporation. "General Policy and Guidelines: Large or Sensitive Projects." Washington, D.C., March 8, 1971.
U.S. Information Agency, Research and Reference Service. "Latin American Attitudes toward the Alliance for Progress and the Role of Private Investment." Reproduction, December 1965.
Upton, T. Graydon. Address to Forum of the Americas, jointly sponsored by the Chamber of Commerce of San Diego and Time-Life Broadcast. San Diego, California, May 16, 1967.
Weintraub, Sidney. "An Overview of U.S. Policy towards Latin America." Address to meeting of Esso executives. Boca Raton, Florida, January 29, 1971.

Appendix

Corporate Members of Council of the Americas
July 31, 1970

Addressograph-Multigraph Corporation
Allegheny Ludlum Steel Corporation
Aluminum Company of America
Aluminum Limited
American Broadcasting Company (ABC) International Television, Inc.
American Can Company
American & Foreign Insurance Company
American Home Products Corporation
American International Oil Company
American International Underwriters Corporation
American Machine & Foundry Company (AMF)
American Smelting and Refining Company
American Standard Company
Anaconda Company
Anderson, Clayton & Company
Anglo-Lautaro Nitrate Company Ltd.
Armco Steel Corporation International
Arthur Andersen & Company
Asiatic Petroleum Corporation
Atlantic Richfield Company
Bacardi Corporation
Bank of America
Bank of the Southwest
Bankers Trust Company
Bechtel Corporation
Belco Petroleum Corporation
Bethlehem Steel Corporation
Booz, Allen & Hamilton International, Inc.
Borden Company
Borg-Warner Corporation
Braniff Airways International
Bristol-Myers Company
Brown & Root, Inc.
Business International, Inc.
Canadian International Power Company, Ltd.
J. I. Case Company

Caterpillar Tractor Company
Celanese Fibers Group Company
Cerro Corporation
Chase Manhattan Bank
Chemetron Corporation
Chemical Bank and New York Trust Company
Chrysler Corporation
Cities Service Company
Clark Equipment Company
Coca-Cola Export Corporation
Columbia Broadcasting Systems, Inc. (CBS) Television Services
Combustion Engineering, Inc.
Container Corporation of America
Continental Bank International
Continental Can Company International
Continental Grain Company
CPC International, Inc.
Corning Glass International
Crown Zellerbach Corporation International
Cyanamid International
Cyprus Mines Corporation
Czarnikow-Rionda Company
Deere & Company
Del Monte Corporation
Delta Steamship Lines, Inc.
Deltec Group
Dow Chemical Company
Dun & Bradstreet International, Inc.
E. I. DuPont de Nemours & Company
Eastman Kodak Company
Eaton, Yale & Towne, Inc.
Ebasco International Corporation
Ernst & Ernst
Firestone Tire & Rubber Company
First Boston Corporation
First National Bank of Boston
First National Bank of Chicago
First National Bank of Miami
First National City Bank
First Wisconsin National Bank of Milwaukee
Ford Motor Company
Fresnillo Company
General Electric Company
General Foods Corporation
General Motors Overseas Operations
General Telephone & Electronics Corporation International
General Tire & Rubber Company International
Gillette Company
B. F. Goodrich Company
Goodyear Tire and Rubber Company International
W. R. Grace & Company
Gulf Oil Corporation
Hanna Mining Company
Harnischfeger Corporation
Harris Trust & Savings Bank of Chicago
Haskins & Sells
H. J. Heinz Company
Hercules Inc.
Hewlett-Packard Company
Hooker Chemical Corporation
Industrial Development International
Insurance Company of North America
International Basic Economy Corporation
International Business Machines (IBM) World Trade Corporation
International Harvester Export Company
International Mineral & Chemical Corporation
International Mining Corporation
International Nickel Company, Inc.
International Packers Ltd.
International Paper Company
International Telephone and Telegraph (ITT) Corporation
International Textbook Company
Interpublic Group of Companies, Inc.
Johnson & Higgins
Johnson & Johnson
S. C. Johnson & Son, Inc.
Kaiser Aluminum & Chemical Corporation
Kellogg Company
Kennecott Copper Corporation
Kimberly-Clark Corporation
King Ranch, Inc.
Koppers Company, Inc.
Kraft Foods
Kuhn, Loeb & Company
Latin American Resources, Inc.
Lehman Bros. Corporation
Lincoln National Life Insurance Company
Arthur D. Little, Inc.
Loeb, Rhoades & Company, Inc.
Lone Star Cement Corporation
Lumbermens Mutual Casualty Company
Lybrand, Ross Bros. & Montgomery

Maestro Import Industries, Inc.
Manufacturers Hanover Trust Company
Marcona Corporation
Marsh & McLennan International, Inc.
Merch & Company, Inc.
Merchants National Bank of Mobile
Mobil Oil Corporation
Monsanto Company
Moore-McCormack Lines, Inc.
Morgan Guaranty Trust Company of New York
Morton International, Inc.
Mosler International S.A.
National Cash Register Company
National Lend Company
Norlin Corporation
North American Rockwell Corporation
North American Utility Construction Corporation
Northern Trust Company
Norton Company
Otis Elevator Company
Owens-Illinois, Inc.
Pan-American Life Insurance Company
Pan American World Airways, Inc.
Parker Pen Company
Peat, Marwick, Mitchell & Company
Pepsico International, Inc.
Pfizer International, Inc.
Phelps Dodge International Corporation
Philip Morris International, Inc.
Joshua B. Powers, Inc.
PPG Industries, Inc.
Price Paper Corporation
Price Waterhouse & Company
Puerto Rican Cement Company, Inc.
Quaker Oats Company
Ralston Purina Company International
RCA Corporation International
Reader's Digest Association, Inc.
Republic Steel Corporation
Rexach Construction Company, Inc.
Rheem Manufacturing Company
Richardson-Merrell Inc.
Roberts & Holland
Rohm & Haas Company
Ruder & Finn International, Inc.
St. Joseph Lead Company
Charles A. Sayous, Inc.
Schering Corporation
Joseph E. Seagram & Sons, Inc.
Sears, Roebuck and Company
Sinclair Company International
Singer Company
Smith Kline & French Overseas Company
Southern Peru Copper Corporation
Sperry Rand Corporation
Squibb Beech-Nut International
Standard Fruit & Steamship Company
Standard Oil Company of California
Standard Oil Company of New Jersey
C. V. Starr & Company
Stauffer Chemical Company
Sterling Products International, Inc.
Sun Oil Company
Texaco Inc.
Texas Gulf Sulphur Company
J. Walter Thompson Company
3-M Company
Time-Life International
Times of the Americas
Union Carbide Pan America, Inc.
Union Oil Company of California
United Corporation
United Fruit Company
United Shoe Machinery Corporation
United States Steel International, Inc.
Upjohn Company International
Vision, Inc.
Warner-Lambert Company International
Wells Fargo Bank
Westinghouse Electric Corporation International
Whirlpool Corporation
White, Weld & Company
Whitney National Bank of New Orleans
Xerox Corporation
Arthur Young & Company

TABLE A-1

Communication with Congress on Foreign Aid[a]

Attitudes	Total Sample N=100 (%)	Manu-facturing N=48 (%)	Extractive N=15 (%)	Other N=37 (%)
Communicated	41	38	53	41
Did not communicate	45	46	33	49
Indirect communication	5	4	..	8
No response (not ascertained)	9	13	13	3

a. Totals may not add due to rounding of figures.

TABLE A-2

Communication with Congress on Protection of U.S. Investment[a]

Attitudes	Total Sample N=100 (%)	Manu-facturing N=48 (%)	Extractive N=15 (%)	Other N=37 (%)
Communicated	27	21	33	32
Did not communicate	58	60	47	59
Indirect communication	5	8	..	3
No response (not ascertained)	10	10	20	5

a. Totals may not add due to rounding of figures.

TABLE A-3

Communication with Congress on OPIC[a]

Attitudes	Total Sample N=100 (%)	Manu-facturing N=48 (%)	Extractive N=15 (%)	Other N=37 (%)
Communicated	25	23	27	27
Did not communicate	61	69	60	65
Indirect communication	3	2	7	5
No response (not ascertained)	11	6	7	3

a. Totals may not add due to rounding of figures.

TABLE A-4

Communication and Attitude toward Foreign Aid

Attitudes	Communicated N=41 (%)	Did Not Communicate N=45 (%)
Reverse decline in foreign aid		
Yes (N=37)	46	31
No (N=38)	27	51
Maintain reasonable level (N=14)	17	11
No response (N=11)	10	7

TABLE A-5

Size of Latin American Investment[a]

Attitudes	Investor Small N=19 (%)	Investor Medium N=23 (%)	Investor Large N=38 (%)
Salience of danger of expropriation			
High (N=18)	26	15	18
Medium (N=36)	26	48	29
Low (N=37)	42	27	47
No response (N=9)	5	9	5
Salience of hostility to private enterprise			
High (N=31)	16	27	45
Medium (N=34)	53	27	32
Low (N=27)	26	39	18
No response (N=8)	5	6	5
Latin Americans prefer non-U.S. investors			
Yes (N=55)	53	52	58
No (N=31)	32	33	32
Not necessarily (N=10)	16	6	11
No response (N=4)	..	9	..
Hickenlooper Amendment outlived its usefulness			
Agree (N=76)	63	82	79
Disagree (N=21)	26	15	21
No response (N=3)	11	3	..
Experience with joint ventures			
Experience (N=60)	47	58	68
No experience (N=17)	21	12	13
No response (N=23)	32	30	18
Practicality of joint venture			
Practical (N=68)	79	70	53
Impractical (N=14)	11	12	21
Mixed assessment (N=4)	..	9	21
No response (N=14)	11	9	5

TABLE A-5 (Continued)

Attitudes	Investor Small N=19 (%)	Investor Medium N=23 (%)	Investor Large N=38 (%)
Importance of OPIC to firm			
Important (N=52)	42	64	50
Unimportant (N=37)	47	21	39
Unfamiliar with program (N=8)	5	12	8
No response (N=3)	5	3	3
Private capital primary source of foreign assistance			
Yes (N=62)	68	73	58
No (N=21)	21	9	29
Need both (N=15)	11	15	13
No response (N=2)	..	3	..
Reverse decline in foreign aid			
Yes (N=37)	42	21	47
No (N=38)	32	52	32
Maintain reasonable level (N=14)	21	15	11
No response (N=11)	5	12	11
Communication with Congress on foreign aid			
Communicated (N=41)	32	33	55
Did not communicate (N=45)	63	55	26
Indirect communication (N=5)	..	3	11
No response (N=9)	5	9	8
Communication with Congress on OPIC			
Communicated (N=25)	21	12	39
Did not communicate (N=61)	68	82	53
Indirect communication (N=3)	5	3	3
No response (N=11)	5	3	5
Communication with Congress on protection of U.S. investment			
Communicated (N=27)	32	24	32
Did not communicate (N=58)	68	61	47
Indirect communication (N=5)	..	3	11
No response (N=10)	..	12	11

a. Totals may not add due to rounding of figures.

TABLE A-6

Size of Manufacturing Investment[a]

Attitudes	Investor: Medium Manufacturing N=23 (%)	Investor: Large Manufacturing N=19 (%)
Salience danger of expropriation		
High (N=18)	13	16
Medium (N=36)	48	21
Low (N=37)	35	53
No response (N=9)	4	10
Salience hostility to private enterprise		
High (N=31)	30	47
Medium (N=34)	35	26
Low (N=27)	30	16
No response (N=8)	5	11
Latin Americans prefer non-U.S. investors		
Yes (N=55)	52	63
No (N=31)	35	32
Not necessarily (N=10)	4	5
No response (N=4)	9	..
Hickenlooper Amendment outlived its usefulness		
Agree (N=76)	87	79
Disagree (N=21)	13	21
No response (N=3)	..	..
Experience with joint ventures		
Experience (N=60)	52	63
No experience (N=17)	13	21
No response (N=23)	33	16
Practicality of joint ventures		
Practical (N=68)	60	42
Impractical (N=14)	17	26
Mixed assessment (N=4)	13	21
No response (N=14)	10	11

TABLE A-6 (Continued)

Attitudes	Investor: Medium Manufacturing N=23 (%)	Investor: Large Manufacturing N=19 (%)
Private capital primary source of foreign assistance		
Yes (N=62)	74	53
No (N=21)	9	32
Need both (N=15)	17	16
No response (N=2)	..	..
Reverse decline in foreign aid		
Yes (N=37)	17	53
No (N=38)	52	26
Maintain reasonable level (N=14)	17	11
No response (N=11)	14	10

a. Totals may not add due to rounding of figures.

TABLE A-7

Years of Experience in Latin America[a]

Attitudes	Under 20 Years N=40 (%)	Over 20 Years N=57 (%)
Salience of danger of expropriation		
High (N=18)	15	21
Medium (N=36)	40	32
Low (N=37)	38	37
No response (N=9)	8	11
Salience of hostility to private enterprise		
High (N=31)	33	30
Medium (N=34)	35	33
Low (N=27)	25	28
No response (N=8)	8	9
Latin Americans prefer non-U.S. investors		
Yes (N=55)	65	47
No (N=31)	28	33
Not necessarily (N=10)	5	14
No response (N=4)	3	5
Hickenlooper Amendment outlived its usefulness		
Agree (N=76)	75	77
Disagree (N=21)	20	21
No response (N=3)	5	2
Experience with joint ventures		
Experience (N=60)	55	65
No experience (N=17)	20	13
No response (N=23)	25	23
Practicality of joint ventures		
Practical (N=68)	68	67
Impractical (N=14)	18	12
Mixed assessment (N=4)	10	12
No response (N=14)	5	9

TABLE A-7 (Continued)

Attitudes	Under 20 Years N=40 (%)	Over 20 Years N=57 (%)
Importance of OPIC to firm		
Important (N=52)	63	44
Unimportant (N=37)	33	40
Unfamiliar with program (N=8)	5	11
No response (N=3)	..	4
Private capital primary source of foreign assistance		
Yes (N=62)	63	63
No (N=21)	18	23
Need both (N=15)	15	14
No response (N=2)	5	..
Reverse decline in foreign aid		
Yes (N=37)	38	37
No (N=38)	33	40
Maintain reasonable level (N=14)	15	14
No response (N=11)	15	9

a. Totals may not add due to rounding of figures.

TABLE A-8

Salience of Danger of Expropriation[a]

Attitudes	High N=18 (%)	Medium N=36 (%)	Low N=37 (%)
Hickenlooper Amendment outlived its usefulness			
Agree (N=76)	61	81	78
Disagree (N=21)	33	17	19
No response (N=3)	5	3	3
Practicality of joint ventures			
Practical (N=68)	77	75	51
Impractical (N=14)	11	8	24
Mixed assessment (N=4)	11	11	11
No response (N=14)	..	6	14
Importance of OPIC to firm			
Important (N=52)	72	53	49
Unimportant (N=37)	17	36	41
Unfamiliar with program (N=8)	6	11	8
No response (N=3)	6	..	3
Communication with Congress on protection of U.S. investment			
Communicated (N=27)	28	17	32
Did not communicate (N=58)	67	67	51
Indirect communication (N=5)	6	6	5
No response (N=10)	..	11	11

a. Totals may not add due to rounding of figures.

TABLE A-9

Salience of Hostility to Private Enterprise[a]

Attitudes	High N=31 (%)	Medium N=34 (%)	Low N=27 (%)
Hickenlooper Amendment outlived its usefulness			
Agree (N=76)	68	74	85
Desagree (N=21)	29	26	7
No response (N=3)	3	..	7
Practicality of joint ventures			
Practical (N=68)	48	71	81
Impractical (N=14)	19	18	7
Mixed assessment (N=4)	19	6	7
No response (N=14)	13	6	4
Importance of OPIC to firm			
Important (N=52)	58	50	56
Unimportant (N=37)	32	41	30
Unfamiliar with program (N=8)	10	6	11
No response (N=3)	..	3	4
Communication with Congress on protection of U.S. investment			
Communicated (N=27)	26	26	22
Did not communicate (N=58)	65	56	63
Indirect communication (N=5)	3	3	11
No response (N=10)	6	15	4

a. Totals may not add due to rounding of figures.

TABLE A-10

Importance of OPIC to Firm[a]

Attitudes	Important N=52 (%)	Unimportant N=37 (%)	Unfamiliar with Program N=8 (%)
Communication with Congress on OPIC			
Communicated (N=25)	35	19	..
Did not communicate (N=61)	60	68	100
Indirect communication (N=05)	4	3	..
No response (N=09)	2	11	..

a. Totals may not add due to rounding of figures.

Latin American Monographs—Second Series

Number 1 (1965): *Fidel Castro's Political Programs from Reformism to "Marxism-Leninism"*
by Loree Wilkinson

Number 2 (1966): *Highways into the Upper Amazon Basin*
by Edmund Eduard Hegen

Number 3 (1967): *The Government Executive of Modern Peru*
by Jack W. Hopkins

Number 4 (1967): *Eduardo Santos and the Good Neighbor, 1938–1942*
by David Bushnell

Number 5 (1968): *Dictatorship and Development: The Methods of Control in Trujillo's Dominican Republic*
by Howard J. Wiarda

Number 6 (1969): *New Lands and Old Traditions: Kekchi Cultivators in the Guatemalan Lowlands*
by William E. Carter

Number 7 (1969): *The Mechanization of Agriculture in Brazil: A Sociological Study of Minas Gerais*
by Harold M. Clements, Sr.

Number 8 (1971): *Liberación Nacional of Costa Rica: The Development of a Political Party in a Transitional Society*
by Burt H. English

Number 9 (1971): *Colombia's Foreign Trade and Economic Integration in Latin America*
by J. Kamal Dow

Number 10 (1972): *The Feitosas and the Sertão dos Inhamuns: The History of a Family and a Community in Northeast Brazil, 1700–1930*
by Billy Jaynes Chandler

Number 11 (1973): *The Moving Frontier: Social and Economic Change in a Southern Brazilian Community*
by Maxine L. Margolis

Number 12 (1973): *San Rafael—Camba Town*
by Allyn MacLean Stearman

Number 13 (1974): *The Afro-Asian Dimension of Brazilian Foreign Policy, 1956–1972*
by Wayne A. Selcher

Number 14 (1975): *Population and Energy: A Systems Analysis of Resource Utilization in the Dominican Republic*
by Gustavo A. Antonini, Katherine Carter Ewel, and Howard M. Tupper

NUMBER 15 (1975): *Rubén Darío and the Pythagorean Tradition*
by Raymond Skyrme

NUMBER 16 (1976): *The Embattled Colossus: Economic Nationalism and United States Investors in Latin America*
by Robert H. Swansbrough